"*Christianity and World Religions* fills a great nee̲ ̲
ingly live together with people of other faiths, Christians are largely ignorant of the history and content of some of the most important religions. As a result, they tend to live in a fool's paradise. Derek Cooper supplies abundant information on the worldview of five major religions, and adds wise suggestions for interacting with their adherents. Ideal for classroom or small-group study, the book is both very learned and yet also accessible to the nonexpert. In the bargain, assiduous readers will find themselves more confident as they reach out to their neighbors."

—**William Edgar,** Professor of Apologetics, Westminster Theological Seminary, Philadelphia

"Only the best-informed writers can summarize diverse religious traditions in a brief but insightful manner. That is precisely what Derek Cooper has done in this book. More than a factual survey, each chapter explores the founding stories of various world religions and the resulting beliefs and practices. While helping us communicate the truth of the gospel within our religiously diverse neighborhoods, the author treats each religion with care and its adherents with respect. Especially for its size, this book fills an important gap."

—**Michael Horton,** J. Gresham Machen Professor of Systematic Theology and Apologetics, Westminster Seminary California

"Cooper's book clearly and carefully explains many of the complexities and nuances of world religions—no small task. But even better is how Cooper encourages Christians in the United States to interact meaningfully with real-live adherents of other religious traditions. Readers, especially those with little interreligious experience but with a heart to learn and serve, will be enriched and enriching to new friends of other faiths."

—**J. Nelson Jennings,** Director of Program and Community Life, Overseas Ministries Study Center; Associate Editor, *International Bulletin of Missionary Research*

"*Christianity and World Religions* is a special book. It is certainly information written for our times and communicated in such a way that it will appeal both to those who have some understanding of the great religions of the world and to those who have very little understanding. It is an easy read, not because the material is easy but because of the author's engaging, clear, and concise style. Any Christian who regularly reads the newspaper will want to read this book in order to relate to current events and to neighbors from different religious backgrounds."

—**Paul D. Kooistra,** Coordinator, Mission to the World, PCA

"In adopting the compelling motif of 'rival stories of the world,' Derek Cooper has written a conversational, eminently accessible introduction for Christian students to other religious traditions. Charmingly reminiscent of Paul in Athens (Acts 17), this introduction beautifully exhibits a deep-rootedness in Christian confession, conviction, and practice and a generosity of spirit toward other traditions. Peppering his book with engaging personal anecdotes and supplementing the text with helpful charts, tables, and sidebars throughout, Cooper has authored a truly helpful guide for thoughtful Christians seeking meaningful points of contact with their non-Christian neighbors."

—**Michael Lodahl,** Professor of Theology and World Religions, Point Loma Nazarene University, San Diego

"*Christianity and World Religions* is a clear and concise exposition of many of the world's prominent religions. Derek Cooper's discerning and winsome exploration also provides practical recommendations on how to engage adherents of these traditions. This volume will be welcomed by all Christians seeking to be more faithful, knowledgeable, and effective witnesses in our increasingly multifaith society."

—**Paul Louis Metzger,** Professor of Christian Theology and Theology of Culture, Multnomah Biblical Seminary, Portland, Oregon

"Derek Cooper's *Christianity and World Religions* is a timely and accessible resource for Christians (let alone a general public) who are largely uneducated about the stories, history, beliefs, and scriptures of major world religions. Cooper's intent is not to preach but to prepare the disciple of Christ to share the good news in a biblically and theologically informed manner that respects the devotees of other religions without compromising the identity and saving work of the God revealed in Jesus Christ. This text functions very well as a handbook of religions and Christian responses and as an introductory textbook in a Christian-oriented class on world religions."

—**Dennis Okholm,** Professor of Theology, Azusa Pacific University, Azusa, California

"Derek Cooper reminds the Christian reader that loving one's neighbor—inclusivist, exclusivist, pluralist, universalist, and particularist alike—as one loves oneself means taking the time to understand one's neighbor's beliefs, values, and joys. Cooper's book is designed for Christian readers who not only want to know more about their neighbors' beliefs but also want to share their own faith commitments. Study questions and guides for attending the services of other religions will challenge Christians and enable them to respectfully engage those with whom they share the world."

—**Brandon Withrow,** Assistant Professor of the History of Christianity and Religious Studies and Director of the Master of Arts (Theological Studies) Program, Winebrenner Theological Seminary, Findlay, Ohio

Christianity & World Religions

ADDITIONAL AIDS FOR TEACHERS AVAILABLE.

For information concerning Quizzes / Final Exam questions

and answers, e-mail marketing@prpbooks.com.

Christianity & World Religions

An Introduction to the World's Major Faiths

DEREK COOPER

PUBLISHING

P.O. BOX 817 • PHILLIPSBURG • NEW JERSEY 08865-0817

Unless otherwise indicated, Scripture quotations are from The Holy Bible, English Standard Version, copyright © 2001 by Crossway Bibles, a division of Good News Publishers. Used by permission. All rights reserved.

Italics within Scripture quotations indicate emphasis added.

ISBN: 978-1-59638-446-0 (pbk)
ISBN: 978-1-59638-579-5 (ePub)
ISBN: 978-1-59638-580-1 (Mobi)

Cover images: cross © istockphoto.com / malerapaso; collage (clockwise from top): Statue of Ganesha © Photowee / dreamstime.com, Torah in Hebrew © Chert61 / dreamstime.com, Buddhist monk with begging bowl © Chatchai Somwat / dreamstime.com, Daoist temple © Iiiiimax / dreamstime.com, statue of the Hindu goddess Kali © Kirat Jadeja / dreamstime.com, Siamese Buddha statue © Erinpackardphotography / dreamstime.com, Hassan II Mosque © Pniesen / dreamstime.com, Confucius © Lieska / dreamstime.com

Cover, page design, and typesetting by Dawn Premako

Printed in the United States of America

Library of Congress Cataloging-in-Publication Data

Cooper, Derek, 1978-
  Christianity and world religions : an introduction to the world's
major faiths / Derek Cooper.
      p. cm.
  Includes bibliographical references and index.
  ISBN 978-1-59638-446-0 (pbk.)
  1. Christianity and other religions. 2. Religions. I. Title.
  BR127.C635 2012
  261.2--dc23
                        2012026413

This book is dedicated to the countless individuals who have sat attentively in classes and churches as I discussed Christianity and world religions. You have forced me to ask better questions, think more critically, and learn more about this topic than I ever imagined.

Brief Contents

Contents

CHAPTER 3   CONFUCIANISM AND DAOISM: THE STORIES OF ORDER AND NATURE

PART 2: : CHRISTIAN RESPONSES TO THESE STORIES

Acknowledgments

I WOULD LIKE TO THANK the many people who have taken time to read over portions of this manuscript or who have provided feedback about the topic of this book. These include Dennis Brice, Ed Cyzewski, Yonah Gross, Mike Hollenbach, Jongbum (Daniel) Kee, Greg Klimovitz, Stephen Kriss, David Lamb, Miguel Lau, Hae Rhim (Philip) Park, Stephen Taylor, and Dustin Youngstrom.

Many cheers go to Lydia Putnam and Kelly Pfleiger at Biblical Seminary. Lydia kindly requested countless interlibrary loans for me during the writing of this book, while Kelly graciously helped me with graphics.

I am grateful to the staff at P&R Publishing for their support of my work. It has been great working with you.

I also want to thank the many individuals and groups over the years who have graciously received me into their mosques, synagogues, and temples, and who have sat patiently with me as I asked many questions about their religions and as I inquired about their views and perspectives on Christianity.

Finally, it is always a privilege to thank my beautiful, ever-charitable, and long-suffering wife, Barb! As deadlines approached and time was short, I worked longer hours than usual and was away from home more than either of us wanted. She is a ray of hope and joy in my life, for which I am eternally grateful. To my three wonderful children—Gabriela, Mia, and Eli—who still do not understand why Daddy spends so much time pressing keys on the computer, thank you for your patience when I was busy and for your timely distractions when I was overly focused on work! I love you all!

Introduction

Other faiths used to belong to other lands. At home rival religious claims could safely be ignored. Today things are different.

John Habgood

The existence of and communication among world religions is the most significant challenge to and opportunity for the Christian church in the new millennium.

Veli-Matti Karkkainen

WHEN THE APOSTLE PAUL entered the city of Athens in AD 50, his soul was greatly troubled. Everywhere he looked he saw false representations of the true God. Although his spirit was deeply "provoked" within, as the book of Acts describes (Acts 17:16), the apostle to the Gentiles did not summarily pronounce judgment on the town and walk away, shaking the dust from his sandals. Nor did he indifferently turn a blind eye to what he was experiencing. Instead, he engaged the religions he encountered.

As a Jewish Christian, Paul first entered the synagogue and shared with the people the story of Jesus the Messiah and his resurrection from the dead. Afterward he shared the same message with the non-Christian townsfolk who happened to be in or around the marketplace. Paul next turned his attention to the Athenian philosophers, who used to "spend their time in nothing except telling or hearing something new" (Acts 17:21). Paul's riveting story about the God of the universe who appointed his Son to die and be resurrected three days later was so attention-grabbing that some of the leading philosophers in the town invited him to speak before the Areopagus, the meeting place of the influential political and religious leaders of the town.

After Paul shared the story about the true God of the world, people in the audience responded in one of three ways. The first group immediately rejected Paul's message. The story about God's bringing to life his appointed heir and Son was too far-fetched to believe. Within their rival story of how the world was created and how the gods would maintain it, they could not make sense of Paul's fanciful message. The second group, some of whom perhaps eventually entered the Christian fold, were touched by this strange story but wanted to process the apostle's message before becoming disciples. The final group, who immediately received the message with faith, accepted the story that Paul recounted and were probably baptized soon thereafter.

Reflecting on the Biblical Message Today

Every time I read through the book of Acts and the episode where Paul enters Athens and preaches the gospel, I still get goose bumps. I quickly imagine what Paul must have felt as he walked through the sun-drenched and dust-filled roads of one of the most ancient and religious cities of the world. It was no doubt similar to the way Martin Luther must have felt the first and only time he visited Rome. After weeks of walking and wandering through countless towns and villages in Western Europe, sleeping and eating sparingly, he enters the center and glory of the Christian world—Rome. However, instead of seeing devoutness, faithfulness, and sacrificial living, he sees greed, godlessness, and gluttony. His heart breaks, and within a few years he would renounce his orders as an Augustinian monk in the Catholic Church and move in a very different theological direction.

Paul, although a Roman citizen and a traveler of the world, was not impressed with the mighty city of Athens. Nor did he waste any time. He immediately began surveying the religious panorama and traveling to the major religious sites and temples in the town. This inevitably took him to the highest point in the city, to the Acropolis. Here the Greeks and Romans had worshiped rival deities to the God of the Bible for hundreds of years. Temples in honor of and statues dedicated to deities such as Zeus and Athena were in active use, and the area was bustling with religious activity. After taking the religious pulse of the city, the apostle began sharing the story of Jesus with any and all who listened.

Fig. I.1. The Parthenon in Athens, Greece, which was a temple dedicated to the goddess Athena and by which the apostle Paul would have passed in his travels.

Closer to Home

Paul's heroic engagement with the religious practices and stories in Athens could be relegated to the type of scene that could happen only in the Bible. But that would be a mistake. The world in which we live today is perhaps closer to the world Paul inhabited than it has been for hundreds of years. Indeed, the world is becoming smaller each day—as technology advances, international opportunities expand, and immigration increases. Now, more than ever, people of different ethnic and religious identity are living as neighbors.

At the seminary where I teach, in a typical suburban setting in the United States, there is great ethnic and religious diversity. Within a few miles of the school, there are booming Hindu, Buddhist, and Muslim populations. Week after week, these groups attend religious meetings by the hundreds, and the statistics only indicate further growth among these populations. When I teach Christianity and world religions at the seminary, I require students to attend two different non-Christian religious services. For the initial trip, I take them with me, so they can gain enough confidence for a second trip to a different religious site on their own. Time after time, I hear the same response after they research and locate non-Christian meeting places in their communities: "I can't believe there is a mosque just miles from the church I attend!" or "Who would have ever thought there is a Buddhist temple just minutes from my house!"

Despite the prevalence of non-Christian populations in North America and their continual growth, it has been my experience that Christians know very little about other faiths. It is not surprising, therefore, that they have minimal engagement with these communities and the individuals who inhabit them. This is true not only for laypeople but also for Christian pastors and leaders. When I teach students Christianity and world religions, I begin each class with a pop quiz, which gauges the students' knowledge of other religions. It probably does not come as a surprise that no one has ever passed! Although after the quiz we have a good laugh about our religious illiteracy, this quiz signals a great need. The simple fact is that most Christians cannot explain the difference between a Sunni and a Shiite Muslim, or what a Hindu believes is the goal of existence, or what are the essential teachings of the Buddha.

Now, one could make the argument that learning about other religions is not an important endeavor. In theory, I am willing to grant this. In practice, however, I do not accept this. Here is why: It has been my overwhelming experience that Christians who learn about other religions interact more with people who follow these other religions. In other words, if you know nothing about Islam and have no desire to learn anything about it, there is a good chance that you do not know any Muslims or have any interaction with them. However, if you do know the essentials of Islam, if you have ever read a portion of the Qur'an, or if you have ever visited a mosque, there is a very good chance that you personally know and interact with Muslims.

Those Christians who do know about other religions are in a greater position to share Christ's love for them and thus to love their neighbors as themselves. I am amazed and humbled at the stories I hear from students after taking a class on world religions. Just recently, a Presbyterian pastor in one of my classes chose to visit a mosque for his assignment. There he was warmly received and the imam—the Muslim pastor of the community—invited him for lunch later that week. At lunch, the imam asked the pastor if he would be willing to teach the youth group (numbering more than 100) in his community what Christians believed about Jesus! What an amazing opportunity—all of which happened because a Christian was willing to learn more about another religion and venture outside his comfort zone.

Now, I know what you may be thinking: *I picked up this book to learn more about other religions, not to attend a Muslim service or have lunch with an imam!* If this describes you, you have not picked up the wrong book: Please keep reading! The primary objective of this book is to get a guided tour of the world's most influential religions. Whatever the outcome of learning about other religions may be, we will leave this in the hands of our great and all-wise God. For the time being, it is my prayer that God would use this book to help Christians learn about other religions, so that we can, as Peter exhorts, "always [be] prepared to make a defense to anyone who asks [us] for a reason for the hope that is in [us]" (1 Peter 3:15).

PART 1

The Six Rival Stories of the World

The last several decades have witnessed a dramatic increase in the power of stories to structure and give meaning to life. Indeed, stories are important vehicles used to transmit ideas. One of the primary objectives of this book is to understand the rival stories of the world. As is probably assumed, there are many more competing stories than we have time to address in this book. But we will focus on what I believe are the six most influential religious stories that rival the Christian story.

The first part of this book will discuss the essentials of the six rival stories of the world in five chapters. Each chapter will contain six parts: (1) the beginning of the story, (2) the religion's historical origin, (3) religious writings, (4) beliefs,[1] (5) worship practices, and (6) a point of contact with the religion. Because this is an introductory book, we will focus on the main points of each of these religions. At the same time, I include many details about each religion that will give us an informed overview of the religious stories of the world.

---

1. In a couple of chapters, parts 3 and 4 have been reversed.

Hinduism: The Story of Diversity and Devotion

Hinduism is by far the most complex religion in the world, shading under its enormous parasol an incredibly diverse array of contrasting beliefs, practices, and denominations.

Linda Johnsen

Hinduism is not organized in the way we see most religions in the world. It does not have a particular founder, savior, book, leader, or holy place. It has no specific day of the week to observe, or call to prayer, or certain ritual that everyone must observe. It is decentralized and localized in a way in which it allows anyone to observe the basic principles that are best for him or her.

Stephen Knapp

There can be as many Hindu Gods as there are devotees to suit the moods, feelings, emotions and social backgrounds of the devotees.

Sri Ramakrishna

Part 1: The Beginning

In a beginning, says Hinduism—not *the* beginning—the universe was full of water. In the middle of the water was an ever-growing egg, which was surrounded by the four elements of wind, fire, water, and sky. In the middle of the egg was Vishnu, one of the three most powerful gods in the Hindu pantheon. Vishnu was floating on the egg in the water and took the form of Brahma, the god of creation, who then created everything. When it is time to destroy this present world

3

before creating the next, Vishnu will take the form of Shiva, the god of destruction. Together these gods—the Hindu trinity—create, sustain, and destroy the universe.[1]

In a beginning—so goes another Hindu creation story—the universe was but a soul or *atman*. Because it desired a mate, it became as big as a man and a woman who were embracing, and divided its body in two. Together they produced humankind. Afterward the soul of the woman became a cow, and the soul of the man became a bull. From their union cows were born. The soul of the cow proceeded to turn into every female animal species, just as the soul of the bull transformed itself into every male animal species until all animals, "down to ants," were created. Eventually the original soul created everything else in the world in a similar way. At the conclusion of the creation account, it was discovered that the soul was actually Brahman—Pure Awareness or the Supreme Reality. This reinforces the idea that everything is either directly or indirectly connected to Brahman.[2]

In a beginning—so goes just one more Hindu creation story— there was nothing in the universe. In fact, the universe was not there either! The only thing that existed was the Brahman or Divine Essence, which was without beginning or end. Lord Vishnu manifested himself on the water, where he slept on a great egg. While he was asleep, a lotus flower appeared out of his navel, and it grew and grew. From that lotus flower emerged the god Brahma—not to be confused with Brahman, of which Brahma is just one manifestation.

Brahma was curious about the origin of this lotus flower, and began asking himself the basic questions of life: "Who am I and where have I originated? What is the purpose of my existence?"[3] So he traveled for a hundred years to find the origin of the lotus flower; when he could not find it, he took another hundred years to return to his original home. Eventually he fell asleep from exhaustion. When he awoke, the four-armed Lord Vishnu was standing before him, and ordered him to perform meditation. Brahma did not realize that Vishnu was the origin of the lotus flower that bore him, so he was put off by this other being ordering him around! Immediately the two got into a fight and continued fighting until they saw the image of the god Shiva standing before them. They agreed to stop fighting

1. This creation story is based on the "Vishnu Purana," in *The Vishnu Purana*, trans. H. H. Wilson (Calcutta, 1894).

2. This creation story is based on the "Brihadaranyaka Upanishad," in *The Bible of the World*, ed. Robert Ballou (New York: Viking Press, 1939), 38–41.

3. The "Shiva Purana," in *Shiva Purana*, trans. B. K. Chaturvedi (New Delhi: Diamond Pocket Books, 2006), 10.

so that they could locate the origin of the shadow. They searched for
thousands of years, to no avail.

Fig. 1.1. Statue
of the Hindu
god Vishnu on a
temple wall.

Similar to the case before, the two gods Vishnu and Brahma ceased
searching and decided to pray. After a hundred years of praying, the
five-faced and ten-armed Shiva appeared before them. It was good
that they were all together, they agreed. Shiva made an important
announcement:

> We are all three parts of the same entity. We are one and the same
> though having different forms. Brahma is the creator, Vishnu is the
> preserver, [and] I am the destroyer . . . . There is another being named

Rudra who will originate from my body. But understand that Rudra and I will not be different.[4]

Once each of their roles had been established, creation began. In this way, these three supreme Hindu gods created humankind and everything that exists.

So go three of the more interesting creation stories of Hinduism. There are many more creation stories—thousands more. If you are anything like me, you may be wondering how it's possible to have multiple creation accounts. Isn't there only one? In Hinduism there are two ways to answer this question. The first is that there are myriad accounts of creation. And none of these is perceived as "contradicting" another. Rather, each of these stories refracts the tiny light of a much greater reality. Unlike Western expressions of Christianity, Hinduism is much more accepting of diversity and paradox.

The other part of the answer is that there are innumerable beginnings and ends of creation. Hindus believe the world has been created and destroyed countless times. So it is theoretically possible that one creation story contains one actual creation account, while a different one contains another. In Hindu thinking, the universe is billions of years old, and it goes through continual cycles of creation and destruction that repeat themselves just like the four seasons. As one Hindu practitioner explains:

> Hindus experience time as cyclical, not progressing forward toward a final point as folks believe in Judaism, Christianity, and Islam. This concept is important because it leads to a completely different understanding of human history and of our role in the divine plan.[5]

According to Hinduism, when our present world cycle ends, another will be created. These cycles will continue in perpetuity. The cycle we are currently in is called *Kali*. Some believe this cycle began in 3102 BC at the time of the great Indian epic, the Mahabharata.[6] Characterized by darkness, vice, and short life spans (only 120 years for human beings), the Kali cycle lasts 432,000 years. It will eventually be replaced by a longer and more stable cycle. In line with Hindu thought, most of us who are alive today will eventually experience this new cycle—although we will do so in a different reincarnation of ourselves!

4. Ibid., 10–11.
5. Linda Johnsen, *The Complete Idiot's Guide to Hinduism*, 2nd ed. (New York: Alpha, 2009), 8.
6. John Keay, *India: A History* (New York: HarperCollins, 2000), 3.

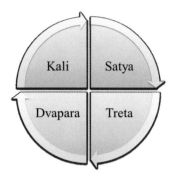

Fig. 1.2. The four cycles of Hinduism.

As far as these different cycles of creation and destruction are concerned, no one knows exactly when the earth was created. Nor is there any founder or apparent origin of Hinduism. Instead, practitioners of Hinduism assert that this religion has always existed, and is therefore called in Sanskrit—a Hindu religious language similar to Latin in Christianity—*Sanatana Dharma* or "the eternal religion." This is a shocking declaration to some Christians, who believe that our Judeo-Christian heritage is the sole claimant of being the world's oldest religion. On the contrary, Hindu practitioners understand their views and values to reside within the fabric of the universe itself. The laws and principles of Hinduism, it is believed, are interconnected with the laws of the cosmos. And regardless of which cycle we may find ourselves in—or even in what planet or solar system—these principles are eternally true.

Part 2: Historical Origin

As I mentioned above, Hinduism does not have an easily traceable historical origin. Whereas, for instance, historical figures like Siddhartha Gautama (d. 483 BC) and Muhammad (d. AD 632) serve as convenient beginning points for Buddhism and Islam, respectively, Hinduism has the distinction of having no founder or religious leader. Thus, rather than turning to a specific historical figure to demarcate its origin, it is better to understand Hinduism as a melding together of four common periods—or, as one religious scholar describes these periods, a series of geological layers.[7] In this configuration, we could classify all the great diversity that we call "Hinduism" into four clearly identifiable layers or traditions—all of which, it is important to note, are

7. Stephen Prothero, *God Is Not One: The Eight Rival Religions That Rule the World—and Why Their Differences Matter* (New York: HarperCollins, 2010), 139.

legitimate expressions of this religion or way of life: (1) Indus, (2) Vedic, (3) Wisdom, and (4) Devotion.

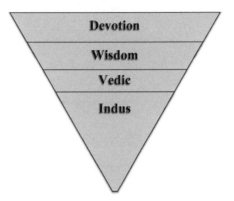

Fig. 1.3. The four traditions or "layers" of Hinduism.

First Hindu Layer: Indus Civilization

The first tradition, or perhaps pre-tradition, of Hinduism is traced back to a people who lived in current-day Pakistan and northwest India. They are called Aryans or Indo-Aryans. As a group, the Aryans thrived about four thousand years ago, and they are mentioned in the oldest Hindu scriptures, the Vedas. The Aryan society was a highly developed one, whose geographical reach encompassed the entirety of Greater India—a land that included modern-day countries such as India, Afghanistan, Bangladesh, Nepal, and Pakistan. It is debated whether this society was indigenous to Greater India or whether it came from a different location. Either way, it was through this culture that the term *Hindu* originated. The story of how this people group came to be known as Hindus goes like this:

> One of the neighboring countries [of the Aryans], Persia, had a common border with ancient India, which at that time was known as Aryavarta—the land of the Aryans. This common border between Persia and ancient India was the river Indus, called in Sanskrit, Sindhu. The Persians could not pronounce Sindhu correctly; they pronounced it Hindu. They also called the Aryans, living on the other side of the river Sindhu, Hindus; thus the religion of the Aryans became known as Hinduism.[8]

With the rise of Christian missionaries from Europe and North America in the nineteenth century, the names *Hindu* and *Hinduism* stuck, and they

---

8. Swami Bhaskarananda, *The Essentials of Hinduism: A Comprehensive Overview of the World's Oldest Religion* (Seattle: Viveka Press, 2002), 2.

have become synonymous with essentially all the people from Greater India who are not Muslim. Over time the term also came to encompass those in this region who were not Buddhist, Jainist, Sikh, or Christian.

Second Hindu Layer: Vedic Period

It is from the Aryans that the second tradition of Hinduism emerges. Known as the Vedic period, this era is perhaps best associated with the influence of the caste system—with the Brahmins or priestly class at the top of the rung. As a passage from the Rig Veda, the oldest of the Vedas, explains:

> One fourth of Brahman constituted all beings, while three fourths of him are immortal and stand above. With the one fourth below, he extended on all sides into animate and the inanimate . . . His face became Brahman. His arms were made into the Kshatriya, his thighs became the Vaishya; from his feet the Shudra was born. (RV 10.90.3–4, 12)[9]

At the top of the caste system were the Brahmins, who were seen as being constituted out of Brahman itself, which is Pure Awareness or Supreme Reality—what we as Christians might call an impersonal god. This priestly class was significant because it was the only group that could perform vital cultural and religious rituals and pronounce sacred mantras to the gods for sustenance and balance in the world.

CASTE	RANK	DESCRIPTION (AND *DHARMA*)
Priests (*Brahmins*)	Highest	Traditionally assigned to studying and teaching the Vedas, and performing vital rituals
Warriors (*Kshatriyas*)	Second highest	Assigned to protect and govern people. Includes politicians, princes, military, and police officers
Merchants (*Vaishyas*)	Second lowest	Assigned to take care of business. Includes the middle class, such as teachers, merchants, and businesspeople
Servants (*Shudras*)	Lowest	Assigned to serve those in the three castes above. Includes farmers and manual laborers
Untouchables (*Dhalits*)	No class	The people who have no status and cannot participate fully in their religion

9. Wendy Doniger, trans., *The Rig Veda* (London: Penguin, 1981), 61.

Below the priestly (Brahmin) class were the remaining castes: warriors, businesspeople, menial laborers, and finally the untouchables—those who do not even qualify as being part of this system. In association with each caste, there is a *dharma* or responsibility. For the warriors, it is to protect; for the businesspeople, it is to take care of business and finance; and for the menial laborers, it is to serve. Largely acknowledged but frequently misunderstood, the caste system or *varna* ("color") has played an extremely influential role in the history of Hinduism for centuries.

It was during the Vedic period that the first of the four Vedas or sacred scriptures, the Rig Veda, was composed. These texts date to the time of Moses.[10] In the Vedic period, the two main gods worshiped were Agni, the god of fire, and Indra, the god of storms. Although each of the Hindu traditions today traces its origin back to the Vedic period, this era's most notable gods like Agni and Indra "have lost their importance and now play only a quite subordinate role."[11] Indeed, I have never met a Hindu who believed them to have any real importance in their lives or in Hindu thought.

Third Hindu Layer: Philosophical Tradition

Instead of focusing on the Vedic gods and the vast rituals that only the top three classes in the caste system can participate in, the third tradition of Hinduism—which emphasizes wisdom and philosophy—gives prominence to different gods and concepts that have been connected with the Hindu religion ever since this time. This includes concepts such as reincarnation, karma, and *advaita* or non-duality, the doctrine that all is one and nothing is separate from another being. Rather than turning to manifestations of the Divine Essence or Brahman, practitioners of this third tradition of Hinduism turn internally to the Brahman within each person.

Over the years, Hindus have distilled the vast teaching of this tradition into four truths called The Great Contemplations or The Great Utterances, which ultimately lead to one essential concept: I and Brahman are one. This is often a hard teaching for my students to grasp, so accustomed as we are to think of the creator as "wholly other"—as one Christian theologian asserts—and completely distinct from creation. Whereas Christians believe that God created humankind in his image—

10. William Young, *The World's Religions: Worldviews and Contemporary Issues* (Upper Saddle River, NJ: Pearson Prentice Hall, 2005), 59.

11. Hans Kung et al., *Christianity and World Religions: Paths to Dialogue with Islam, Hinduism, and Buddhism* (New York: Maryknoll, 2001), 151.

but not out of his own body—so Hindus influenced by this philosophical tradition, by contrast, believe that Brahman resides in every sentient being like a drop of water comes from the sea. In this way, you and I are one with all of creation.

Truth	Sources
Consciousness is Brahman.	*Aitareya Upanishad* 3.3 of Rig Veda (RV)
I am Brahman.	*Brihadaranyaka Upanishad* 1.4.10 of Yajur Veda (YV)
You are Brahman.	*Chandogya Upanishad* 6.8.7 of Sama Veda (SV)
The self and Brahman are one.	*Mandukya Upanishad* 1.2 of Atharva Veda (AV)

Fourth Hindu Layer: Devotional Hinduism

Although it is important and helpful to recognize the earlier forms of Hinduism, today the most common form of Hinduism is what may be referred to as devotional or *bhakti* Hinduism. In contrast with Brahmin priests performing rituals or gurus pursuing union with the Supreme Reality by renouncing the world or endlessly meditating, devotional Hinduism is about the average man or woman devoting his or her life to a god without leaving the comforts of life. This form of Hinduism is encapsulated by a well-known chapter in the Bhagavad Gita, which is a section of a much larger epic poem called the Mahabharata. In this chapter in the Gita, Lord Krishna informs his pupil Arjuna:

> Whosoever desires to worship whatever deity (using whatever name, form, and method) with faith, I make their faith steady in that very deity. Endowed with steady faith they worship that deity, and fulfill their wishes through that deity. Those wishes are, indeed, granted only by Me. (7:21–22)[12]

The meaning of this passage is straightforward. All you have to do in this life is choose whichever god you want to be devoted to and then be obedient to him or her. It need not matter whether this god is Krishna, Jesus, Allah, a planet, or even a person—since each of these is seen as a representation of the same True Reality: Brahman. Your sincere devotion to this incarnation or expression of god is all that is needed.

12. Shri Purohit Swami, trans., *Bhagavad Gita: Annotated and Explained* (Woodstock, VT: SkyLight Paths, 2010), 63.

The majority of Hindus in the world practice devotional Hinduism. As one contemporary author writes, "Hinduism today is a way of devotion."[13] To devotional Hindus, their gods are real, personal, and faithful. In fact, I have witnessed practicing Hindus dedicate as much devotion, care, and love to their personal god as I have seen in many other religions—including Christianity. One of the most famous Hindu devotional worshipers was a Brahmin priest and guru named Ramakrishna (1836–86), who lovingly spent hours a day worshiping the goddess Kali. As one English Hindu practitioner writes about Ramakrishna and his devotion to Kali:

> [Ramakrishna's] absolute trust in and devotion to the Mother [goddess Kali] led him from stage to stage of ecstasy, empowerment, and revelation of her nature in all its dazzling and paradoxical formal and formless aspects until, at last, he came to know her to be as inseparable from Brahman the absolute reality "as burning is from fire."[14]

Fig. 1.4. *Murti* (or sacred statue) of the Hindu goddess Kali, stepping on her husband Shiva in a temple in Malaysia.

13. Prothero, *God Is Not One*, 153.

14. Swami Nikhilananda, trans., *Selections from the Gospel of Sri Ramakrishna: Annotated and Explained* (Woodstock, VT: SkyLight Paths, 2002), viii.

Part 3: Religious Writings

Unlike Islam or Christianity, whose scriptural canons are closed and relatively small, the sacred writings of Hinduism are enormous and ongoing. It is not unheard of for gurus to compose new scriptural texts in the present, although they do not carry the same weight as the more historical and established writings. As I mentioned above, at the foundation of the structural basis of Hindu sacred texts are the Vedas. One author writes succinctly, "The four Vedas form the core of our religion."[15] The traditional author, or at least compiler, of the Vedas (as well as the older Hindu scriptures) was Vyasa, a man believed to have lived over five thousand years ago.[16]

	Writings	Content
Heard **(Shruti)**	*Vedas*	Four sacrificial and ritual works
	Brahmanas	Instructions for priests
	Sutras	Instructions for all people
	Laws of Manu	Instructions for all people
	Upanishads	Philosophical meditations
Received **(Smrti)**	*Mahabharata*	Epic of war between tribes
	Bhagavad Gita	Vital section of Mahabharata
	Ramayana	Epic story about Rama
	Puranas	Stories about various gods*

* Modified from Winfried Corduan, *Pocket Guide to World Religions* (Downers Grove, IL: InterVarsity Press, 2006), 70.

Somewhat similar to the notion of two types of canonical writings in Catholicism—first and most important, the proto-canonical or first-canonized writings (which virtually every Christian tradition accepts), and second, the deutero-canonical or second-canonized writings (which Protestants call the Apocrypha and reject as not divinely inspired)[17]—Hinduism has two sets of sacred texts. The oldest scriptures are called *shruti* ("that which is heard"), since they were believed to have been intuited by seers. These seers were spiritual masters who supposedly entered deep states of consciousness to hear the words of the universe to write down in their scriptures. The other group is called *smrti* ("that which is received"), since they were conceived, formulated, and written

15. Sri Chandrasekharendra Saraswati, *The Vedas*, 7th ed. (Mumbai: Bhavan's Book University, 2009), 3.

16. Johnsen, *Hinduism*, 48.

17. Michael Gorman, ed., *Scripture: An Ecumenical Introduction to the Bible and Its Interpretation* (Peabody, MA: Hendrickson, 2005), 11.

by humans.[18] Although these distinctions are still maintained, some in the second group of religious writings are just as famous and beloved as those in the first. It is difficult to date many of these texts, although many Hindus claim they are the most ancient of religious writings.[19]

The four Vedas ("knowledge"), like the Torah or first five books of the Jewish and Christian Bibles, are foundational. Although they are rarely read today by modern Hindus, they contain vestiges of the Vedic period from many thousands of years ago. The Vedas are composed in Vedic, an ancient form of Sanskrit, and include countless hymns directed toward a variety of gods as well as sacrificial rituals for Brahmin priests to perform. For the uninitiated, the Vedas are difficult to understand. They require a teacher to explain the spiritual or inner meaning of the literal words. The other main group of writings in the first order of canonized scriptures is the Upanishads ("sitting nearby"), which were written by the philosophers and contain stories between teachers and their pupils as well as mystical interpretations or reflections on the Vedas. There are more than two hundred Upanishads, although one hundred eight are usually grouped as the core ones.

In addition to the first order of canonized Hindu scriptures, there are a number of beloved sacred texts in the second order. We saw one group of these writings, the Puranas ("of ancient times"), in the beginning of the chapter when I discussed creation myths. These are traditionally eighteen in number, although, of course, the fluidity of the Hindu canon allows for more. These contain creation stories or myths. The Ramayana ("Rama's journey") and Mahabharata ("great telling of India") are both epics, and are very long books. The first is about the god Rama, who is an incarnation or avatar of the god Vishnu, and his ventures to recover his wife Sita from a demon. The latter is a story about two rival clans who wage war against each other and find themselves in difficult situations requiring wisdom and sound ethics. A small section of this epic—which is otherwise about four times as long as the entire Bible!—is called the Bhagavad Gita ("song of god"). In this beloved book, the god Krishna serves as a spiritual guide to the warrior Arjuna. And Arjuna, realizing what an amazing opportunity he has to speak face-to-face with a god, asks to see what the Supreme Reality looks like—a request that Krishna obliges.

Part 4: Beliefs

As may be gathered, Hinduism is one of the most diverse of world religions. Unlike Islam, for instance, which requires assent to key articles

---

18. Winfried Corduan, *Pocket Guide to World Religions* (Downers Grove, IL: InterVarsity Press, 2006), 70–71.

19. Johnsen, *Hinduism*, 48.

of faith such as belief in one omnipotent God—known as Allah or "the God"—as well as the finality of Allah's messenger Muhammad, Hinduism is not nearly as dogmatic. To an outsider, one can get the impression that anything goes with Hinduism. Although not exactly true, the religion does have different scriptures, different gods, different worship practices, different postures toward one's purpose or goal in life, and different ways to pursue whatever goal of life one wants to observe. As history of religions scholar Huston Smith writes:

> If we were to take Hinduism as a whole—its vast literature, its complicated rituals, its sprawling folkways, its opulent art—and compress it into a single affirmation, we would find it saying: You can have what[ever] you want.[20]

Hinduism is less about a set of stringent doctrines and timeless beliefs and more about what one makes of it. In this sense, one scholar quite rightly points out, "There is nothing that you can say about Hindus or Hinduism without some form of qualification."[21]

Compare Hinduism with Buddhism, for example. Although there is great diversity within Hinduism's largest religious offshoot, there is probably less than in Hinduism—no doubt because Buddhism has a definite historical founder who serves as a measuring rod of orthodoxy (right belief) and orthopraxy (right practice). Hinduism does not.[22] At the same time, it is not quite true to imply that anything goes within Hinduism. Although there are not necessarily religious leaders evaluating one's beliefs to determine whether one is "in" or "out," there are some shared beliefs and attitudes. Below is a list of nine commonalities within the Hindu religion. Although not every Hindu would agree with these articles—again, Hinduism is perhaps the most diverse of all the major religions—these articles nevertheless serve as a good starting point for discussion about Hindu core beliefs.

Nine Beliefs of Hinduism[23]

1. Hindus believe in one all-pervasive Supreme Being [Brahman] who is both immanent and transcendent, both Creator and Unmanifest Reality.

20. Huston Smith, *The World's Religions: Our Great Wisdom Traditions* (San Francisco: HarperCollins, 1991), 13.
21. Stephen Jacobs, *Hinduism Today: An Introduction* (London: Continuum, 2010), 6.
22. Gavin Flood, *An Introduction to Hinduism* (Cambridge: Cambridge University Press, 1996), 10.
23. See the following website: http:// www.hinduismtoday.com.

2. Hindus believe in the divinity of the four Vedas, the world's most ancient scripture, and venerate the Agamas as equally revealed. These primordial hymns are God's word and the bedrock of *Sanatana Dharma*, the eternal religion.

3. Hindus believe that the universe undergoes endless cycles of creation, preservation, and dissolution.

4. Hindus believe in karma, the law of cause and effect by which each individual creates his own destiny by his thoughts, words, and deeds.

5. Hindus believe that the soul reincarnates, evolving through many births until all karmas have been resolved, and *moksha*, liberation from the cycle of rebirth, is attained. Not a single soul will be deprived of this destiny.

6. Hindus believe that divine beings exist in unseen worlds and that temple worship, rituals, sacraments, and personal devotionals create a communion with these *devas* and gods.

7. Hindus believe that an enlightened master, or *satguru*, is essential to know the Transcendent Absolute, as are personal discipline, good conduct, purification, pilgrimage, self-inquiry, meditation, and surrender in God.

8. Hindus believe that all life is sacred, to be loved and revered, and therefore practice *ahimsa*, noninjury, in thought, word, and deed.

9. Hindus believe that no religion teaches the only way to salvation above all others, but that all genuine paths are facets of God's Light, deserving tolerance and understanding.

The nine beliefs above serve as a good rubric from which to discuss the core elements of Hindu thinking. Because discussing all nine of these articles would require a book in and of itself, we will limit our discussion in this section to the first article: the Supreme Being. This immediately distinguishes the Hindu religion from, on the one extreme, Buddhism, which classically denies a personal god, and, on the other extreme, Islam, which asserts the existence of *the* only God: Allah. It has been estimated that there are 330 million gods within Hinduism, but there is no requirement to believe in one or another. In this way, there is great diversity. In fact, there are several potential beliefs concerning the nature and number of gods:

1. There is one God, and all the other "gods" are mere manifestations of the one true God.

2. There are many gods.
3. There is no god, just our own imaginations conceiving of different gods.

For Christians, this is strange and does not make sense. How can different people be of the *same religion* when one person believes in many gods, while another person believes in one—or none! I distinctly remember having a conversation with a group of Hindu believers from India at a Hindu temple when I asked how many gods there are. Without blinking, they responded in unison: "We believe in one god!"

"Then how," I rejoined, "are there so many different gods in Hinduism?"

Again in unison, they replied: "There is one supreme God that cannot be fully known or understood. The gods we talk about on earth and give devotion to are simply manifestations of that one supreme God."

This gets to the core of a common misconception about Hinduism. Although there are countless "gods"—whether Shiva or Vishnu or Ganesha or Parvati or Hanuman—these gods are commonly understood by Hindus as representations of the true God, whom we cannot fathom. This is why one Hindu can worship Shiva, while another worships Kali. Although each person seems to be worshiping a different god, the person is really worshiping only the one true God, who is manifest through Shiva or Kali or whomever. How do you decide which god to worship? It depends. Some people worship specific gods because of the town or village they live in or because of their family or place in the caste system.

More pragmatically, some worship a particular god because of that god's association with a specific thing. I remember one conversation I was recently having with a Hindu priest about this very topic. He said that perhaps the most popular deity in his temple was the goddess Lakshmi. I asked him why, and he was quick to reply: "Because most of the people in our temple would like more money, so it's natural to worship her, who has cascades of gold coins rushing down from her hands!" In the temple where he presided, he said, it is not that some people prefer Shiva or some people prefer Vishnu—two of the most popular gods in the Hindu pantheon. Instead, people worship this god or that god based on their need of the moment. Are you about to go on a business trip? Then ask for guidance from Ganesha, the god of venture and journey. Are you in need of money? Then ask Lakshmi!

Fig. 1.5. Statue of Ganesha, one of the most beloved Hindu gods.

Part 5: Worship Practices

Unlike Christians, who have historically worshiped on Sunday mornings, Hindus do not have a prescribed service or time of worship, a practice that is called *puja* ("reverence"). In fact, most Hindus have their own personal shrines at home and do not necessarily attend a temple on a regular basis. They are able to perform *puja* at home on their own (or, for wealthier families, with the aid of a priest). They will feed, clothe, and give worship to these household gods on a daily basis. These gods are small statues called *murtis* ("embodiment") that are imbued with the divine through a ceremony by a priest, and Hindu practitioners need to make use of the priest and temple only on special occasions—such as for festivals, for individual requests, or for making or fulfilling vows. For those who do attend a Hindu temple, a religious service typically includes a congregational *puja* three times a day where the priest performs a special ceremony or ritual.[24] Individuals are also able to make use of the temple through the rituals of the priest for a fee. The highlight of many services is *darshan* ("sight"), when a person is "seen" by the god that he or she is devoted to—or even by a guru—in order to receive a transaction of blessing.

In terms of worship practices, there are three main paths or *yogas* ("yokes") to God,[25] which we discussed in a section above. Depending on which religious path one takes, this compels one to live a certain way.

24. Winfried Corduan, *Neighboring Faiths: A Christian Introduction to World Religions* (Downers Grove, IL: InterVarsity Press, 1998), 208.

25. There is sometimes added a fourth way, called *raja yoga*, which is for the advanced and focuses on the mind and meditation.

Although the term *yoga* in the West generally conjures up the image of a fit person trying to make a workout spiritual as well as physical, this type of yoga in Hinduism, called *hatha yoga* ("path of persistence"), is not common or particularly spiritual.[26] As the related term *yoke* in English suggests, *yoga* means yoking or uniting something to something else—in the case of Hinduism, yoking one's soul or *atman* ("self") to the Supreme Reality or Brahman. For all practical purposes, the different ways of yoking one's soul to Brahman are paths that one can follow. Because there are several paths to the same destination, the paths are not mutually exclusive. They can be combined or they can be roads that individuals take at different phases of their lives.

The Different Types of Yoga as Illustrated in the Bhagavad Gita

Of the three established paths of uniting one's soul to the divine, the first one, called *karma yoga* ("path of action"), is about action or works. Specifically, it is the selfless action that one performs according to one's duty or station in life—including one's place within the caste system. It is about sacrificing your own ego or self in order to become one with and to be used by the divine. If you are a stay-at-home mother, for example, this means that you are to perform those duties that come with this line of work, and to do so cheerfully and without complaint. You are to understand your work without regard for your own benefit or advantage. You work for your husband, your children—and for your god. By doing so, you are able to be a channel of the divine and you are working out your own karma or deeds. In the beloved Bhagavad Gita, *karma yoga* is the type of yoga that is traditionally understood to be the first of three in that book. Although the protagonist Arjuna is demoralized because he does not want to fight his cousins, the god Krishna explains to him that it is his duty as a warrior in the caste system to fight—regardless of the consequence. By so doing, he is able to be a channel of the divine and to fulfill his purpose on earth. In short, the importance of living within the boundaries of the caste system in Hinduism cannot be overestimated.

As I have amply discussed above, the second type of yoga is by far the most common in Hinduism today. Called *bhakti yoga* ("path of devotion") or devotional Hinduism, this form of Hinduism is about showing love and devotion to a god or goddess of your choosing (among the millions of gods and goddesses available!). There are four major denominations or

26. Smith, *The World's Religions*, 27.

schools of thought within devotional Hinduism. In a manner of speaking, they recognize different gods as supreme:

1. The school of Vishnu (Vaishnavism), which venerates Vishnu, his wife Lakshmi, and Vishnu's incarnations (such as Krishna and Rama).
2. The school of Shiva (Shaivism), which venerates Shiva, his wife Parvati, and their son Ganesha.
3. The school of Shakti (Shaktism), which venerates goddesses such as Kali and Durga, who are both consorts of Shiva.
4. The school of Smarta (Smartism), which venerates any number or combination of gods.

TYPE	DESCRIP-TION	SECTION	EXCERPT FROM BHAGAVAD GITA
Works (*Karma Yoga*)	The (selfless) action one performs according to one's *dharma* or duty without desire of reward	Chaps. 1–6	"Perform all your actions with mind concentrated on the Divine, renouncing attachment and looking upon success and failure with an equal eye." (2.48)
Devotion (*Bhakti Yoga*)	Devotion to one's god (in this case, Krishna as the avatar of Lord Vishnu)	Chaps. 7–12	"Listen, O Arjuna! And I will tell you how you shall know me in my full perfection, practicing meditation with your mind devoted to me, and having me for your refuge." (7.1)
Knowledge (*Jnana Yoga*)	Distinguishing between what is real and unreal	Chaps. 13–18	"The one who can see the Supreme Lord in all beings, the Imperishable amid the perishable, this is the one who really sees." (13.27)*

* Shri Purohit Swami, trans., *Bhagavad Gita: Annotated and Explained* (Woodstock, VT: SkyLight Paths, 2010), 19, 59, 109.

Of all the different forms of Hinduism, *bhakti yoga*, or the way of loving attachment and devotion, is the path most like Christianity. As Christians direct our love, faith, and worship to God through the person of Jesus Christ, so *bhakti* practitioners direct their love and devotion to a particular god—whether Krishna, Kali, Vishnu, or another. And also like Christianity, the person who practices this type of yoga directs his or her love and adoration to a god who is personal and personable. This devotion is demonstrated by repeating the god's name, by offering the god fruit or flowers, and by offering worship and prayers to him or her.

The third type of Hindu religious practice is *jnana yoga* ("path of knowledge") or philosophical Hinduism. This is the path for the very spiritual. The goal is discrimination between what is real and what is unreal, and what is true and what is not true. The way toward discriminating between these things is by meticulous study and reflection. Through practice, one is then able to understand and apply the notion that we, as living beings, are not different from the Supreme Reality, and that I am not different from you. Like separating oil from water when poured into a glass, a *jnana yogi* has to separate the true and infinite self from the transient self. One common exercise for this type of yoga is practicing thinking and saying that it is not you, for instance, who is reading this book; rather, it is Josh or Janet—or whomever—who is reading this book! By doing so, you are able to detach yourself from the impermanent and thereby unify yourself to the permanent.

Part 6: Point of Contact

One way to think about the Hindu religion is to understand it as the journey of the soul. Like a hermit crab that uses a shell for a time before inevitably taking on a new one, Hinduism asserts that a soul or *atman* endures year after year, century after century, millennium after millennium. For one century it may be a man; for a millennium it could be another sentient being. This cyclical view of reality clashes with the Christian worldview. As Christians, we agree that life is a journey, but we do not see it as an endless cycle of death and rebirth. Thanks to Jesus Christ, who has conquered death, we do not have to fear what will happen to us after we die physically. We have entrusted our lives to the One who is Lord of both body and soul.

For Christians, the way we receive the benefits of Christ's death (and his conquering of death) is by trusting in him for the forgiveness of our sins. As the New Testament authors explain, "all have sinned and fall short of the glory of God" (Rom. 3:23), except, that is, for Jesus—who is the only One who was "without sin" (Heb. 4:15). We therefore turn to Jesus for our salvation. In Hindu thought, by contrast, one's sins do not warrant the sacrificial death of God's son; nor is salvation given prominence. What is more important for Hindus is not salvation from sin but liberation from the continual cycle of death and rebirth—what is called *samsara* ("continuous flow"). Liberation from this cycle comes about by uniting with the divine. This is accomplished by devoutly and resolutely following one of the major paths we discussed above. By following such a path, one will either ensure a better birth in the next reincarnation of oneself or, as an advanced guru, learn how to escape *samsara* and be forever united to Brahman. The latter is very difficult to do, so the average Hindu is resigned to seeking a better birth in the next lifetime.

Because of the great tolerance and syncretism of Hinduism, it is not uncommon for Christians to share their faith in Jesus with Hindus, and for Hindus to cheerfully add Jesus to their pantheon of gods. I remember having a conversation with a Hindu woman about my Christian faith in Jesus, and why it is important to worship him. "But I do worship Jesus," she said. "I have a statue of Jesus at my home that I pray to every day!" As Ramakrishna, one of the great Hindu teachers of the past few centuries, whom I mentioned above, once stated, "Truth leads to unity, ignorance to diversity." What Rama-krishna meant is that all religions, although seemingly different, are actually the same and lead to the same God. As Christians, we certainly believe in the unity of the body of Christ, but we deny that Jesus is only one of many ways to God. On the contrary, we believe that Jesus is "*the* way" (John 14:6) to God. There is not another path or yoga to the Father (1 John 5:12).

In the end, Hinduism is certainly a fascinating religion—one that is vibrant, diverse, and deeply spiritual. It is for this reason that it continues to attract practitioners in the West who are spiritually bankrupt and weary of the materialism and consumerism of our everyday lives. It is also attractive to many in the West because of what Christian author Os Guinness calls "the ABC (or 'anything but Christianity') mood" of the West, which fancies any religion that is fresh and lively—provided that it is not Christianity![27] As the West continues to come into more contact with the East, religions such as Hinduism—and the worldviews they espouse—will only become more prominent. It is for this reason that it is important to know more about this juggernaut of a religion—out of which, by the way, the term *juggernaut* originated[28]—so that we can know how to discern its teachings as well as how to respond to Hindus and fellow believers with gentleness and respect about the great hope that lies in us as Christians.

27. Os Guinness, *The Call: Finding and Fulfilling the Central Purpose in Your Life* (Nashville: Word Publishing Group, 2003), 145.

28. The term originated from a large craft used by Hindus in special ceremonies that carried *murtis* or Hindu gods. See Young, *The World's Religions*, 75.

Discussion Questions

1. Imagine what it would be like to view life as an unending cycle of reincarnation—life, death, and rebirth. How would this affect the way you approached each day? How would it affect your future planning?

2. In contrast with Christianity, Hinduism has thousands of creation stories. In the three Hindu stories included in this chapter, what differences are there between the Hindu gods and the God of the Bible in Genesis? Do these differences matter?

3. Given the popularity in the West of *hatha yoga*—or what most Americans would simply call *yoga*, conjuring up images of healthy, flexible people in aerobic garb—is it appropriate for Christians to engage in yoga for exercise purposes? Does considering the fact that *hatha yoga* is not particularly spiritual affect your opinion?

4. Some Hindus worship Jesus as a god. Does this open up the possibility of Christian dialogue and witness with Hindus? How does a Christian convey the ultimacy of Christ as the one "way"? What obstacles would there be to overcome in such a conversation?

5. The caste system is often viewed negatively by Westerners because of its lack of opportunity for social mobility. Many in the caste system believe that their station in life is their "fate," and that it cannot be changed. What kind of hope can the gospel of Jesus Christ offer to people in the caste system? Specifically, what hope does it offer to those living in the lowest, "untouchable" echelons of the caste system? What passages of the Bible come to mind?

Further Readings

Bhaskarananda, Swami. *The Essentials of Hinduism: A Comprehensive Overview of the World's Oldest Religion*. Seattle: Viveka Press, 2002.

Doniger, Wendy, trans. *The Rig Veda*. London: Penguin, 1981.

Flood, Gavin. *An Introduction to Hinduism*. Cambridge: Cambridge University Press, 1996.

Johnsen, Linda. *The Complete Idiot's Guide to Hinduism*. 2nd ed. New York: Alpha, 2009.

Keay, John. *India: A History*. New York: HarperCollins, 2000.

Purohit Swami, Shri, trans. *Bhagavad Gita: Annotated and Explained*. Woodstock, VT: SkyLight Paths, 2010.

Rodrigues, Hillary. *Introducing Hinduism*. London: Routledge, 2006.

chapter 2

Buddhism: The Story of Enlightenment

Suffering, the origin of suffering, the destruction of suffering, and the Noble Eightfold Path that leads to release from suffering—that is the safe refuge, that is the best refuge. A person is delivered from all pains after going to this refuge.

The Buddha

Rather than portray Buddhism as a philosophy or a way of life, as it is so often characterized in the West, I prefer to view Buddhism as a religion to which ordinary people have turned over the centuries for the means to confront, control, or even escape the exigencies of life.

Donald Lopez Jr.

Buddhism is older than Christianity, older than Islam, deeper than the Ganges River [referring to Hinduism] and the Mekong [in Southeast Asia]. Today, more than five hundred million people worldwide practice Buddhism, and it manifests in many different forms. But whatever shape it takes, it always strives to free human beings from the life of suffering. It is a philosophy of emancipation.

Stephen Asma

The designation Buddhist without further qualification conveys virtually no insight into what a person believes or practices. There are as many schools of Buddhism as there are Christian Protestant denominations, but the teachings of many of these schools appear to be irreconcilable beyond a very general core.

Winfried Corduan

Part 1: The Beginning

If Hinduism is the religion of infinite creation stories, Buddhism is the religion of none. According to Buddhist teaching, there is no beginning to the universe. Instead, what we call the universe is simply the combined experiences and actions of the universe's inhabitants as well as the physical elements that house these inhabitants. The life spans and living conditions of these residents are determined by the law of cause and effect—karma ("action").

There are traditionally understood to be six realms in which the inhabitants of the universe live. Known as the Wheel of Life, these realms represent the places where all beings are born and reborn based on their actions in former lives.[1] Aside from the fact that Buddhism views these realms to be cyclical rather than linear as in the (Christian) West, these realms are not completely different from the medieval Catholic construal of the universe as containing four levels: heaven, purgatory, earth, and hell.

The highest realm in the Buddhist universe or Wheel of Life is that of the gods.[2] However, the luxury and prosperity of gods' lives covers their eyes to the truth of suffering, and thus they are eventually reborn in another realm. The next level, where we currently reside, is the realm of potential enlightenment.[3] Here, humans are able either to seek awakening or to be consumed with the desire to acquire and possess. The next realm is that of the titans (demigods or demons), who are always fighting with the gods because they want to be like them. Next comes the realm of the ghosts. The ghosts are pitiable creatures whose necks are so thin that food is unable to pass to their perpetually hungry stomachs. The residents of the ghost realm live there because of their jealousy and greed in their former lives, although they were not so bad as to end up living in hell. The animal realm is marked by comfort, ignorance, and apathy. Finally, those living in the hell realm

1. As the Buddha said, "Some people are reborn. Evildoers go to sorrowful existences. Doers of good go to happy ones. Those who are free from all worldly desires attain nirvana" (9.11), in *Dhammapada: Annotated and Explained*, annot. and rev. Jack Maguire (Woodstock, VT: SkyLight Paths Publishing, 2005), 41.

2. This reference to "gods" does not mean Creator Gods as in Judaism or Islam but rather beings who have reached this level based on good karma.

3. As a Tibetan Buddhist monk explains, "Generally, there are three ways in which we can use our precious human life to realize its potential. We can use it to ensure that in future lives we will be born as a human being with all the conditions necessary for a happy and meaningful life; we can use it to attain complete liberation from suffering; or we can use it to attain full enlightenment, or Buddhahood, for the sake of all living beings." See G. K. Gyatso, *Introduction to Buddhism: An Explanation of the Buddhist Way of Life* (Glen Spey, NY: Tharpa Publications, 2008), 40.

are tormented by fire or frozen in ice. The residents of this regrettable realm likely led angry and abusive former lives.[4]

Fig. 2.1. The Wheel of Life in Buddhism.

Often portrayed at the center of this ever-turning Wheel of Life are a pig, a rooster (or bird), and a snake. Together these animals symbolize ignorance, attachment, and aversion, respectively, and are sometimes called the Three Poisons. As long as these types of vices or poisons are present in a living being, karma will dictate that he, she, or it will be born again in one of these different realms. It is only after desire or attachment is suspended that one's karma runs out like a shooting star, and one ceases to be imprisoned by the laws of cause and effect—which is the goal of enlightened human beings.

The question may arise concerning where karma originated, since karma is the source of power that holds everything together and continually gives birth to life and rebirth. Getting to the bottom of where or how karma originates, however, is a futile task. Like the God of the Bible, karma does not have a beginning. It has always existed. At the same time, however, although it is true to say that the universe—like karma—does not have a beginning as we understand this concept in the West, the universe does go through cycles.

Like Hinduism, Buddhism teaches that the universe develops through four periods or stages: creation, abiding, destruction, and nothingness.[5] The universe is always in one of these cycles. We, for instance, are living during the second stage, when beings inhabit the different realms discussed above. After the universe is destroyed and becomes nothingness, karma—like the rustling of leaves in a windstorm—will blow into this nothingness and living beings will once again begin to

4. Damien Keown, *Buddhism: A Very Short Introduction* (Oxford: Oxford University Press, 2000), 30–36.

5. Huston Smith and Philip Novak, *Buddhism: A Concise Introduction* (New York: HarperSanFrancisco, 2003), 19.

inhabit the universe. Or, to change images, after the universe is destroyed, karma—like a powerful magnet—will force all the bits of nothingness to unite. Then the period of abiding will be inaugurated.

It is sometimes difficult to understand the concept of how nothing can produce something or how something can come from nothing. As Christians, particularly Westernized Christians, we tend to think in a very linear fashion and highly value logical thinking. It is not easy for many of us to conceptualize—let alone visualize—how something can simultaneously exist yet not exist. This is a theme that my Buddhist friends point out to me regularly. Perhaps, then, there is an easier way to understand how Buddhism can say that the universe has *no* beginning while at the same time say that it *does* have a beginning.

The answer lies with the Buddha himself. As noted Buddhist practitioners and scholars Huston Smith and Philip Novak assert, "Buddha preached a religion that skirted speculation."[6] In other words, the Buddha intentionally refused to speculate about the origin of the universe and when or why or how the universe was created. Such questions, the Buddha thought, were fruitless. More to the point, the Buddha believed that attempts to probe these types of questions distracted a person from the ultimate issue of life: how to ease and altogether eliminate suffering. This was the only real question worth asking. An anecdote from the Buddha's life illustrates his aversion to the question of the universe's beginning:

> Should anyone say that he does not wish to lead the holy life under the Blessed One,[7] unless the Blessed One first tells him, whether the world is eternal or temporal, finite or infinite; whether the life principle is identical with the body, or something different; whether the Perfect One continues after death, etc.—Such a one would die, [unless] the Perfect One could tell him this.
>
> It is as if a man were pierced by a poisoned arrow and his friends, companions, or near relations called in a surgeon, but that man should say: I will not have this arrow pulled out until I know who the man is that has wounded me: whether he is a noble, a prince, a citizen, or a servant; or: whether he is tall, or short, or of medium height. [Surely], such a man would die, [unless] he could adequately learn all this.
>
> Therefore, the man who seeks his own welfare should pull out this arrow—this arrow of lamentation, pain, and sorrow.[8]

6. Ibid., 25.

7. Although this statement may give the impression that the Buddha relied on God ("the Blessed One"), this is just a figure of speech. The gods, if they existed at all, really had nothing to do with achieving enlightenment. They are referred to sometimes in early Buddhist thought simply because they are residues of Indian (Hindu) thought.

8. Dwight Goddard, *A Buddhist Bible*, 2nd ed. (Boston: Beacon Press, 1966), 35.

The arrow to which the Buddha refers is suffering. It is a poisoned arrow that directly leads to death. All that is important in this life is *the present*, namely, understanding that the arrow kills but that it can be eliminated. Theorizing about the past is pointless.

When understood in this context, we can see how Buddhism teaches that the universe has no beginning. For even if a person discovered exactly how or when or why the universe came into existence, this information would not bring us any closer to the reality of suffering and the attempt to eliminate it. In this way, we may say, the Buddha was hardly an abstract teacher or a theoretician. Rather, he was from beginning to end a practitioner—focused on the here and now rather than the there and then. As the Buddha said to his disciples, "greed for [speculation] tends not to edification."[9] What is most important is what is right in front of us: suffering.

Part 2: Historical Origin

Religious scholar Stephen Prothero summed it up best when he wrote that "Buddhism begins with a fairy tale."[10] Indeed, the lack of interest in a creation story in Buddhism is abundantly made up for by a rich and fanciful array of stories about the Buddha's life. Because these stories were written down by various groups of followers hundreds of years after the Buddha's death, there is a good degree of diversity in these writings and a fine line between historical fact and poetic license.

What Siddhartha Encountered	What It Symbolized
Sick person	Life is frail.
Old man	Age masters everyone.
Corpse	We will all die.
Ascetic	Liberation can occur.

The story of the Buddha's life begins when a prince of the warrior caste named Siddhartha Gautama (563–483 BC) was born to the Shakya tribe in present-day Lumbini, Nepal. Just as Jesus' birth was attended by praises from the angelic hosts (Luke 2:13–14), so Siddhartha's birth was attended by "thousands of waiting-women looking on with joy in their

9. E. A. Burtt, *The Teachings of the Compassionate Buddha* (New York: Mentor Books, 1955), 32.
10. Stephen Prothero, *God Is Not One: The Eight Rival Religions That Run the World—and Why Their Differences Matter* (New York: HarperCollins, 2010), 169.

hearts."[11] Although born as a human being, Siddhartha "did not enter the world in the usual manner, [for] he appeared like one descended from the sky." He entered the world in full awareness because he had meditated for eons (in countless previous lifetimes) before his present birth. He took seven steps after being born, and his first words indicated his purpose in this life: "For enlightenment I was born, for the good of all that lives. This is the last time that I have been born into this world of becoming."[12]

Despite the auspicious circumstances surrounding Siddhartha's miraculous birth and the fact that his mother received the best medical care available at the time, his mother Maya died from complications shortly after giving birth to her prized and remarkable son. To protect his son partly from the pains of the world and partly from the prophecy stated over Siddhartha after his birth by a Brahmin (Hindu) priest that he would be a great world king if he was not exposed to suffering (otherwise, he would be a holy man), Siddhartha's father Shuddhodana made every effort to provide all that Siddhartha would ever need or desire in order to influence the likelihood of his becoming a ruler. But his plan backfired. Instead of becoming a great king, Siddhartha would become a holy man.

Unfulfilled in life even with the best that money and power could provide, including a beautiful wife and loving son, Siddhartha bid farewell to his life of luxury and comfort at the age of twenty-nine. The impetus for this decision occurred over the course of four successive trips during which he encountered the realities of sickness, aging, death, and liberation, respectively. Known as the Great Signs, these excursions that Siddhartha took with his chariot driver awakened him to the fact that suffering left its mark like a handprint on everything in this world. He also realized that he had lived completely secluded and sheltered from this reality. His only hope was to understand what it all meant so that he could help others, and to this end he left everything in pursuit of awakening.

The next six years of Siddhartha's life were as exhausting as they were ineffective. He first studied with two Hindu (*raja*) gurus, but eventually learned all they could teach him. Siddhartha then joined a group of ascetics—those who believe they can master themselves spiritually by manipulating their physical bodies like a blacksmith beats down and forms a piece of metal. Instead of attaining spiritual enlightenment, however, the great prince only managed to starve himself nearly to death. Siddhartha was so emaciated by his ascetic

---

11. Edward Conze, ed. and trans., *Buddhist Scriptures* (London: Penguin, 1959), 35.
12. Ibid., 36.

lifestyle that, as he later stated, "when I thought I would touch the skin of my stomach I actually took hold of my spine."[13]

Fig. 2.2.
Siamese
Buddha statue
in Thailand.

Everything changed for Siddhartha as he sat down one afternoon under the Bodhi ("enlightenment") Tree in Bodh Gaya in India. After accepting a bowl of rice porridge from a country girl—the eating of which signaled his renunciation of asceticism—he entered the lotus (sitting) position and vowed not to get up until he had attained enlightenment. As in the case of Jesus when he battled with the devil for forty days in the desert before the inauguration of his ministry, Siddhartha warred with Mara, the Lord of Death.[14] Mara tempted Siddhartha in many ways,

13. Clarence Hamilton, *Buddhism: A Religion of Infinite Compassion* (New York: Liberal Arts Press, 1954), 14.
14. Conze, *Buddhist Scriptures*, 48.

but each time the prince responded with concentration and resolve. Eventually Mara was defeated.

Alone under the tree, Siddhartha went deeper and deeper into meditation. Like a bucket of water penetrating the deepest levels of the well, Siddhartha reached the limits of what one's mind can see and apprehend. He first saw all his countless previous lives and deaths and rebirths, which made him mindful of all living beings. He then traced the cause of the endless cycle of death and rebirth (called *samsara*) to ignorance. This empowered him to recognize that karma ceases to have command over a being once ignorance is destroyed. And once karma is destroyed, a living being ceases to be imprisoned by the perpetual cycle of life.

As the dawn rose from the night, Siddhartha awoke with the universe and became forever known as the Buddha, "the Awakened One." The Buddha knew all things because he was one with everything. Although he attempted to get up, the peace, calm, and joy of his realization kept him seated under the tree for a week—and altogether for forty-nine days. At the end of this time, two of the principal Hindu gods, Brahma and Indra, implored the Buddha to share his realization with the universe:

> O Buddha, Treasure of Compassion, Living beings are like blind people
>   in constant danger of falling into the lower realms.
> Other than you there is no Protector in this world.
> Therefore we beseech you, please rise from meditation equipoise and
>   turn the Wheel of Dharma.[15]

This is exactly what the Buddha did. He turned the Wheel of Dharma by teaching others what he realized in meditation. Like Jesus the Christ, Siddhartha the Buddha soon attracted disciples—eventually becoming a traveling guru who always tempered public teaching with private meditation. Also like Christ, the Buddha comforted, counseled, challenged, encouraged, and discipled. Upon his death at the age of eighty in Kushinagar, India (the result of natural causes after he healed from accidental food poisoning),[16] the Buddha's disciples surrounded him one last time. Because he had taught them all that was necessary

The lotus flower symbolizes purity. For just as a lotus flower is born in the mud but blossoms atop the water, so we are born in suffering but can attain purity of mind.

15. Gyatso, *Introduction to Buddhism*, 10. As the author explains, "The reason why Buddha's teachings are called the *Wheel of Dharma* ["Protection"] is as follows. It is said that in ancient times there were great kings . . . who used to rule the entire world. These kings had many special possessions, including a precious wheel in which they would travel around the world. Wherever the precious wheel went, the king would control that region. Buddha's teachings are said to be like a precious wheel, because wherever they spread, the people in that area have the opportunity to control their minds by putting them into practice" (10–11).

16. See the original story in E. J. Thomas, trans., *Buddhist Scriptures* (New York: E. P. Dutton & Company), 112.

for them to know, his last earthly statement was just a summary of his overall teaching: "Decay is inherent in all things; be sure to strive with clarity of mind (for nirvana)."[17]

Council	Year	Country
1st	483 BC	India
2nd	387 BC	India
3rd	250 BC	India
4th	1st c. BC 1st c. AD	Sri Lanka Kashmir

Because the Buddha achieved nirvana (or "extinction" of existence as we know it) after his death through his achievement of enlightenment while on earth, he was no longer bound by the law of cause and effect (karma) and so was not reborn. His legacy, however, continued. For even while alive, the Buddha established the first religious monastic community in the world—the *Sangha* ("community"), a group of monks and nuns who put into practice what the Buddha taught. Like Muhammad, the Buddha did not indicate a successor. Instead, as his last words conveyed, it was the responsibility of each individual to discover the truth and test the Buddha's words against his or her own experiences.

As time went on, several Buddhist councils were formed to determine what the Buddha actually taught as well as to determine the parameters of Buddhist thought and practice. The first council, which occurred soon after the Buddha's death, was convened in order to recall and then memorize the Buddha's teaching since he, like Jesus, did not write anything down. These recitations became known as the Pali Canon or Tripitaka. The second council, meeting about a century later, convened as a result of a division within Buddhism. The dispute arose between those who followed a strict interpretation of the Buddha's teaching and those who followed a less strict approach.

Roughly another century later, the third council met to adjudicate how to handle the alarmingly high number of Buddhists who became practitioners of the religion after the emperor of northern India, a man named Ashoka (304–232 BC), converted to Buddhism.[18] In the same way that Emperor Constantine's conversion to Christianity in the early fourth century made Christianity more widespread among the Roman masses

17. Keown, *Buddhism*, 28.
18. Karen Armstrong, *The Buddha* (London: Penguin, 2004), vii.

and more susceptible to theological divergence, so Emperor Ashoka's conversion to Buddhism in the third century BC led to increased conversions to Buddhism. This caused certain Buddhists to be suspicious of the newcomers' orthodoxy and sincerity, and the third council met to discuss these matters. It was during this time that Buddhism spread beyond Greater India and into other parts of Asia. There it would flourish and grow more in influence than in India. Finally, two of the last initial Buddhist councils met in the first century BC and AD, respectively, to write down (rather than retain only in oral tradition) the Buddha's teachings as well as codify commentaries written by earlier monks on these sayings.

Part 3: Beliefs

Buddhism, like its parent religion Hinduism, is extremely diverse. In this way, Buddhists come in all shapes and sizes. Some, for instance, do not believe in a god, while others worship gods. Some believe that the Buddha was a great human teacher, while others believe that the Buddha was divine. Religious scholar Winfried Corduan summarizes this diversity of Buddhist thought well:

> The designation Buddhist without further qualification conveys virtually no insight into what a person believes or practices. There are as many schools of Buddhism as there are Christian Protestant denominations, but the teachings of many of these schools appear to be irreconcilable beyond a very general core.[19]

Because Buddhism is so varied, it is customary to divide the religion into denominations or major schools of thought. This is the approach we will adopt.

Two Main Traditions: Theravada and Mahayana Buddhism

The first school of thought in Buddhism is called Theravada Buddhism ("way of the elders"). Sometimes called Hinayana ("the small vehicle"), Theravada Buddhism is the oldest, most traditional, and most conservative of the many strands of Buddhist thought and practice. It is the denomination most similar to what the Buddha taught, and is most dominant in Southeast Asian countries such as

---

19. Winfried Corduan, *Neighboring Faiths: A Christian Introduction to World Religions* (Downers Grove, IL: InterVarsity Press, 1998), 220.

Myanmar (Burma), Thailand, and Cambodia. Although there are both monks and laypeople in Theravada Buddhism, the monks are primary. It is commonly believed that only they can achieve enlightenment, and the role of the layperson is to support them as they do so. Daily life as a monk includes meditating, begging for food in the morning, performing chores, and following strict rules outlined by the *Sangha* or Buddhist community. Lay Theravadins, by contrast, provide food and clothing to the monks, maintain temples, and follow ethical guidelines that are less strict than those for the monks.[20]

	DENOMINATION	
	Theravada	Mahayana
Liberation	Achieved alone	Aided by divine powers
View of God	Atheistic	Pantheistic
Dominant	Thailand, Cambodia	Vietnam, Korea, Japan
Virtue	Wisdom	Compassion
Model	*Arhat* (Monk)	*Bodhisattva* (Savior)
Ritual	Meditation and study	Petition and prayer
Profession	Monk	Layperson
Focus	Inward	Outward
Buddha	Saint	Savior*

* Huston Smith, *The World's Religions: Our Great Wisdom Traditions* (San Francisco: HarperCollins, 1991), 13.

The second major school of thought in Buddhism is called Mahayana Buddhism ("greater vehicle"). It originated as a reaction against Theravada Buddhism—which its adherents believed to be too strict and narrow—and is most dominant in East Asian countries such as China, South Korea, and Japan. It is the larger of the two major Buddhist traditions. Whereas the focus of Theravada Buddhism is monks, the focus of Mahayana Buddhism is the laypeople. Anyone, monk or layperson, is able to achieve enlightenment. Other emphases in the Mahayana tradition are that the Buddha is understood as more than a saint or example; he is also a godlike figure. In addition to seeing the Buddha

20. The five rules are: (1) no killing, (2) no stealing, (3) no sexual misconduct, (4) no intoxicants, and (5) no lying. See Donald Lopez Jr., *The Story of Buddhism: A Concise Guide to Its History and Teachings* (New York: HarperCollins, 2001), 367.

as a god in a different realm, Mahayanists developed a theology of various saviors called *bodhisattvas* ("enlightened beings"). These are buddhas in the making, so to speak, who attempt to save all beings from ignorance.

Unlike Theravada Buddhism, which is more narrow and restricted in terms of thought and practice, Mahayana Buddhism is varied and vast. It can be subdivided into many additional schools of thought. One of these is called Pure Land Buddhism. It focuses on Amitabha ("Infinite Light"), a Buddha who created a paradise in heaven for average people to enter so that they could concentrate on enlightenment after death without all the distractions of life on earth. I once visited a Buddhist temple that was part of this school of thought. Most of the service was focused on two things: meditation and chanting. The chanting consisted of reciting the phrase *namu amida butsu* ("I worship the Buddha Amitabha") for many minutes at a time. The chanting of this phrase is believed to bring one closer to this Buddha. And one's faith in Amitabha enables one to attain the Pure Land after death.

Another school of thought in Mahayana Buddhism is called Zen Buddhism. This form is perhaps most popular in the West. Its spontaneity, spirituality, and simplicity have garnered a keen following in America, and it has made its way firmly into popular culture. Zen Buddhism, as its name means, focuses on meditation. Its aim is to crack the shell of our own egos. It is about opening up the "third eye" of our beings. As Japanese Zen Buddhist scholar and practitioner D. T. Suzuki explains:

> Zen [Buddhism] . . . wants us to open up our "third eye" . . . to the hitherto undreamed-of region shut away from us through our own ignorance. When the cloud of ignorance disappears, the infinity of the heavens is manifested, where we see for the first time the nature of our own being.[21]

A Buddhist monk once explained to me the purpose and goal of meditation. In essence, he said, Buddhists meditate because they seek to purify the dirty water inside them. Like digging a well, he said, meditation allows a person to go deep into the recesses of who we are and find the clean, natural, and unpolluted water. To do so, we must move beyond our five senses (seeing, hearing, smelling, tasting, and feeling), our mind (awareness), and our ego (the illusory part of

21. D. T. Suzuki, *Zen Buddhism* (New York: Three Leaves Press, 2006), 4.

ourselves that believes we actually exist), so that we can enter the original mind, which leads us to enlightenment.

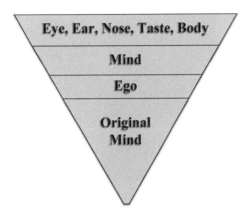

Fig. 2.3. Passing through the stages of Buddhist meditation.

The last major school of thought in Mahayana Buddhism is called Tibetan (or Vajrayana) Buddhism. It has become increasingly accepted and even trendy in the West because of the glowing personality of and widespread media attention focused on the Dalai Lama ("Ocean Teacher"), who is believed to be the fourteenth reincarnation of the *bodhisattva* Chenrezig (or Avalokitesvara). Because of his role as a *bodhisattva*, the Dalai Lama recites a daily prayer that is more than a thousand years old: "As long as space remains, as long as sentient beings remain, until then, so too may I remain, and dispel the miseries of the world."[22] Like other branches of Mahayana Buddhism, Tibetan Buddhists believe in *bodhisattvas*—including the Dalai Lama—who vow to delay nirvana and be reincarnated countless times until all living beings attain enlightenment.

Important Buddhist Teachings

In addition to some of the major Buddhist schools of thought, there are many terms and concepts that are important in Buddhism. Although not every school of thought adheres to all these concepts, we will highlight those that are most common. We will begin where the Buddha began: with the Four Noble Truths, which he taught to his first disciples after his attainment of enlightenment under the Bodhi Tree.

22. *The Dalai Lama: Essential Writings*, selected with an introduction by Thomas Forsthoefel (Maryknoll, NY: Orbis, 2008), 31.

Dependent Origination (or Arising)
1. "Old age and death depend on birth."
2. "Birth depends on existence."
3. "Existence depends on attachment [or clinging]."
4. "Attachment depends on desire [or craving]."
5. "Desire depends on sensation [or feeling]."
6. "Sensation depends on contact."
7. "Contact depends on the [six senses]."
8. "The [six senses] depend on consciousness."
9. "Consciousness depends on ignorance."*

* See *Samyutta Nikaya* 12.2, in *The Bible of the World: An Anthology of the Sacred Books of the Ten Principal Religions* (New York: Macmillan, 1961), 260–61.

The first of the Four Noble Truths is that all of life is marked by suffering. This does not mean that life is always gloomy—on the contrary, life can be full of joy and happiness—but it does mean that suffering is part and parcel of living. For no matter how much happiness we may experience at the moment, this happiness will eventually deflate like a balloon. That's because we are trapped in a continual cycle of aging, sickness, and death—what we call *samsara*—and we are almost powerless within this system. Death is not an escape. Rather, it is the trigger that shoots us into another body where we will experience suffering all over again.

The second of the Four Noble Truths is that we are trapped in *samsara* because we desire things and attach ourselves to them. This represents an inherent problem for the simple reason that life is forever changing and impermanent. So any attachment we make to something will necessarily cause us to suffer, since everything is always changing. There is an entire chain of events—often a sequence of nine to twelve—that leads one to desire or make an attachment to something.

Let's say you like a specific brand of coffee. When you first encountered it, you liked the smell of it as well as its color. When you drank it, you enjoyed the taste and the effects it produced in your body. Over time you became attached to it and desired it weekly, if not daily. Eventually, because everything is always in a state of change and because everything is always related, something happens—whether you move to a different part of the country that does not import that brand of coffee, your doctor puts you on a diet that excludes caffeine, the coffee company goes out of business because of fraud, or the coffee beans that produced the coffee were destroyed during a hurricane. In any case, your desire for coffee will eventually result in suffering. This is the doctrine of dependent origination, the notion that everything is connected to something else—and that suffering is inevitable.

The last two of the Four Noble Truths go together. While the third truth teaches that suffering—the root cause of which is ignorance—can be eliminated, the last of the truths explains that suffering can be eliminated only by practicing the Noble Eightfold Path. The fact that there is a solution to the problem of suffering is the good news. However, the bad news is that this is incredibly difficult to do. The first path of the eight, for instance, sounds innocuous enough: we must have right beliefs. But this is much more challenging than we might initially think. That's because having right beliefs means seeing the world as it truly is—an extremely difficult thing to do. For instance, it took the Buddha years to see things as they truly were when he was Siddhartha Gautama—despite eons of lifetimes of practice before that lifetime! The remaining seven paths to enlightenment build on the first: right thoughts, right speech, right conduct, right livelihood, right effort, right mindfulness, and right meditation.

To condense the Noble Eightfold Path into a paragraph, the attaining of enlightenment entails the following: (1) seeing things as they truly are and understanding the reality of and cause of suffering, (2) thinking accordingly, (3) speaking the truth, (4) acting and doing according to this teaching, (5) living in a manner that does not disrupt other life, (6) spending one's time doing good things and not becoming attached to anything, (7) being aware of one's thoughts at all times, and (8) focusing one's mind and concentrating.[23]

The last important teaching of Buddhism that we will discuss is that of no-self or *anatta*. This is sometimes a difficult concept to understand. Traditional Buddhism contends that living beings (including deities) do not have souls, for the simple reason that souls are nonexistent. Souls, in other words, are imaginary. Such a radical notion, which would have been scandalous within an Indian context of myriad divinities, was a direct assault on Hindu thinking. In fact, the implications of this belief are just as provocative today as they were twenty-five centuries ago: Not

23. For an explanation of the Noble Eightfold Path, see the *Samyutta Nikaya* (SN) 45.8, in *A World Religions Reader*, ed. Ian Markham and Christy Lohr (Oxford: Wiley-Blackwell, 2009), 95–96.

only do deities not exist, but *we* do not even really exist. I do not exist, and you do not exist.

If that's the case, we might be wondering, what *does* exist? Buddhists have an answer. In short, they assert, living beings are composed of five different *skandhas* ("aggregates"). These five aggregates are matter, sensations, perceptions, thoughts, and consciousness.[24] Matter is an external thing such as a body part, while sensations are the feelings we have as we interact with this matter. The sensations we have through our contact with matter cause perceptions or the recognition of things. This leads to thoughts and the decisions we make as a result. Finally, our consciousness is our overall awareness of everything.

Together these "aggregates" or bundles of energy constitute our existence, and they are held together by, you guessed it, karma! When desire or attachment is broken, karma disbands like a withered rope and we cease to exist. Clinging to the notion of our own independent existence only tightens and strengthens the knot of *samsara*. As long as we believe that we exist and that we have a soul, we will be forever trapped in the cycle of suffering, sickness, and death. We will be free only after we recognize and accept that self-existence is an illusion.

Part 4: Religious Writings

The Buddha taught often but wrote nothing. As with Jesus, his parables, lessons, and discourses were immediately memorized by his disciples and only later put into writing. This occurred in the first century BC.[25] As is the case with Christianity, which has three different scriptural canons depending on whether a person is associated with Orthodoxy, Catholicism, or Protestantism, so there are different canonical scriptures in Buddhism based on the major schools of thought or denominations in Buddhism. The teachings of the Buddha serve as the core scriptures for each of these denominations, but the Buddha's teachings have been transmitted slightly differently in each of these schools of thought. What's more, unlike Christianity, which believes the Bible to be inspired by God, the Buddhist scriptures generally contain the words of the Buddha and his disciples—who were people and not gods. Indeed, just as the Buddha taught his disciples to question even him and to discover the truth for themselves, so the scriptures in Buddhism are guidelines to be used inasmuch as they are practical and functional.

---

24. Prothero, *God Is Not One*, 184.
25. Lopez, *The Story of Buddhism*, 106.

Scriptures of Theravada Buddhism

Pali Canon	Contents
Vinaya Pitaka ("Discipline Basket")	Rules for monks and nuns; stories about the Buddha's first disciples
Sutta Pitaka ("Saying Basket")	Sayings of the Buddha and his disciples
Abhidamma Pitaka ("Higher Truth Basket")	Sayings and summaries of the Buddha from his disciples

We will begin our discussion with the oldest of the Buddhist denominations. Known as Theravada Buddhism, this tradition looks to the Pali Canon as its standard collection of writings, so called because Pali is the language used—a language very similar to what Siddhartha spoke. The Pali Canon is often called the Tripitaka ("Three Baskets"), since it was kept in three separate receptacles or baskets when composed in written form.[26] The Tripitaka contains many sayings of the Buddha along with sayings and commentaries written by his disciples and later monks.

The first basket, called the Vinaya Pitaka or "Discipline Basket," contains three major works.[27] These texts focus on the conduct of monks and nuns, provide rules for etiquette for the *Sangha* (the Buddhist community), and contain stories of the Buddha's enlightenment. One of the stories I find most interesting in the Vinaya texts includes a report of the Buddha's interaction with his first disciples. After attaining enlightenment under the Bodhi Tree and remaining there for forty-nine days, the Buddha encountered five ascetics in a deer park and shared with them his testimony:

> I have overcome all foes; I am all-wise; I am free from stains in every way; I have left everything and have obtained emancipation by the destruction of desire. Having myself gained knowledge, whom should I call my master? I have no teacher; no one is equal to me; in the world of men and of gods no being is like me. I am the holy One in this world, I am the highest teacher, I alone am the absolute Sambuddha [or fully enlightened being]; I have gained coolness (by the extinction of all passion) and have obtained Nirvana.[28]

26. Armstrong, *The Buddha*, xiv.

27. The names of the three works in this first division of canonical books in the Pali Canon are *Suttavibhanga* ("Rule Analysis"), *Khandhaka* ("Collections"), and *Parivara* ("Accessory"). See the Pali Text Society at http:// www.palitext.com for translations of the works in the Pali Canon included here and below.

28. *Sacred Books of the East*, Vinaya Texts, vol. 13, pt. 1, ed. Max Muller, trans. T. W. Rhys David and Herman Oldenberg (Oxford: Clarendon Press, 1881), 91.

Notice in this passage that the Buddha "obtained emancipation" only after destroying desire. This resulted in nirvana or "extinction." If the candle represents Siddhartha and the flame represents his desire, what he did in meditation under the Bodhi Tree was to extinguish the flame.

The next group of writings in the Pali Canon is the Sutta Pitaka or "Saying Basket." There are five groups of writings in this division.[29] Known as the Suttas ("teachings") or Nikaya ("collections") texts, these writings contain thousands of sayings from the Buddha and his disciples. The last group of Nikaya texts contains hundreds of direct sayings from the Buddha and is called the Dhammapada ("Eternal Path"). It is perhaps the most beloved of all Buddhist scriptures, and without doubt my favorite Buddhist text to read. A few verses from the chapter on thirst reinforce the Buddha's emphasis on desire in his teaching:

> Those who are slaves to passion follow the stream of desires, as a spider runs down the web it has made. When they have ceased to do this, at last they make true progress, free from cares and leaving all pains behind (24.14).
>
> Give up what is ahead, give up what is behind, give up what is between, when you go to the other shore of existence. If your mind is altogether free, you will not again enter into birth and decay (24.15).
>
> If you allow yourself to be tossed by doubts and swayed by strong passions, and if you yearn only for what is sensually pleasing, your thirst will grow greater and greater, and you will make your bonds stronger and stronger (24.16).[30]

As was the case with the Vinaya text quoted above, this passage from the Dhammapada explains that the goal of existence is to be released from the desire to have or possess. By giving up and releasing "what is ahead" (our future rebirth), "what is behind" (our previous lives), and "what is between" (our current lives), we are then ready to "go to the other shore of existence," namely, nirvana. When we do so—and our minds are therefore "free"—we will exit the system of death and rebirth called *samsara*.

The last group of writings in the Pali Canon is called the Abhidamma Pitaka or "Higher Truth Basket."[31] This division contains seven

---

29. The names of the five works in this second division of canonical books in the Pali Canon are *Digha Nikaya* ("Collection of Long Discourses") or DN; *Majjhima Nikaya* ("Collection of Middle-Length Discourses") or MN; *Samyutta Nikaya* ("Connected Discourses") or SK; *Anguttara Nikaya* ("Increased by One Collection") or AN; and *Khuddaka Nikaya* ("Short Collection") or KN.

30. *Dhammapada*, 105–6.

31. The names of the seven works in this last division of books in the Pali Canon are the *Dhammasangani* ("Psychological Ethics"), *Vibhanga* ("Book of Analysis"), *Dhatukatha* ("Discourse

works that discuss various issues related to the Buddha's teaching. The following is an excerpt from the Kathavatthu:

> Enlightened ones speak without anger or arrogance, with a mind not boiling over, without vehemence, without spite. Without envy they speak from right knowledge. They . . . delight in what's well said and do not disparage what's not [said well]. They don't study to find fault, don't grasp at little mistakes, don't put down, don't crush, [and] don't speak random words. For the purpose of knowledge, for the purpose of [inspiring] clear confidence, counsel that's true: That's how noble ones give counsel. That's the noble one's counsel. Knowing this, the wise should give counsel without arrogance.[32]

Because those who are enlightened have risen above the pettiness and transience of the world, they do not act angrily or arrogantly. At the same time, because they have discovered the truth, they are content to share this truth with others—but always in a way that is humble, kind, and practical.

Scriptures of Mahayana Buddhism

Although Mahayana Buddhism generally accepts the different scriptures above, its followers have additional writings. What's more, and somewhat confusing to outsiders, some of the scriptures that Mahayanists affirm that are similar to those of Theravadins differ slightly because they are transmitted in another language or found in another version.[33] To add even more confusion, different groups or traditions within Mahayana Buddhism have their own scriptures or at least emphasize certain writings over others. For this reason, we will take a very general survey of Mahayana scriptures.

In addition to the scriptures in Theravada Buddhism, the thousands of other texts that Mahayana Buddhists affirm are often called *sutras* ("threads" or "discourses" in Sanskrit). These *sutras* are customarily attributed to the Buddha or his disciples, although they were written down hundreds of years later and are the product of later Buddhist communities. One such *sutra* is called the Shurangama ("indestructible") Sutra,

---

of Elements"), *Puggalapannatti* ("Designation of Human Types"), *Kathavatthu* ("Points of Controversy"), *Yamaka* ("Pairs"), and *Patthana* ("Conditional Relations").

32. "Kathavatthu Sutta: Topics for Discussion" (AN 3.67), trans. (from the Pali) Thanissaro Bhikkhu, *Access to Insight* (July 3, 2010), http://www.accesstoinsight.org/tipitaka/an/an03/an03.067 .than.html.

33. This is why some people may refer to what are called the Agamas ("scriptures"), which contain many of the same writings as the Pali Canon. One difference is that the Agamas were originally thought to have been written in Sanskrit rather than in Pali, but they have been transmitted to us in the Chinese or Tibetan language.

which is popular in Chinese Buddhism. As we learned about Mahayana Buddhism above, this text lauds buddhas in the making to become *bodhisattvas* who, rather than attaining enlightenment and escaping the cycle of death and rebirth, voluntarily abstain from the attainment of nirvana out of compassion for others:

> I [Buddha] urge all Saints and holy men to choose to be reborn in order to deliver all sentient beings. You should make use of all manner of transformations, such as disciples, laymen, kings, lords, ministers, virgins, boy-eunuchs, and even as harlots, widows, adulterers, thieves, butchers, peddlers, etc., so as to be able to mingle with all kinds of people and to make known the true emancipation of Buddhism.[34]

In other words, the Buddha teaches, people are not to pursue attainment just for their own release from the cycle of death and rebirth (*samsara*) but rather to sacrifice themselves for the good of others. They are to make this sacrifice so that they can teach others how to attain enlightenment, which is the highest form of compassion that one can show.

Another *sutra*, called the Lankavatra ("Island Castle") Sutra, is a Mahayana writing I find informative. It focuses on the concept of nirvana in relation to the *bodhisattva*. The book represents a discourse between the Buddha, who always refers to himself as *Tathagata* ("One who has come and gone") in Buddhist writings—just like Jesus referred to himself as "the Son of Man" in the Gospels—and a *bodhisattva* named Mahamati. In the following excerpt the Buddha explains to Mahamati about those who are not able to enter nirvana:

> There are two classes of those who may not enter the Nirvana of the Tathagatas [Buddhas]: there are those who have abandoned the Bodhisattva ideals, saying, they are not in conformity with the sutras, the codes of morality, nor with emancipation. Then there are the true Bodhisattvas who, on account of their original vows made for the sake of all beings, say, "So long as they do not attain Nirvana, I will not attain it myself," voluntarily keeping themselves out of Nirvana. But no beings are left outside by the will of the Tathagatas; some day each and every one will be influenced by the wisdom and love of the Tathagatas of Transformation to lay up a stock of merit and ascend the stages. But, if they only realised it, they are already in the Tathagata's Nirvana[;] for, in Noble Wisdom, all things are in Nirvana from the beginning.[35]

34. Shurangama Sutra, quoted in *The World's Great Scriptures*, ed. Lewis Browne (New York: Macmillan, 1961), 193.

35. Lankavatra Sutra, quoted in ibid., 200.

Here we learn something important about nirvana. Not only is it available to all—save those *bodhisattvas* who either broke their vow or delay it until all beings are liberated—it is only a matter of time before everyone will eventually attain this truth. And more interestingly, we are already in nirvana, if we only realized it.

I want to discuss one last Buddhist scripture that continues to garner a good deal of attention in the West. It is popularly called the Tibetan Book of the Dead. Sacred to the Tibetan Buddhist tradition, which is an offshoot of the Mahayana tradition, this book gives direction to those who are about to die. It focuses on the *Bardo* (or "intermediate existence"), a Tibetan term that refers to the gap between death and life. The following excerpt guides a person who is soon to expire:

> Since you do not have a material body of flesh and blood, whatever may come—sounds, lights, or rays—are, all three, unable to harm you: you are incapable of dying. It is quite sufficient for you to know that these aspirations are your own thought-forms. Recognize this to be the *Bardo*.
>
> O nobly-born, if you do not now recognize your own thought-forms, whether of meditation or of devotion you may have performed while in the human world—if you have not met with this present teaching—the lights will daunt you, the sounds will awe you, and the rays will terrify you. Should you not know this all-important key to the teachings—not being able to recognize the sounds, lights, and rays—you will have to wander in the *Samsara*.[36]

Part 5: Worship Practices

Worship practices within Buddhism vary widely depending on one's tradition, one's station in life, where one lives, and the individual's own preferences or habits. Although we in the West almost make Buddhism synonymous with meditation, not all Buddhists meditate. In fact, a great many do not. Instead, some Buddhists may venerate a statue of the Buddha, while still others may chant the Buddha's name or light incense in front of an image. This can be done at home or at a temple. For those Buddhists who do meditate, they usually do so silently in a seated position for a consecutive set of minutes or even hours.

Most of the services I have attended at Buddhist temples include chanting, meditation, teaching or *dharma* talk, and scripture reading. Unlike churches that have pews and seating during worship, many

---

36. Modified from W. Y. Evans-Wentz, trans., *The Tibetan Book of the Dead* (Oxford: Oxford University Press, 1957), 104.

Buddhist houses of worship have practitioners sit on the floor or stand during worship. If standing, Buddhists may circumambulate (or walk around) a statue of the Buddha or his relics (if in a stupa or "heap," which is a mound-like structure that contains relics of the Buddha) as well as bow and prostrate themselves.

If you should attend a Buddhist service, one of the first things you will be asked to do is, like Moses at the burning bush (Ex. 3:5), remove your shoes. You will then be greeted by a waft of incense, large statues, colorful designs, and beating drums. You may also see Buddhist practitioners standing in front of an image or statue of the Buddha, reciting prayers and bowing down—perhaps reciting the three refuges three times: "I take refuge in the Buddha. I take refuge in the *dharma*. I take refuge in the *Sangha*." This refers to one's devotion to the Buddha, his teachings, and the Buddhist community, respectively.

If traveling to South Asian countries like Thailand or Myanmar where Theravada Buddhism is prevalent, you will no doubt notice the many monks dressed in saffron robes who surround temples and carry bowls for begging from Buddhist laypeople. Although it may be tempting to enter into a conversation with monks or at least make eye contact as you walk past them, they typically keep to themselves and will not approach you. Instead, lay Buddhists provide food daily for the Theravadin monks in an exchange of merit. In a country where Mahayana Buddhism is present, practitioners may stop by the temple for a few minutes throughout the day or visit the temple only on special occasions, such as holidays or funerals.

Fig. 2.4.
(Theravadin)
Buddhist monk
with begging
bowl.

Part 6: Point of Contact

With such variety of beliefs and practices, it is sometimes difficult to know where a Christian would begin a conversation with a Buddhist. Should we talk about reincarnation? Death? The notion that we do not have souls? Although these are all good topics for conversation, I would like to focus on two important Buddhist topics in particular. The first relates to the *bodhisattva*. As you recall from our discussion above, a *bodhisattva* is a person who abstains from attaining nirvana so that he or she can help all other living beings attain enlightenment. Speaking metaphorically, a *bodhisattva* is one who arrives home (nirvana) after a long journey (life), but instead of entering his home, he intentionally pauses at the door and instead helps everyone else through the door and vows to enter the home only after every other being has entered safely.

As Christians, we cannot help but notice some interesting parallels between a *bodhisattva* and Jesus. Our Lord and Savior Jesus Christ is the One who literally gave up his own life so that he could give life to others. Through his sacrificial death on the cross, we have access to eternal life. Just as Buddhists believe that the *bodhisattva* made a vow to emancipate all people, so Jesus, the second person of the Trinity, left his abode at the right hand of the Father and incarnated himself.

> Have this mind among yourselves, which is yours in Christ Jesus, who, though he was in the form of God, did not count equality with God a thing to be grasped, but emptied himself, by taking the form of a servant, being born in the likeness of men. And being found in human form, he humbled himself by becoming obedient to the point of death, even death on a cross. Therefore God has highly exalted him and bestowed on him the name that is above every name, so that at the name of Jesus every knee should bow, in heaven and on earth and under the earth, and every tongue confess that Jesus Christ is Lord, to the glory of God the Father. (Phil. 2:5–11)

Rather than remain in God's presence and allow humanity to suffer endlessly, Jesus humbled himself on the cross. So whereas a *bodhisattva* delays nirvana by allowing himself to be reincarnated, Jesus allowed himself to be violently and shamefully killed so that he could provide salvation to the world.

The second topic I want to highlight is that of desire. Whereas not all Buddhists believe in a figure called a *bodhisattva*, most Buddhists affirm that desire produces suffering. So this is a good place to begin. Below is an excerpt from an Indian-born Hindu in the nineteenth century, Sundar Singh (1899–1927), who renounced Hinduism as a teen and converted to Christianity. In one of his books, he discusses how Christians can converse with Hindus about desire:

> Some say that desire is the root cause of all pain and sorrow. According to this philosophy, salvation consists in eliminating all desire, including any desire for eternal bliss or communion with God. But when someone is thirsty, do we tell him to kill his thirst instead of giving him water to drink? To drive out thirst without quenching it with life-sustaining water is to drive out life itself. The result is death, not salvation. Thirst is an expression of our need for water and a sign of hope that spiritual peace exists. Something can satisfy our thirsty souls. When the soul finds God, the author of that spiritual thirst, it receives far greater satisfaction than any thirsty man who receives water. When the soul's desire is satisfied, we have found heaven.[37]

I am drawn to Singh's assertion that "thirst is an expression of our need for water and a sign of hope that spiritual peace exists." As Christians, we believe that Jesus is the true living water. We affirm that Jesus, just as he spoke to the woman at the well, is the only thirst-quencher on this earth. Whereas Buddhists believe that thirst should be overcome and mastered, we believe that thirst is a natural state of being that signals our need to be quenched. Our desire for water, in other words, does not need to be overcome. Rather, our desire for water needs to be brought to completion—we, again like the woman at the well (John 4:1–30), have to come to Jesus to quench our spiritual thirst and not overlook how God made humanity in such a way that our bodies oftentimes alert us to spiritual needs that need to be realized rather than overcome.

Discussion Questions

1. How would the Buddha's vision of life on earth being marked ultimately by suffering affect one as a follower of his path? Can hope beyond escape really exist in this worldview? What is the Christian understanding of suffering?
2. Buddhism is distinct in its disinterest in the beginning of the world. Are stories of origin important? If so, why? In what ways does what one believes or knows about the past affect the present and the future?

37. *Sadhu Sundar Singh: Essential Writings*, selected with an introduction by Charles Moore (Maryknoll, NY: Orbis, 2005), 38.

3. Most Westerners, whether professing Christians or not, believe that people contain a "spirit" or a "soul." Classical Buddhism, in contrast, holds a core belief of *anatta* or "no-self"—no one really exists. How different is this concept from the basic belief of Western philosophy: "I think, therefore I am"? How can you interact with someone who thinks so differently?

4. As suggested in the final section of the chapter, two key opportunities for conversation between Buddhism and Christianity exist in the concept of a *bodhisattva*'s relation to Christ as Savior and discussion on desire. How could a Christian best engage in these conversations? In addition to the passages listed above, what other biblical examples could one use to begin this dialogue?

5. What lesson does Buddhism have for Western Christians? Why do you think Buddhism has become so attractive to many in the West? What does Buddhism offer in this regard that is distinct from Judaism, Christianity, or other traditional religions in the West?

Further Readings

Dalai Lama. *The Dalai Lama: Essential Writings.* Selected with an introduction by Thomas Forsthoefel. Maryknoll, NY: Orbis, 2008.

Dhammapada: Annotated and Explained. Translated by Max Muller. Annotated and revised by Jack Maguire. Woodstock, VT: SkyLight Paths Publishing, 2005.

Gyatso, G. K. *Introduction to Buddhism: An Explanation of the Buddhist Way of Life.* Glen Spey, NY: Tharpa Publications, 2008.

Keown, Damien. *Buddhism: A Very Short Introduction.* Oxford: Oxford University Press, 2000.

Lopez, Donald, Jr., ed. *Buddhist Scriptures.* London: Penguin, 2004.

Lopez, Donald, Jr. *The Story of Buddhism: A Concise Guide to Its History and Teachings.* New York: HarperCollins, 2001.

Smith, Huston, and Philip Novak. *Buddhism: A Concise Introduction.* New York: HarperSanFrancisco, 2003.

chapter 3

Confucianism and Daoism: The Stories of Order and Nature

Circling around each other like yin and yang themselves, Taoism and Confucianism represent the two indigenous poles of the Chinese character.

Huston Smith

Daoism emerged in the midst of Confucian civilization, so Daoist jazz has from the beginning been contrasted with the classical music of Confucianism. Whereas Confucians argue that human beings become fully human by becoming social, Daoists say that we become fully human by becoming natural.

Stephen Prothero

Daoism teaches that the only way to the unity [Heaven and Earth] is to follow natural law, while Confucians believe that it is by self-cultivation and the instruction of sages that humans come into harmony with Heaven.

Xinzhong Yao

Part 1: The Beginning

Confucianism

One day Confucius was sitting in his study. His disciple Zeng Zi was attending to him. Confucius asked Zeng Zi, "Do you know by what

51

virtue and power the good emperors of old made the world peaceful, the people to live in harmony with one another, and the inferior contented under the control of their superiors?" Ever humble and rising from his seat, Zeng Zi replied, "I do not know this, for I am not clever."

Confucius, taking a teaching posture, then replied to his student, "The duty of children to their parents is the fountain [through which] all other virtues spring, and also the starting-point from which we ought to begin our education. Now take your seat, and I will explain this. Our body and hair and skin are all derived from our parents, and therefore we have no right to injure any of them in the least. This is the first duty of a child. To live an upright life and to spread the great doctrines of humanity [so that our parents] win [a] good reputation [and we] reflect great honour upon our parents: This is the last duty of a son. Hence the first duty of a son is to pay . . . careful attention to every want of his parents. The next is to serve his government loyally; and the last is to establish a good name for himself."[1]

Filial piety is one of the most important concepts in Confucianism. It means demonstrating proper respect to your elders, particularly your parents and grandparents when living and your ancestors when dead.

So goes the opening section of one of the five "classics" of Confucianism. It is no creation story, but it does include the main features of Confucian thought—rites, relationships, and right conduct. Together these form the heart of Confucianism. As for rites, Confucianism does leave room for religious rites, but its focus is on the here and now. In the story above, the primary rites we must perform as children are those that honor our parents when alive and venerate them when dead. This takes us to relationships, which are inherently related to rites. Confucianism is typically centralized around five key relationships—the relation of a son to his father being paramount. This is often called filial piety, which is the very title of the book quoted above. It should not be overlooked that filial piety is seen in the passage as the glue that binds society together.

Finally, there is right conduct. By this I mean that a person is supposed to act the right way at all times. In the passage above, it means that a son is supposed to conduct himself in such a way that he never dishonors his parents, his family, or himself. This is because in Confucianism you do not live for yourself. Rather, you are always connected to someone else and always exist in a web of (hierarchical) relationships. The goal of a Confucian is self-cultivation, which, when understood in the context above, is always simultaneously communal cultivation. We cultivate ourselves and, by so doing, cultivate the world and bring peace and order to it.

1. This comes from "The Book [or Classic] of Filial Piety," in *The World's Great Scriptures*, ed. Lewis Browne (New York: Macmillan, 1961), 261–62.

Daoism

It was a typical day at the Hangu Pass in China. Yin Shi, the commander of the Pass, watched people enter and exit the state of Zhou as he had many times before. But this day was different. A very old man riding a water buffalo soon caught his attention. The old man was apparently leaving China in the direction of India. After stopping and inquiring of the man, Yin Shi learned that it was Li Er, otherwise known as Lao Tzu, the wise yet ever humble archivist of King Wu's library. The commander could not resist asking the old man to have a cup of tea with him. "You must possess extraordinary knowledge," Yin Shi exclaimed as he poured the tea. The old man, always calm and temperate, replied:

> The Tao is about returning to simplicity, not pursuing knowledge. While there are certainly many books in the archives, by themselves they are powerless to capture the essence of the Tao.[2]

The conversation between these two men proceeded for some time. In addition to speaking of the Dao[3]—the impersonal force of the universe—they also spoke of the impending war in China, which was one of the main reasons for the old man's departure. The commander, in turn, lamented how attached he was to his job and property to leave with the old man. "Such is the nature of desires and attachments," Lao Tzu responded. "That which you desire tends to bind you; relinquishing or reducing the desire tends to free you." After they finished their tea, Lao Tzu prepared to leave, but the commander had one last request. "It is a pity that you are leaving, Master, for I and many others can learn much from you," said Yin Shi. "Would you consider writing down some notes for us, so we can cultivate the Tao on our own?" Seeing no reason to refuse, the old man wrote down all his wisdom, gave the copy to the commander, and rode off into the sunset on his water buffalo, never to return.[4]

Like the story from the life of Confucius above, the story at the Hangu Pass is not about the creation of the universe. Nor is it about the Daoist pantheon—although such a pantheon does indeed exist. Instead, it focuses on the story of the creation of the *Daodejing* ("The

---

2. Derek Lin, trans., *Tao Te Ching: Annotated and Explained* (Woodstock, VT: SkyLight Paths Publishing, 2006), xiii.

3. Because of different translational systems from Chinese into Romanized English, words such as *Dao* (or *Tao*) and *Daoism* (or *Taoism*) begin with either a *d* or a *t*. All spellings in this book follow the Pinyin System and so begin with a *d*, unless they are direct quotations.

4. This story is taken from Derek Lin's recounting of the legend of the *Daodejing*. See *Tao Te Ching*, xii–xv.

Way and Its Power"), which is so important because it is focused on the Dao. And the Dao is the underlying reality of Daoist thought. It is the "way" of existence and the way of the universe itself. As Derek Lin explains:

> The original conception of the Tao was simply the observation that reality has a certain way about it. This "way" encompasses all existence: life, the universe, and everything. A Christian may call it God's will; an atheist may call it the laws of nature. These are labels pointing to the same thing, and the Tao is simply the most generalized label imaginable, applicable to both perspectives.[5]

Such is the nature of the Dao, which—if you recall from the previous two chapters—is very similar to the (Indian) Hindu and Buddhist concepts of karma. For like karma, the Dao is impersonal, irresistible, uncontainable, and uncreated. The Dao is always in front of and around us, and we do well to live according to its way.

As we step back and reflect on the stories above, you probably noticed that these stories had little, if anything, to do with how or why the universe was created. It's not that Confucians and Daoists do not have such stories—for surely they do—but I do not think it important to include them here because the emphasis of these religions or ways of life is elsewhere. In short, Confucians emphasize the here and now, while Daoists emphasize living according to the Dao. Although noticeably different from the three Abrahamic religions in the West, both Confucianism and Daoism include all the dimensions and endeavors of human life. In this way, the major difference between the two has less to do with deciding whether one is a religion or a philosophy of life—scholars continue to debate and question whether Confucianism and Daoism are actually religions—and more to do with the reality that both of them seek to address all the dimensions of life, the religious and spiritual dimension included.

Part 2: Historical Origin

The story of Confucianism and Daoism is, to a certain extent, the larger story of China. Just as Hinduism and Buddhism originated in India and played a significant role in shaping and reflecting India's religious heritage, so Confucianism and Daoism remain the most enduring and influential expressions of China's religious

5. Ibid., xvii.

history and culture. For our purposes, we will classify the history of Confucianism and Daoism into five major eras: (1) Pre-Origins, (2) Early, (3) Medieval, (4) Modern, and (5) Contemporary. These categories—although neither exact nor exhaustive—are helpful markers of Confucian and Daoist history.

Pre-Origins

The oldest recorded dynasty in China is the Shang Dynasty, which lasted from 1751–1045 BC.[6] The Shang religion had well-developed notions of spirits and religious practices before Confucianism and Daoism dominated Chinese thought. In the words of religious scholar Huston Smith, "Heaven and Earth were considered a continuum" in ancient China.[7] While Earth contained living human beings, Heaven contained deities and human ancestors who were ruled by a supreme ancestor named Shang Ti ("Ruler on High"). Shang Ti, who later evolved into the Jade Emperor (the Daoist god), "ruled over a celestial hierarchy, modeled after the government bureaucracies, with deities in charge of [different] 'ministries.'"[8] Because the realms of Heaven and Earth were linked, it was incumbent on humans to make sacrifices to dead ancestors—who, in turn, acted as intermediaries between Heaven and Earth. This was often done by sacrifice in the home. It was also customary for earthly inhabitants to divine insight from Heaven (*Tian*), which was an impersonal force that also granted emperors, called the Sons of Heaven, the privilege of ruling Earth.

The Shang rulers acted forcefully and were alone believed to have communion with Heaven. This all changed, however, when the leader of the Zhou people, a man named King Wu (ruled 1046–43 B.C.), marched to the capital of the Shang Dynasty and took control. In order to justify his unprecedented actions, Wu declared that Heaven had been dissatisfied with Shang tyranny, and so sought a new king to rule over the land. This marked the beginning of a new religious culture, in which the "Mandate of Heaven" rested on rulers inasmuch as they ruled justly.[9]

The Zhou Dynasty gained control of the Shang Dynasty in 1045 BC and was soon apportioned to various rulers and chieftains.

Although the first Chinese dynasty was the Xia, the first dynasty with historical records was the Shang Dynasty, which lasted from c. 1751–1045 BC.

The Warring States Period (480–221 BC) was a time of great societal turmoil. The supposed founders of Confucianism and Daoism—Confucius and Lao Tzu—lived around this time period.

6. Unless otherwise noted, dates come from John and Evelyn Berthrong, *Confucianism: A Short Introduction* (Oxford: Oneworld, 2000).

7. Huston Smith, *The World's Religions: Our Great Wisdom Teachers* (New York: HarperSanFrancisco, 1991), 183–84.

8. William Young, *The World's Religions: Worldviews and Contemporary Issues* (Upper Saddle River, NJ: Pearson Prentice Hall, 2005), 114.

9. David Curtis Wright, *The History of China*, 2nd ed. (Santa Barbara: Greenwood, 2001), 18.

Over time, this Chinese feudalism created a great surge of political and social unrest. Later in this period's history, a time called the Warring States Period (480–221 BC), there was constant battle among the Chinese states. Although these battles were initially chivalrous, they eventually degenerated into mass slaughters of tens of thousands of innocent people.[10] In fact, as David Curtis Wright points out, "The Chinese out of the Warring States period . . . [were] the first in the world to use chemical and especially poison gas weapons on the battlefield."[11]

Early Period

Out of this bloodshed and mass upheaval, Confucianism and Daoism emerged. This period owes its influence to Confucius and Lao Tzu as well as their followers. Confucius (551–479 BC) or "Master Kong" lived immediately before the Warring States Period. It was his aim to remedy the mounting disorder in China in a way that would bring about harmony and peace. As for his actual line of work, Confucius was never successful during his lifetime. Like a brilliant artist who lived ahead of his time, Confucius offered his counsel to various rulers but no one heeded his advice, despite the fact that Confucius was wise and astute. Indeed, as the Analects record:

> The Master said: "At fifteen I set my heart on learning, at thirty I was established, at forty I had no perplexities, at fifty I understood the decrees of heaven, at sixty my ear was in accord, and at seventy I followed what my heart desired but did not transgress what was right." (2.4)[12]

Although we tend to think of Confucius as the founder of Confucianism, it is clear that he had no ambition to innovate. "I transmit," he stated succinctly, "but do not create" (7.1).[13] Instead, Confucius was interested in reviving the old sage tradition of China and inviting this tradition to usher in an era of peace, harmony, and social cohesion. He was just one of many rival sages who sought to bring order and stability to the disordered and unstable society in which he lived.

10. Smith, *The World's Religions*, 160.
11. Wright, *The History of China*, 43.
12. *The Analects*, trans. with introduction and notes by Ronald Dawson (Oxford: Oxford University Press, 2008), 6.
13. Ibid., 24.

孔子
Confucius

Fig. 3.1.
Drawing of
Confucius.

One of these rival sages was a sixth-century BC contemporary[14] known as Lao Tzu or "Old Man." Lao Tzu believed the best way to address all the political turmoil of the Warring States Period was by not addressing it! In this way, Lao Tzu and the text that came to be associated with him, the Daodejing, serve as a direct response to and attack on Confucius and his line of thinking. As the Daodejing explains, for example, "When the Tao fades away," there are only categories such as "benevolence" and "justice."[15] When interpreted in its historical context, this passage criticizes two key terms (*ren* and *yi*) in Confucian thought that arbitrarily seek to make and maintain distinctions about what things are and how

14. Some scholars doubt that Lao Tzu actually lived, but was rather a "fictional name used to give a voice to ideas within an influential lineage of teachers." Ronnie Littlejohn, *Daoism: An Introduction* (London: I. B. Tauris, 2009), 9.

15. Lin, *Tao Te Ching*, 37.

Daoism was,
in many ways,
a criticism of
Confucianism.

we are supposed to relate to them. According to this mind-set, "fighting and struggling over these human-made distinctions are the sources of all strife in the world."[16]

Indeed, Confucius' agenda for order is commonly referred to as "the rectification of names." This phrase describes the response Confucius gave to the question of what he would "give priority to" if he were able to "run the government." Without batting an eye, the Master proclaimed: "What is necessary is to rectify names" (13.3).[17] By this phrase he meant that the most immediate and lasting way to order society and provide stability was by recognizing what things were, calling them accordingly, and then acting in accordance with their names and roles. There was a proper way to act in all situations, and it was the responsibility of all people to play their part.

Although artlessly simple, it is amazing how strongly certain Asian cultures have preserved the concept of the rectification of names. I have noticed this most tangibly in the thought of South Koreans, where Confucian influence has been long-lasting. I have taught many Korean students over the years, and for the longest time, I experienced great difficulty when trying to organize group discussions—for the Korean students never spoke or participated. As I began to study Confucianism in detail, I eventually discovered that many of the difficulties I experienced as a teacher of Korean students arose because of Confucianism! According to Confucian thought, for example, it is the role of a teacher to impart information; it is the role of a student to listen attentively and remain silent. Therefore, when I asked Korean students to speak in class, I was, in a very small yet tangible way, defying hundreds of years of conventional Confucian thinking, which believed that teachers alone were allowed to speak in class!

Medieval Period

The next major division of Confucian and Daoist history lasted from the Han Dynasty (206 BC–AD 220) to the Six Dynasties (316–589). These are the periods in Chinese history during which Confucianism became the official ideology of the state and when Daoism became an official religion. These two schools of thought were seen as crucial links to the stability of this time period, which contrasted with the instability of the Warring States Period. Two important developments of Confucianism during this time were its creation of the first university and the

---

16. Littlejohn, *Daoism*, 16.
17. *Analects*, 49.

inauguration of the Confucian Temple, where sacrifices were made to Confucius and his disciples.[18]

There were also key developments in Daoism. The first was a cult established around Lao Tzu. Some Daoist groups began identifying the "Old Man" as Lord Lao, who was the personification of cosmic harmony.[19] Over time, there emerged many schools of thought in Daoism, including the Way of Great Peace, the Celestial Masters, the Way of Highest Clarity, and the Way of Numinous Treasure. The first two of these movements arose at generally the same time period in the Han Dynasty. They were both theocratic governments where the civil and religious leaders were the same, and they both revered Lao Tzu as an integral personage in their pantheon.[20] The other two movements emerged at a later time and were later incorporated into a more united expression of Daoism.

Modern Period

The fourth major division of Confucianism and Daoism correlates with the momentous changes these systems of thought faced between the Six Dynasties and the Qing Dynasty (AD 1644–1911). Particularly during the Sung Dynasty (AD 960–1279), Confucianism, Buddhism, and Daoism found themselves increasingly in contact with each other. This occurred as Buddhism became integrated into Chinese culture just as Confucianism and Daoism became integrated into other Asian cultures. Not surprisingly, the influence of these systems of thought on each other was as enduring as it was divisive.

For instance, although Confucianism coheres well with Daoism and Buddhism, Confucianists during the Sung Dynasty had difficulty with several Buddhist concepts. Part of this difficulty resulted from the fact that Buddhism was imported (from India) rather than indigenous to China (like Confucianism and Daoism). In short, Buddhists had completely different worldviews. Indeed, many of the Buddhist concepts—the law of cause and effect, the high regard for celibacy, and the notion that we do not exist—stood in stark contrast with Confucian thought, which largely believed that we are responsible for our own actions, that all people should marry and have children, and that all human beings do exist as a result of a very real substance called *chi*.[21]

18. Rodney L. Taylor, *Confucianism* (London: Chelsea House Publications, 2004), 12.
19. Livia Kohn, *Introducing Daoism* (London: Routledge, 2008), 32–33.
20. James Miller, *Daoism: A Short Introduction* (Oxford: Oneworld, 2003), 8.
21. Lee Dian Rainey, *Confucius and Confucianism: The Essentials* (Oxford: Wiley-Blackwell, 2010), 164.

In addition to its influence on Confucianism, Buddhism also influenced the development of Daoism. Particularly during the Tang Dynasty (AD 618–907), Daoism became an official religion in China—partly because of "a nationalistic reaction against the foreign religion of Buddhism."[22] Despite the Tang Dynasty's attempt to rally around indigenous Chinese religion, however, the influence of Buddhism persisted. This can be seen in the formation of the Way of Complete Perfection during the Sung Dynasty, for it was essentially a combination of "Daoist emphasis of the body with Buddhist-style meditation practices and a Confucian insistence on spiritual and ethical integrity."[23] This syncretization or mixing together of the three religions eventually gave way to the famous Chinese saying, "Every Chinese wears a Confucian cap, a Daoist robe and Buddhist sandals."[24]

Contemporary Period

The last division of Confucianism and Daoism refers to the contemporary period. Because of unprecedented changes in East Asia, particularly in China, during the past century, these two religions entered perhaps the most precarious stages of their histories. The period emerged in the early part of the twentieth century as China struggled to enter the modern world and progress into a leading world empire. The birth pangs China experienced as it sought to grow into the modern world led to the view that Confucianism and Daoism—and religious systems in general—were the cause of China's societal and governmental problems during this transition.

While the initial blow to Confucianism and Daoism came during the disestablishment of the Qing Dynasty in 1911 and the subsequent establishment of the Republic of China, the rise of the Communist Party and its takeover of the government in the middle of the twentieth century served as these religions' final defeat. The People's Republic of China was established by Mao Zedong (1893–1976), otherwise known as Chairman Mao, in 1949. The Cultural Revolution that followed in the 1960s–1970s dealt decisively with Confucianism and Daoism by desecrating their temples, killing or exiling sympathizers (including Daoist priests), destroying their books, statues, art, and images, and prohibiting their festivals. By the time Chairman Mao died in 1976, these two religions "seemed completely dead."[25]

> Buddhism, Confucianism, and Daoism are known as the Three Great Teachings due to their prominence and intermixing in Chinese culture.

22. Miller, *Daoism*, 11.
23. Ibid.
24. J. J. Clarke, *The Tao of the West: Western Transformations of Taoist Thought* (London: Routledge, 2000), 22.
25. Rainey, *Confucius and Confucianism*, 181.

Interestingly, however, neither Confucianism nor Daoism died. Not only did they endure, but Confucianism in particular has been regarded by many as the source of the economic prosperity in the twentieth century of many Asian territories, including Japan, Hong Kong, Singapore, and South Korea. Governments in many Asian countries, including secular China, eventually began teaching Confucianism and Daoism in schools.

All this is to say that Confucianism and Daoism are alive and well today—though certainly not dominant and prevailing.[26] Although they are both recuperating from the extreme hardships they experienced during the Cultural Revolution, they are poised for growth and adaptation in the new Western cultures in which they increasingly find themselves. This adaptation, however, focuses more on Confucianism and Daoism's philosophical ideas and concomitant practices than it does their religious beliefs and structures.

Part 3: Beliefs

Over the centuries, Confucianism and Daoism have become so interconnected that they are difficult to separate. It is not that these two religions or ways of life are identical or even similar. They have very different aims, practices, and beliefs. In this way, it is more appropriate to speak of Confucianism and Daoism as the religious yin and yang of many East Asian countries such as China and Taiwan. Although different, they are complementary. What's more, these two ways of life have historically been integrated into other religious systems, most notably Buddhism. "Traditionally," the saying goes, "every Chinese was Confucian in ethics and public life, Taoist in private life and hygiene, and Buddhist at the time of death."[27] Part of the complementariness of Confucian and Daoist thought, as we explored above, arises from the fact that they both originated in China at the same time. So it is most natural to begin our discussion of the beliefs of these two religions with what they hold in common before moving on to some of their differences.

One of their first commonalities is their understanding of the concept of *chi* (or *qi*), which is vital life energy. One of the earliest and most articulate explanations of *chi* comes from a man named Zang Zai (AD 1020–71), who is often considered the founder of Neo-Confucianism. An excerpt from one of his writings illustrates this concept:

---

26. Ibid., 182; Miller, *Daoism*, 3.
27. Smith, *The World's Religions*, 189.

> Heaven [*yang*] is my father and Earth [*yin*] is my mother, and even such a small creature as I finds an intimate place in their midst. Therefore, that which extends throughout the universe, I consider as my body and that which directs the universe I consider as my nature. All people are my brothers and sisters, and all things are my companions.[28]

As this text illustrates, *chi* is understood as the supreme reality or source of the universe. This *chi* or primal energy unites all human beings since we are created from it.[29]

Another commonality between Confucianism and Daoism is their holistic understanding of the relatedness of Heaven and Earth. Although Confucianism is sometimes portrayed as unspiritual and this-worldly, Confucius himself never denied the existence of Heaven. Instead, Confucius shifted people's attention from Heaven to Earth, as Huston Smith explains, "without dropping Heaven from the picture."[30] Both of these religions assumed that it was necessary to keep peace and stay in regular communication with Heaven. They just did this in different ways.

Confucianism

Confucianism is often understood as a set of ethics that extols certain virtues and emphasizes key relationships. Five of the best-known virtues are humaneness, rightness, ritual or propriety, wisdom, and faithfulness. The first of these virtues, humaneness, deals with how a human being relates to another person. Confucius states in the Analects, for instance, "If one sets one's heart on humaneness, one will be without evil" (4.4).[31] What's more, while the second virtue, rightness, means acting with a sense of justice, the next refers to ritual or propriety. An excerpt from the Analects exemplifies the important concept of ritual:

> When the Master entered the grand temple, he asked about every single thing. Someone said: "Who says that the son of the man from Zou knows the ritual? When he enters the grand temple, he asks about every single thing." When the Master heard this, he said: "This is the ritual." (3.15)[32]

28. "The Western Inscription," in Rainey, *Confucius and Confucianism*, 164.

29. Xinzhong Yao, *An Introduction to Confucianism* (Cambridge: Cambridge University Press, 2000), 102–3.

30. Smith, *The World's Religions*, 185.

31. *Analects*, 13.

32. Ibid., 10.

Higher Position	Virtue	Lower Position	Virtue
Father	Humaneness	Son	Filial Piety
Ruler	Rightness	Subject	Loyalty
Husband	Ritual	Wife	Obedience
Older sibling	Wisdom	Younger sibling	Humility
Friend	Faithfulness	Friend	Faithfulness*

* This chart has been modified from Winfried Corduan, *Pocket Guide to World Religions* (Downers Grove, IL: InterVarsity Press, 2006), 53.

Although originally having religious overtones and denoting an act performed by means of sacrifice, the word *ritual* eventually expanded in meaning to signify all the basic principles of the universe—whether the religious, naturalistic, legal, or relational. The fourth virtue, wisdom, is a common virtue in society. Confucius defines wisdom as this: "When you understand something . . . recognize that you understand it; but when you do not understand something . . . recognize that you do not" (2.17).[33] Finally, the last virtue in Confucianism is faithfulness, which refers to being truthful in all circumstances.

The five key relationships are directly related to the five virtues above as well as five corresponding virtues. This line of thinking is based on the principle that each relationship is structured and united around a specific virtue for each person in the relationship—including the superior and the inferior. The first of these relationships is between a father and a son. It is centered on the virtues of humaneness and filial piety. The second relationship, between a ruler and a subject, is exemplified by the virtues of rightness and loyalty. The third relationship refers to the rituals and obedience shown in the marriage of a husband and a wife. Next comes the relationship between older and younger siblings, where wisdom and humility are needed. Finally, the last relationship in Confucianism refers to that between friends, where faithfulness is most important.

Together these relationships—and their corresponding virtues or crucial characteristics—provide structure and stability to an otherwise disordered society. It is important to keep in mind that there are generally two virtues or concepts that undergird each of these relationships. The first is humaneness, which, as we learned above, is about observing a general sense of kindness and benevolence. The second is filial piety. This concept, often evident in Asian cultures like Japan, Korea, Vietnam, and Taiwan, means that younger people show deference to older people. Formally it means that

33. Ibid., 7.

younger people bow to older people and give them proper respect, while practically it means that the society looks to older people for wisdom and seeks to honor them as they age and venerate them after they die.

Daoism

Whereas Confucianism is about rites and relationships, Daoism is about living according to the Dao. This means "going with the flow" in the best use of the phrase—not going against the way of nature or giving up on life but letting go of attempting to organize, strategize, strive, and achieve. It is action that is not founded on purpose, motive, or ambition. As one Daoist scholar explains:

> The way to be with the Dao is through nonaction . . . and natural-ness . . . . [I]t means letting go of egotistic concerns—what Daoists call "passions and desires"—in favor of finding a sense of where life, nature, and the world are headed. It means to abstain from forceful and interfering measures that cause tensions and disruption in favor of gentleness, adaptation, and ease. Then one can attain success, contentment, and long life.[34]

The notion of nonaction or noninterference can be best explained with a metaphor. Let us imagine a swimmer. A swimmer is a person who acts so instinctively in the water that she intuits where to go and adjusts her course depending on the swimming conditions. She does not fight the conditions but responds to them in the appropriate way. This is, Daoism suggests, an ideal way to live life. When a person acts in accordance with the Dao, everything flows as it should. But when we ignore or reject the Dao, we divide yin and yang and are forced to create man-made concepts and categories like "good" and "ugly" to guide our thoughts.

Another important concept in Daoism (as well as in all traditional Chinese thought, including Confucianism) is yin and yang. The yin and the yang represent the fundamental elements of the universe. Although they are always intertwined, they are fundamentally different. Yin is associated with earth, cold, wet, passive, dark, mysterious, and feminine, while yang is associated with heaven, hot, dry, active, bright, clear, and masculine. Neither of these is "good" or "bad," "right" or "wrong," or "better" or "worse." Instead, they are complementary phases of the vital energy or *chi* of the universe. They sum up all of life's opposites or polarities. Whereas the original symbol for the yin and yang was a tiger

---

34. Kohn, *Introducing Daoism*, 24.

(yin) and a dragon (yang), today the best-known symbol of the yin-yang structure is the circle containing black and white curved halves, with a white or black dot placed in each curve. This circular image is called the *Taiju* diagram, which means "Supreme Ultimate."[35] The symbol illustrates that nothing is either completely "evil" or "good"; rather, each of these values or concepts is relative to the person who holds them.

Fig. 3.2.
Chinese yin and yang symbol, known as the *Taiju* diagram.

Related to the yin and yang is the concept of *chi*. This is the vital energy that runs through all beings. Stated differently, it is the dissolution of *chi* that leads to death. Westerners are perhaps most familiar with the concept of *chi* through acupuncture, which is a procedure using needles and massage therapy to stimulate the flow of *chi* to different pressure points and places in the body. There are also many physical exercises and martial-arts practices that one can perform in order to generate the positive flow of *chi* in our bodies. Most popular expressions of Daoism in the West have focused on either acupuncture or martial arts.

Five Elements
Wood
Fire
Earth
Metal
Water

In addition to these key expressions of Daoist thought, Daoism has been presented to Westerners most notably through the television and movie industry. There are a growing number of movies, for instance, that center on the "five elements" or "five phases" of yin and yang—wood, fire,

35. Littlejohn, *Daoism*, 21.

earth, metal, and water. In Daoist thought, these elements or materials serve as checks and balances to keep the world in harmony. They are in a constant rhythm or cycle, which can be seen in the following classic interplay: Wood serves as fuel for fire; fire creates earth or ash; earth produces metal; metal, in the depths of mountains, attracts clouds and stimulates rainfall or water; and water nourishes wood.[36] The elements illustrate the interconnectedness of the world.

The last important aspect of Daoism has to do with its religious beliefs. This is the most neglected feature of Daoism in the West. Whereas we tend to think of Daoism as a "grab bag of philosophical observations,"[37] which it is, we need to balance this view with its religious heritage and practices. When we do so, we notice that Daoism contains a host of divine figures and other supernatural beings. Today, Daoism is chiefly divided into the Celestial Masters and the Complete Perfection schools of thought, which differ on many issues but centralize on their view that *chi* must be preserved and retained. The Celestial Masters school was founded by Zhang Ling in the second century AD when a deified Lao Tzu appeared to him. Practicing the oldest of the established forms of Daoism, Celestial Masters priests today make a living by performing rituals that call on the spirits to help people secure such things as wealth, well-being, and honor.[38] The way of Complete Perfection began when two of the Eight Immortals appeared to twelfth-century master Wang Zhe in order to initiate him into the cultivation of *chi*.[39]

> Religious Daoism today is chiefly divided into the Celestial Masters and the Complete Perfection schools of thought. Though different in many areas, they both believe that *chi* must be preserved and retained.

Name	Description of the Immortal
Zhongli Quan	Leader and master of elixir
Lu Dongbin	Scholar, calligrapher, poet, healer
Li Tieguai	Crippled, living in beggar's body
Cao Guojiu	Official and uncle of a Sung emperor
He Xiangu	Woman carrying lotus flower
Han Xiangzi	Former Confucian carrying a flute
Zhang Guolao	Old man riding a donkey
Lan Caihe	Male or female carrying fruit*

* Ronnie Littlejohn, *Daoism: An Introduction* (London: I. B. Tauris, 2009), 157–58.

36. Kohn, *Introducing Daoism*, 69.
37. Stephen Prothero, *God Is Not One: The Eight Rival Religions That Rule the World—and Why Their Differences Matter* (New York: HarperCollins, 2010), 284.
38. Miller, *Daoism*, 8–9.
39. Ibid., 11–12.

In addition to these two main schools of thought, there are many deities in Daoism. At the top of the pantheon is a figure named the Jade Emperor. This god rules the heavenly realm like a bureaucrat. He allocates responsibilities to lesser gods who, in turn, report back to him about the affairs on Earth. Although the Jade Emperor is the leading god, the most popular gods in the Daoist pantheon are probably the Eight Immortals. Statues of these Eight Immortals, headed by Zhongli Quan, are prevalent in many temples across Asia.

There are many fanciful stories about how these six men, one woman, and one man-woman became immortals. However, what they most represent to countless Daoists is a tangible and inclusive reminder—for the immortals include all ages, genders, and vocations—that all people can achieve immortality. In fact, it is an ancient view in Daoism that whoever attains a perfect balance of *chi* may become immortal. In this way, one of the primary goals of Daoism—if, in fact, we can indulge in such a Westernized concept when speaking about a goal-opposed religion—is the preservation of and increase in *chi*. This can be achieved in various ways, including the application of ancient Chinese medicine, the performance of martial arts, the use of breathing exercises, the eating of certain foods, and the drinking or inner cultivation of an elixir of *chi*.[40]

Part 4: Religious Writings

Confucian Texts

Term	Symbol
Heaven	☰
Earth	☷

Historically, Confucianism contains the so-called Five Classics and the Four Books. Of the Five Classics, the best known is probably the I Ching or Book of Changes, which is equally regarded and venerated as a classic in Daoism. Despite the fact that it is difficult to understand in any objective sense, the Book of Changes continues to be a favorite among Western audiences. For all practical purposes, the book is a divination manual designed to help people make and reason through decisions. The framework behind the Book of Changes is the famed symbols yin and yang—the cosmic forces of reality that are symbolized by a broken

40. Young, *The World's Religions*, 117.

(– –) and unbroken line (—), respectively. These lines are used as building blocks to refer to all number of natural phenomena.

The other writings of the Five Classics are less known. Two of them, the Book of History and the Spring and Autumn Annals, are history books. While the first covers a vast time period from around 2000 to 200 BC, the latter chronicles many important historical and political events dating from 722–481 BC.[41] Another of the classics is the Book of Rites, which is an anthology of anecdotes and ancient prescriptions. The last of the Five Classics is called the Book of Poetry. It is a collection of poems written over the course of several hundred years. Many of the poems read like biblical psalms, though there are clear differences as well. Here is an excerpt:

> Great heaven, unjust, is sending down these exhausting disorders.
> Great heaven, unkind, is sending down these great miseries.
> Let superior men come into office, and that would bring rest to the
>   people's hearts.
> Let superior men execute their justice, and the animosities and angers
>   would disappear.[42]

This passage illustrates the close connection between Heaven and Earth in Confucian thought. Heaven, though impersonal, is understood to be responsible for the state of affairs on Earth by means of the emperor or ruler it mandates. Rather than asking for a god or some other spiritual being to bring stability to earthly disorder, the poet asks Heaven to send down a ruler who will act justly.

In addition to the Five Classics, Confucianism also centers on what is called the Four Books. These books are more readable than the Five Classics, which were used for state examinations in China for hundreds of years. The Four Books developed as core texts later in Confucian history. Two of these books, the Book of Great Learning and the Doctrine of the Mean, are actually different excerpts from the Book of Rites above. They contain many sayings from Confucius and his disciples. A typical saying, taken from the Doctrine of the Mean, reads: "The superior man does what is proper to the station in which he is; he does not desire to go beyond this."[43] What Confucius is underscoring, not unlike the Hindu caste system, which is crucial to the preservation of Indian society, is the importance of recognizing one's status within any number of relationships. Once recognized, a person must observe the niceties expected of that relationship.

41. Yao, *An Introduction to Confucianism*, 61–63.
42. "Book of Poetry," in *The Bible of the World*, ed. Robert Ballou (New York: Viking Press, 1939), 386.
43. The "Doctrine of the Mean," in ibid., 423.

The last two of the Four Books are the Analects and the Book of Mencius. The Analects contain sayings of Confucius as well as those of his disciples. This is the book to read for beginners in Confucian thought. It is brief, accessible, and representative of Confucian teaching. The Book of Mencius derives from a Confucian scholar named Mencius (371–289 BC), who was the premier interpreter of Confucian thought. He is perhaps best known for advancing the theory that human nature is inherently good:

> Everyone has a heart that contains within it compassion, shame, respect, and the knowledge of right and wrong. A heart with the sprout of compassion leads to humanity. A heart with the sprout of shame leads to rightness. A heart with the sprout of reverence and respect leads to ritual. A heart with the sprout of right and wrong leads to wisdom. Humanity, rightness, ritual, and knowledge are not strapped on to us from the outside; we must certainly have them already.[44]

I once had a conversation with a Chinese missionary who lamented how difficult it was for him to discuss the doctrine of original sin with the people he was working with in China. Like Mencius, this group believed human nature is inclined toward goodness. It's certainly true that many people neglect or ignore this inclination, Mencius would reply, but that is because they did not cultivate this leaning and receive a proper (Confucian) education that would have nurtured the good sprouts.

Daoist Texts

Apart from the very important Book of Changes discussed above, there are two primary texts associated with Daoism. The best-known and beloved of these writings is the Daodejing. This is my favorite of the Daoist texts, but one that some find baffling. It begins in a very non-Western and enigmatic way:

> The Tao that can be spoken is not the eternal Tao
> The name that can be named is not the eternal name
> The nameless is the origin of Heaven and Earth
> The named is the mother of myriad things
> Thus, constantly without desire, one observes its essence
> Constantly with desire, one observes its manifestations
> These two emerge together but differ in name
> The unity is said to be the mystery
> Mystery of mysteries, the door to all wonders.[45]

44. The "Book of Mencius," as quoted in Rainey, *Confucius and Confucianism*, 90.
45. Lin, *Tao Te Ching*, 3.

If you are confused at this point, you are in good company. Those of us in the Christian West, who excel in defining and categorizing, are stymied by this type of literature. That is, to a certain extent, the point. The Dao is above defining and above categorizing. If we were to define it, we would limit it; and if we were to limit it, it would not be the Dao. This is the first lesson we must learn as we reflect on the Dao and prepare ourselves to live in conformity to its path.

The second of the classic Daoist writings is called the Zhuangzi (or Chuang Tzu). This is named after the philosopher Zhuang Zhou (c. 370–290 BC), who is believed to be the originator of the work. Like the Daodejing, the Zhuangzi is difficult for Westerners to understand. When I read excerpts of the book to my classes, I often see puzzled faces! Let us look at one of these puzzling excerpts:

> If there was a beginning, then there was a time before that beginning. And a time before the time which was before the time of that beginning. If there is existence, there must have been non-existence. And if there was a time when nothing existed, then there must have been a time before that—when even nothing did not exist. Suddenly, when nothing came into existence, could one really say whether it belonged to the category of existence or of non-existence? Even the very words I have just now uttered—I cannot say whether they have really been uttered.[46]

Before commenting, let us look at just one more passage:

> Once upon a time, I, Chuang Tze, dreamt I was a butterfly, fluttering hither and thither, to all intents and purposes of a butterfly. I was conscious only of following my fancies as a butterfly, and was unconscious of my individuality as a man. Suddenly, I [awoke], and there I lay, myself again. Now I do not know whether I was then a man dreaming I was a butterfly, or whether I am now a butterfly dreaming I am a man.[47]

You may be wondering what just happened in these sample passages from the Zhuangzi! Many of us read these sayings and feel dizzy and lightheaded. As with the Daodejing, that is part of the point. What the Zhuangzi is trying to do is to free our minds from the commonsense approach to life that most of us assume is true and follow because we have been told to do so. The Zhuangzi is attempting to jolt our minds out of ordinary logic and into spontaneous truth. Instead of presenting a perspective of life as formal, predictable, and ritualistic, this expression of Daoism gives

---

46. The "Zhuangzi," in Ballou, *The Bible of the World*, 508.
47. Ibid., 512–13.

a perspective that is mystical, adventurous, and natural. As one translator of the Zhuangzi explains about the purpose of the book:

> If man would once forsake his habit of labeling things good or bad, desirable or undesirable, then the man-made ills, which are the product of man's purposeful and value-ridden actions, would disappear and the natural ills that remain would no longer be seen as ills, but as an inevitable part of the course of life. Thus, in Zhuangzi's eyes, man is the author of his own suffering and bondage, and all his fears spring from the web of values created by himself alone.[48]

The focus of the Zhuangzi is freedom and happiness, which is believed to be attainable once we let go of striving, defining, and desiring.

Part 5: Worship Practices

Confucianism

Probably one of the most distinctive ritual practices of Confucianism is called ancestor worship or ancestor veneration. This is the practice of revering and remembering one's relatives who have died. It is based on the central Confucian virtue of filial piety as well as on the belief that one's spirit continues after death. Many Confucian homes have altars or shrines where this is practiced. Ancestor veneration can be performed in a variety of ways. Just a few include burning money or paper versions of specific objects (whether cars or TVs) for the deceased; offering food and drink; giving greetings and saying prayers; offering incense; and bowing down on the floor ceremonially.[49] These deceased spirits receive and accept these offerings and ensure well-being for the household, and are, in turn, assured of well-being in the afterlife because of the honor they receive from human ancestors on earth.

When (Catholic) missionaries arrived in China in the sixteenth century, they immediately took notice of ancestor veneration. They were concerned that this practice conflicted with the Christian command to worship the one true Lord. The missionaries were forced to decide whether this was a religious or cultural (memorial) practice. One group, the Jesuits, decided that it was cultural and therefore did not conflict with Christian worship, while another group, the Franciscans, decided that

Ancestor worship or veneration is an ancient and important practice in many Asian cultures. It is based on the assumption that one's spirit continues after death and influences the fortune of those living. Many Asian cultures venerate the dead (as well as living parents and grandparents) during the Chinese New Year.

---

48. *Zhuangzi: Basic Writings*, trans. with introduction by Burton Watson (New York: Columbia University Press, 2003), 4.

49. Typically, one bows once to the living and twice to the dead. This goes back to yin and yang. Yang includes one and the living, while yin includes two and the dead.

it was indeed worship. The Franciscans based this on their conviction that the common people were actually worshiping their dead ancestors.[50]

This debate, though seemingly far removed from the West, comes up often when I teach on Confucianism. That's because many of the Korean students I teach, although Christians, are still expected to observe this ritual with their families in South Korea. These students have suffered no little grief over determining to what extent, if at all, they can participate in this practice without, on the one hand, violating their Christian principles and, on the other, forever dishonoring and shaming their families who believe this practice to be integral to the family unit.

Daoism

There are several common religious practices in Daoism. The first is a form of divination. One common practice is consulting fortune-tellers for guidance on health, prosperity, and general issues. This can be done in any number of ways, but one is by picking a flat stick out of many and paying for a fortune-teller to read and interpret the statement related to the stick. Another practice occurs as individuals visit Daoist temples. Whereas many Christians may pray to God for everyday affairs such as securing employment or finding a solution to an issue at work, Daoists may offer incense to the statue of a god, bow down reverently, and ask the god for honor (which is important in Asian cultures), health, or money.

Fig. 3.3.
Daoist temple in the Wadung Mountains in China.

50. Berthrong, *Confucianism*, 140–42.

A third Daoist practice has to do with ancestral tablets and home shrines. Many Asian homes influenced by Daoism contain tablets with the names of dead ancestors. People in these homes light incense to the dead spirits and offer them food, drinks, and flowers. These homes may also have shrines or statues of gods or dead ancestors. These shrines or statues are seen to house these spirits. Some houses contain statues or images of a kitchen god named Zao Jun who resides with his wife in many home kitchens influenced by Daoism. These gods listen to people's daily conversations, record what they say, and report to the Jade Emperor—the head god of Daoism—during the Chinese New Year.

Whereas the practices above are common in Asian countries, the last practice I want to mention is becoming more well known in the West. It is called *fengshui*, and it is also quite evident in Confucianism. This is a term assuming that everything—whether a building, a tomb, a garden, or decorations—has a proper way of being spaced and arranged harmoniously. Observing *fengshui* is an important way to live in balance with *chi*, the five elements, and the spiritual forces of the universe.

Part 6: Point of Contact

A few years ago I came across a Chinese translation of John 1:1: "In the beginning was the Dao, and the Dao was with God." Whereas most English versions translate the Greek word *logos* as "Word," the Chinese give it as *Dao*, which means "way," "path," or "road." This is an easily transferable concept from the East to the West, and I would like to conclude our discussion of Confucianism and Daoism by sharing how we as Christians can share with Confucians and Daoists how Jesus Christ is indeed the Dao.

The place to begin is with the Zhuangzi, one of the most important of the Daoist writings. A section of this text explains the Dao as follows:

> Before heaven and earth came into being, Tao existed by itself from all time. It gave spirits and rulers their spiritual powers. It created heaven and earth. It is above the zenith but it is not high. It is beneath the nadir but it is not low. It is prior to heaven and earth but it is not old. It is more ancient than the highest antiquity but is not regarded as long ago.[51]

I once had a conversation with a Chinese woman in which I asked her whether it were possible that Jesus was the Dao that the Chinese spoke

---

51. Wing-Tsit Chan, trans., *A Sourcebook in Chinese Philosophy* (Princeton, NJ: Princeton University Press, 1963), 194.

about hundreds of years before Jesus Christ came to earth. It was a new concept for her, but one that she considered attentively. I thought this might be the most fitting place to share my faith with her, since there was such an enduring Chinese tradition of understanding the Dao as having existed from the beginning.

Indeed, as the passage I quoted from above explains, the Dao "existed by itself from all time" before Heaven and Earth "came into being." Moreover, just as we read from the Gospel of John, it was Jesus—as the "Word" or "Dao" or whichever translation we use—who created all things. All of this made good sense to the woman, and we continued in conversation. The most difficult concept for her was when I wondered out loud whether it was possible for the Dao to incarnate itself or be made into flesh. Part of the challenge for her was that she understood the Dao to be an impersonal force that does not have personal characteristics. It was quite a stretch for her to think in personal terms about an impersonal reality.

As I think back on this stimulating conversation, I wonder how much this woman thought later about Jesus Christ as the Dao. I also continue to reflect on how the Zhuangzi's discussion of the Dao challenges me to think about how God may have communicated to the Chinese people over the course of their history and within their culture. The concept of the Dao's existing before Heaven and Earth and yet not being "old" serves as a good parallel to how Jesus, though the Creator of all things and therefore more powerful than death, was nevertheless able to be born from a human woman and enter Earth as a man who grew, aged, and died.

Discussion Questions

1. Think about some of the major differences between Chinese thought, as it is informed by Daoism, Buddhism, and Confucianism, and the American worldview. What are some of these contrasts? How does understanding these differences help you to think of ways to engage people from Chinese culture in conversation?

2. Jesus' teaching on "the cost of discipleship" includes the poignant revelation that unless someone "hates" his family members (that is, loves them more than Jesus), he is not worthy to be called Jesus' disciple (Luke 14:26). This idea is hard for Western Christians to comprehend, so one could only imagine its being that much more difficult for someone from an Asian culture, where the Confucianist worldview gives a much different message. How can Christians

better interpret this passage to those from Confucian, Daoist, and other filial piety backgrounds?

3. Confucianism and Daoism's high regard for elderly members of society stands in sharp contrast with Western thought. What can Westerners, including Western Christians, learn from Eastern philosophy about treatment of older members?

Further Readings

The Analects. Translated with an introduction and notes by Ronald Dawson. Oxford: Oxford University Press, 2008.

Berthrong, John and Evelyn. *Confucianism: A Short Introduction*. Oxford: Oneworld, 2000.

Kohn, Livia. *Introducing Daoism*. London: Routledge, 2008.

Lin, Derek, trans. *Tao Te Ching: Annotated and Explained*. Woodstock, VT: SkyLight Paths Publishing, 2006.

Miller, James. *Daoism: A Short Introduction*. Oxford: Oneworld, 2003.

Rainey, Lee Dian. *Confucius and Confucianism: The Essentials*. Oxford: Wiley-Blackwell, 2010.

Wright, David Curtis. *The History of China*. 2nd ed. Santa Barbara: Greenwood, 2001.

Yao, Xinzhong. *An Introduction to Confucianism*. Cambridge: Cambridge University Press, 2000.

chapter 4

Judaism: The Story of Tradition and Identity

The Bible is the cornerstone. The Talmud is the foundation. The edifice that they underpin is Rabbinic Judaism and from the middle of the First Millennium until the nineteenth century, that was the dominant kind of Judaism.

George Robinson

One superficially attractive but actually misleading [notion is that Jews] are united by a common religion. There is a Jewish religion, and for very many Jews it is the focus of their lives . . . . But it would be unrealistic to maintain that it is the Jewish religion that unites the Jewish people. In fact the Jewish religion [is that which] divides the Jewish people today, perhaps almost as much as it divides Jews from non-Jews.

Nicholas de Lange

If you have a sapling in your hand, and it is said to you, "Behold, there is the Messiah"—go on with your planting, and [only] afterward go out and receive him. And if the youths say to you, "Let us go up and build the Temple," do not listen to them. But if the elders say to you, "Come, let us destroy the Temple," listen to them.

The Talmud

Part 1: The Beginning

Thousands of years ago there was a man named Terah who lived in a bustling city on the edge of the Euphrates River in Mesopotamia. One day he charged his oldest son to sell his graven images while he went on a business trip. In the course of the day an elderly man approached the boy with the intention of buying an image. After learning of the man's age, the boy mocked the elder for foolishly thinking—after all his years—that an image made from a tree in only a few days was a suitable god. The man, shocked by the boy's insight, took the sentiment to heart and ceased worshiping idols.

That afternoon a woman came to the boy's shop to offer fine flour to the idols he was in charge of. Afterward the incensed lad took a stick and broke every one of the images except the largest one. He then put the stick in the idol's hand. When his father returned and saw the destruction of his business, he demanded an explanation. The boy replied that each of the little gods had begun fighting the moment the woman entered with the flour because they each wanted to be the recipient of worship. Not surprisingly, the largest of the idols proved victorious and crushed the others. Infuriated at his insolence, the father handed the boy over to Nimrod—the mighty ruler and hunter of old.

Nimrod lauded the boy's refusal to worship idols and instead suggested that fire was the most powerful force on earth. "Actually," the boy replied, "water has power over fire." Nimrod conceded and was prepared to make water his god to be worshiped before the boy pointed out to the great hunter that wind has authority over water. He then explained that people are stronger than wind. Eventually Nimrod tired of the boy's antics and threw him into the fire. Because of his faith in the one true God, however, the boy was saved from the fire without as much as a scratch or burn. Although the archangel Gabriel had offered to help the boy, God himself stepped in to shield him from harm.[1]

So goes the story of Abraham, father of the three great monotheistic religions, as found in Genesis Rabbah, a Jewish commentary on Genesis. Clearly, this is not the story of creation in Genesis—a creation story that we Christians, together with Jews, hold to be the story of the creation of the world. As important as the Genesis account is—and it is important—this is not necessarily the starting point for contemporary Judaism. What *is* the starting point? To answer that question, let us look at a quote from the contemporary Jewish rabbi and scholar Shai Cherry:

---

1. This story is based on Genesis Rabbah or "Midrash on Genesis." See Samuel Rapaport, trans., *Tales and Maxims from the Talmud* (London: Routledge, 1912), 60, 77–78.

Judaism has variously been called a culture, an ethnicity, and a civilization, all terms that struggle to include more than "just" religion.[2]

Judaism today is just as much a culture, an ethnicity, and a civilization as it is a "religion." As a result, I wanted to begin our discussion with a story that encompasses these different aspects of Judaism without focusing just on the religious aspect—as important as that is. As for culture, the story above speaks of Jewish identity. Specifically, it seeks to undermine the (religious) idol worship that tempted so many Jews as the nation lived in close proximity to rival nations in biblical times. In terms of ethnicity, Abraham is commonly regarded in the Jewish tradition as the originator of the Jewish nation and religion. This is apparent not only in the Bible but also in other Jewish literature. Indeed, Genesis Rabbah, the Jewish midrash (or commentary) from which the story above was taken, makes this point strongly:

> Perhaps in the proper order of things Abraham should have been the first man created, not Adam. God, however, foresaw the fall of the first man, and if Abraham had been the first man and had fallen, there would have been no one after him to restore righteousness to the world; whereas after Adam's fall came Abraham, who established in the world the knowledge of God. As a builder puts the strongest beam in the center of the building, so as to support the structure at both ends, so Abraham was the strong beam carrying the burden of the generations that existed before him and that came after him.[3]

Finally, in regard to the idea of civilization, Abraham is seen as the "strong beam" that carried the Jewish civilization forward. In fact, we begin with Abraham not only because he was so pivotal to Judaism but also because he is the father of the three great monotheistic religions in the West: Judaism, Christianity, and Islam. From this one man three powerful stories emerged that have significantly impacted global history.

Part 2: Historical Origin

The story of the Jewish people is one of the most remarkable of all ancient stories. This is because there is perhaps no other people group that has received as much attention and has had as much influence on the world in relation to its actual size. Indeed, as one Jewish scholar points out, the

---

2. Shai Cherry, *Introduction to Judaism: Part 2* (Chantilly, VA: The Teaching Company, 2004), 1.
3. Rapaport, *Tales and Maxims from the Talmud*, 67.

Jewish people, with the exception of modern-day Israel, "are a numerically insignificant minority" in all the places they reside.[4] Although small, the Jewish people have penetrated all parts of the world and have infused their distinct culture into the larger cultures in which they find themselves. The Jewish story is one of trying to maintain one's Jewish identity within the larger context of ethnically and religiously diverse nations.

Origins and Kingdom

We begin our historical overview of Judaism in the beginning of time. The book of Genesis describes the God of Israel as the Creator and Sustainer of the world. This God created two people—Adam and Eve—who gave rise to all humankind. Although they are the first people recorded in history, Abraham is customarily regarded as the founder of the Jewish nation. Indeed, as one historian of the Hebrew Bible quips, "A history of Israel must properly begin with the call of Abram to the father of the chosen nation."[5] The book of Genesis explains that Abraham came from the ancient city-state of Ur, which was a thriving culture. We are told that the Lord God commanded Abraham at the age of seventy-five to leave his home for a place that God would give him (Gen. 12:1–3). Today we call this land Israel or Palestine.

"Know then that it is those of faith who are the sons of Abraham." —Galatians 3:7

Eventually Abraham's descendants became as numerous as God had promised. They grew from twelve sons to twelve tribes. The book of Exodus narrates how the pharaoh of Egypt noticed how fruitful the Jewish people had become and enslaved them in Egypt for hundreds of years. After rescuing his people from Egyptian bondage through Moses, God made a covenant with the Jewish people and regarded them as "a kingdom of priests and a holy nation" (Ex. 19:6). Out of this "kingdom of priests" God consecrated the tribe of Levi as the priestly tribe that would perform the necessary rituals to stay in covenant relationship with this God.

Temple	Built	Destroyed	Destroyer	Scripture
1st Temple	960 BC	586 BC	Babylon under Nebuchadnezzar	1 Kings 6–8; 2 Kings 25:1–21
2nd Temple	515 BC	AD 70	Rome under General Titus	Ezra 6:13–18; Mark 13

4. Nicholas de Lange, *Introduction to Judaism*, 2nd ed. (Cambridge: Cambridge University Press, 2010), 1.

5. Eugene Merrill, *Kingdom of Priests: A History of Old Testament Israel* (Grand Rapids: Baker, 1996), 25.

Several hundred years after the exodus, the twelve tribes of the Jewish nation became isolated and territorial. It was not until the time of King David and his son Solomon in the tenth century BC that the tribes were officially united. David set up his capital in Jerusalem, where the Jewish temple was built. The period under the united kingdom, however, lasted briefly. Over time, stronger world empires such as Assyria and Babylon conquered, destroyed, and divided the tribes and Jewish people groups, which had been weakened by the nation's division into northern (Israel) and southern (Judea) territories after King Solomon's death in the tenth century BC. The Hebrew Bible interpreted the destruction and exile of the Jewish nation as God's condemnation for worshiping idols, acting wickedly, and violating the covenant God had made with the Jews hundreds of years before (2 Kings 17:7–20).

Dispersion

The most enduring defeat and exile of the Jewish people occurred in the sixth century BC at the hands of the Babylonians.[6] The Babylonian armies ravaged Jerusalem, destroyed the temple that God had ordered to be built there, and exiled the wealthiest and brightest citizens into Babylon. This event marked the beginning of the dispersion, the scattering of the Jewish people across the world outside Israel. Although some Jewish people returned to Israel within a century after the Babylonian exile and rebuilt the temple, many did not. In fact, many Jews prospered in exile and experienced better living conditions away from Israel than they did inside their own nation.[7] For those who did return, things were not the same. Not only was the temple only a shadow of its former glory (Hag. 2:3), but the Jewish people were still under the authority of Persia.

Even during New Testament times in the first century AD, despite the fact that the temple had been refurbished and enlarged, there was a common understanding that the people of Israel were still in dispersion. This is the case for two reasons. First, even though some Jews did live in Israel, many did not. Second, the Jewish residents of Israel were under pagan rule—first under Persian and then Greek and Roman rule. The Jewish prophet Jesus of Nazareth lived right before the Jewish nation rebelled against Roman occupation. Jesus, for his

"On the eve of the Passover Yeshu was hanged. For forty days before the execution took place, a herald went forth and cried, 'Yeshu is going forth to be stoned because he has practiced sorcery and enticed Israel to apostasy. Anyone who can say anything in his favor, let him come forward and plead on his behalf.' But since nothing was brought forward in his favor he was hanged on the eve of the Passover." —Talmud (Sanhedrin 43a)

Unless otherwise noted, quotations from the Talmud are taken from Michael Rodkinson, trans., *The Babylonian Talmud* (Boston: The Talmud Society, 1918). Also, some Jewish commentators question whether this comment refers to Jesus of Nazareth.

6. Raymond Scheindlin, *A Short History of the Jewish People: From Legendary Times to Modern Statehood* (Oxford: Oxford University Press, 2000), 20–23.
7. Ibid., 28.

There were several movements in Judaism at the time of the temple's destruction in AD 70: the Sadducees, who were in control of the temple system; the Essenes, who lived ascetic lives away from most Jews; the Zealots or even Sicarii, who advocated Jewish independence against Rome; and the Pharisees, who focused on observing the *halakha* or Jewish laws and customs, and out of whom rabbinic Judaism emerged.

part, encouraged the Jews to live within the kingdom rule of God and to repent (Mark 1:14–15).

In the middle of the first century AD many Jews found themselves increasingly in friction with Rome. Rebellion ensued. The First Jewish War lasted from AD 66–70. It was a watershed moment in Jewish history. The Romans crushed the Jews and destroyed the Jewish temple. But unlike in former times, the temple was never rebuilt. Instead of centralizing around the performance of daily sacrifices by priests, Judaism redefined itself. This redefinition of Judaism came to be called *rabbinic Judaism.*

Rabbinic Judaism, as its name suggests, refers to the Judaism that emerged under the guidance of rabbis or "teachers." Although its origins can be indirectly traced back to Ezra in the fifth century BC, it emerged most fully in the context immediately after destruction of the Jewish temple in AD 70. The Jewish priesthood fell into disuse soon after the temple's destruction because there were no sacrifices to be made. The group that filled this leadership void was made up of rabbis who, instead of making sacrifices in the temple, interpreted Torah. As one scholar explains:

> Rabbinic Judaism centers on the constant study of the Torah and the oral traditions associated with it and involves the meticulous observance of religious regulations, which are understood as constituting a legal system. By placing the study of the Torah at the center of Jewish religious life, the rabbis incidentally laid the foundation for the preoccupation of later Jewish culture with intellectual activities of all kinds.[8]

Seventy years after the destruction of the temple, the Jews rebelled again. Known as the Second Jewish War (132–35), this spirited yet failed attempt to take control of Roman-occupied Judea began hopefully but ended disastrously for the Jews. Simon bar Kokhba (d. 135), the leader of this rebellion, ruled from Jerusalem for three years before undergoing the same fate as his countrymen. Hundreds of thousands of Jews were killed or enslaved. Moreover, the Romans—headed by Emperor Hadrian (76–138 AD)—eradicated all Jewish presence from Jerusalem by exiling Jews on penalty of death, prohibiting circumcision, burning Jewish scrolls, and renaming the area.[9] The sobering outcomes of this war portended the next millennium of the Jewish story—continued exile, dispersion, and maltreatment under more powerful people groups.

8. Ibid., 53.
9. Ibid., 54–55.

Contemporary

Although there was always the option to identify as a Christian or a Muslim during the medieval period, in the late 1700s there were generally three options for Jews, particularly in Europe. The first was to assimilate into the dominant culture. This was a common choice that many Jews took. Although this option downplayed one's Jewish identity, it did provide educational and employment opportunities. Another option was to observe the Jewish traditions and customs as had been done for hundreds of years. Such an approach meant marginalization in the larger culture, but it also gave one identity within the Jewish community. Finally, the last option was a mixing of the two.

Jewish Ethnicities	Descent
Ashkenazi	German / Eastern European
Ethiopian	Sub-Saharan African
Mizrahi	North African / Middle Eastern
Sephardic	Spanish and Arab

This modernizing of Judaism was aimed at gaining "social acceptance without abandoning Jewish identity."[10] Put simply, contemporary Judaism—with its division into Orthodox, Reform, Conservative, and Reconstructionist—emerged out of this larger context. That's because these movements each sought to deal with the rapid changes taking place during the Enlightenment and the rise of modern states. Many Jewish people struggled to understand, on the one hand, how to stay faithful to one's ancient customs while, on the other, how to adapt to an ever-changing world.

The twentieth century has been a momentous period for many in the world but especially for the Jewish people. The two most decisive events in the story of Judaism in this century were the Holocaust and the creation of the state of Israel. As for the first, there was a long history of Jewish persecution in Europe, but this came to a head with the election of Adolf Hitler (1889–1945) as chancellor of Germany in 1933. Within months of his election, Hitler implemented hateful measures against the Jews. The government boycotted Jewish businesses, expelled Jews from civil service, removed their children from

10. Norman Solomon, *Judaism: A Very Short Introduction* (Oxford: Oxford University Press, 2000), 100.

schools, and began the building of concentration camps.[11] Two years later Jews were stripped of their citizenship. Germany aggressively expanded its territory and found allies that forwarded its violent program against the Jews before the Allied forces ultimately defeated Germany and the Axis powers in 1945. But the war had taken its toll. Although difficult to imagine—let alone express in words—in as little as a decade 6 million of the 10 million Jews living in Europe had been murdered.[12]

Ironically, notes Jewish scholar Nicholas de Lange, the anti-Semitism and genocide that the Jews experienced during the Holocaust expedited the formation of a Jewish state in the middle of the twentieth century.[13] The founder of the movement toward Jewish statehood or Zionism was the Austro-Hungarian journalist Theodore Herzl (1860–1904). His passionate plea for the creation of a (secular) Jewish state where Jews could live free from anti-Semitism continued to gain momentum after his death. Although some traditional Jews initially rejected Zionism because they believed it was the Messiah's task—the timing of which only God knew—to gather the Jewish people out of exile and into a Jewish state, this changed after World War II.[14] Within two years of the ending of the war, the United Nations partitioned Palestine into two territories, a Jewish and an Arab state. On May 14, 1948, the state of Israel came into existence.[15] Since that time Zionism and the Zionist movement have continued strong. Indeed, I once had a conversation with a woman in Israel about her religious faith. She told me categorically that she did not believe in religion or God. "However, if pressured into choosing something," she continued after pausing to reflect on our conversation, "Zionism would be my religion."

"The longing to return to the Land of Israel, a yearning that suffuses Jewish prayer and rituals, began to be fulfilled toward the end of the 19th century. The irony is that many of the early pioneers to the Land of Israel were secularists, motivated by politics rather than theology."
—Shai Cherry

Cherry, Introduction to Judaism, 2:21.

Part 3: Religious Writings

There are a variety of religious writings associated with Judaism. Judaism is the world religion that is perhaps most focused on education, learning, and books.[16] Naturally, then, there are a host of writings that are important to this religion and culture. In addition to the Bible, some

---

11. Scheindlin, *A Short History of the Jewish People*, 202–3.
12. Solomon, *Judaism*, 15.
13. De Lange, *Introduction to Judaism*, 42.
14. Leora Batnitzky, *How Judaism Became a Religion: An Introduction to Modern Jewish Thought* (Princeton, NJ: Princeton University Press, 2011), 95.
15. Scheindlin, *A Short History of the Jewish People*, 231.
16. De Lange, *Introduction to Judaism*, 43–44.

of the key writings include the Talmud, prayer books, mystical writings, and interpretive works on the Bible.

The Bible

Law (Torah)	Prophets (Nevi'im)		Writings (Ketuvim)		
	Former	*Latter*	*Poetry*	*Five Rolls*	*History*
Genesis	Joshua	Isaiah	Psalms	Ruth	Daniel
Exodus	Judges	Jeremiah	Job	Song of Songs	Ezra-Nehemiah
Leviticus	Samuel	Ezekiel	Proverbs		
Numbers	Kings	The Twelve Prophets		Ecclesiastes	Chronicles
Deuteronomy				Lamentations	
				Esther	

We begin our discussion with the Hebrew Bible, the oldest and most foundational of the Jewish writings. The Hebrew text used by Jews—the Masoretic Text, which was given its present shape a millennium ago—is the same text that we Christians use in our Bibles. Apart from the name, the only difference is the arrangement. Whereas the Christian Old Testament contains thirty-nine books beginning with Genesis and ending with Malachi, the Hebrew Bible is classified into the three main categories of Law (*Torah*), Prophets (*Nevi'im*), and Writings (*Ketuvim*), which, when put in an acrostic in Hebrew, are referred to as the Tanakh. The main reason that the Christian Old Testament contains more "books" is that the Septuagint—the Greek translation of the Hebrew Scriptures dating to the third century BC—needed extra parchment space when translated into Greek, since Greek letters are larger than Hebrew ones. The Greek translators divided several larger books such as Samuel, Kings, and Chronicles into two.[17]

The Hebrew Bible was written over the course of hundreds of years in many different areas. The foundational section, the Torah or first five books, discusses the establishment of the Jewish nation from the beginning of creation to the time of Moses, who lived sometime between the thirteenth and fifteenth centuries BC.[18] The Prophets discuss the next thousand years of God's interaction with and preservation of the Jewish

17. Norman Geisler and William Nix, *A General Introduction to the Bible* (Chicago: Moody Press, 1986), 23–25.

18. Raymond Dillard and Tremper Longman, *An Introduction to the Old Testament* (Grand Rapids: Zondervan, 1994), 60.

The Hebrew word *Torah* is a broad term that may refer to any of the following: the first five books of the Bible; the whole Hebrew Bible; or the oral tradition given to Moses, that is, the Talmud.

people through the course of the united kingdom, the exile, and the Jewish return to Israel. Finally, the Writings are the most varied of the Hebrew Scriptures. This section contains poems, histories, and prophetic documents that span hundreds of years of Jewish history.

Fig. 4.1.
The Torah in Hebrew.

The Talmud

In addition to the Bible, the most important book in the Jewish canon is the Talmud ("study"). There is a story in the Talmud about when the famed Rabbi Hillel (70 BC–AD 10), whose grandson Rabban Gamaliel taught the apostle Paul (Acts 22:3), answered the secret to life while his student stood on one foot: Like Rabbi Jesus only a few decades later, Hillel said, "That which is hateful to you, do not do to others. That is the whole Torah; the rest is commentary" (Shabbat 31a).

If the Torah can be explained so succinctly, we may be wondering, why is the Talmud so long? The answer is twofold. First, the Torah itself does not spell out all the implications of its commandments and prohibitions. Take the fourth commandment, for instance: "Remember the Sabbath day" (Ex. 20:8). By itself, this commandment does not explain exactly *how* we are to remember the Sabbath and to abstain from work. For example, is starting a fire or taking a walk "work"? In the Talmud the rabbis discuss these issues. (By the way, the rabbinic answer to the first question was "yes," while the answer to the second depended on how far you walked.)

The other reason the Talmud is so long has to do with the time-honored tradition of Jewish debate and argumentation. Unlike Christianity or Islam, Judaism has a long and strong tradition of arguing with God. Jewish scholar and Rabbi Jacob Neusner goes so far as to say that the God of the Torah "expects to be argued with."[19] While all the many rabbinic discussions and interpretations of biblical law have struck some in the Christian tradition as legalistic and too focused on minute details, the Jewish tradition understands these discussions as important ways to preserve the Torah.

According to the Talmud, God gave Moses the "written Torah" and "oral Torah" on Mount Sinai. The written Torah is what came to be recorded in the Pentateuch. The oral Torah, by contrast, was not initially put into writing. Instead, it was passed down and preserved generation after generation. As the following Talmudic excerpt explains:

> Moses received [the oral] Torah at Sinai and handed it on to Joshua, Joshua to elders, and elders to prophets. And prophets handed it on to the men of the great assembly. They said three things: "Be prudent in judgment; raise up many disciples; and make a fence for the Torah." (*Avot* 1:1)

The "fence" that the rabbis made for the Torah is the Talmud. Although its name is a broad term referring to rabbinical commentary, the Talmud is technically composed of two major parts: the Mishnah and the Gemara. Stated differently, the Mishnah plus the Gemara equals the Talmud.

The first part of the Talmud, the Mishnah ("repetition"), contains the sayings and opinions of rabbis from around 300 BC to AD 220. Rabbi Judah HaNasi (AD 138–220), a descendant of Rabbi Hillel and of King David, edited and compiled the definitive version of the Mishnah in the early part of the third century.[20] The Mishnah contains laws, principles, stories, and opinions on any number of civil and religious issues. It is understood to be separate from yet parallel to the Hebrew Bible. Each

---

19. Jacob Neusner, *A Rabbi Talks with Jesus* (Montreal: McGill-Queen's University Press, 2000), 24.

20. Brad Young, *Meet the Rabbis: Rabbinic Thought and the Teachings of Jesus* (Peabody, MA: Hendrickson, 2007), 83.

of its six volumes or "orders" contains several tractates, several chapters per tractate, and several *mishnah* verses or *mishnayot* per chapter.[21]

I once asked one of my classes to read portions of the Mishnah in preparation for a discussion on Judaism. Not one single person understood what he or she was reading! Jacob Neusner, who translated a contemporary version of the Mishnah, captures the disorienting nature of the book well in the eyes of outsiders:

> Falling into the hands of someone who has never seen this document before, the Mishnah must cause puzzlement. From the first line to the last, discourse takes up questions internal to a system that is never introduced. The Mishnah provides information without establishing context. It presents disputes about facts hardly urgent outside a circle of faceless disputants. Consequently, we start with the impression that we join a conversation already long under way about topics we can never grasp anyhow.[22]

Unlike the Hebrew Scriptures, which contain many stories from beginning to end, the Mishnah has no real beginning or ending. The first "order" jumps into commentary concerning when the Shema—the liturgical declaration taken from Deuteronomy 6:4—can be recited in the evening.

The second part of the Talmud is the Gemara ("study"). This section is even more detailed and intricate than the Mishnah. The Gemara, written in Aramaic rather than in Hebrew, "consists largely of detailed and strenuously argued disagreements on the meaning and validity of both Mishnaic and biblical laws."[23] In other words, whereas the Mishnah debates the meaning of the Torah, the Gemara debates the meaning of the Mishnah *and* the Torah. The Talmud is arranged according to *mishnah* verses from the Mishnah followed by *sugyot* or topical commentary from the Gemara. The two different Talmudic versions are the Palestinian (or Jerusalem) Talmud and the Babylonian Talmud. They were completed around AD 350 and 500, respectively.[24]

Other Jewish Writings

In addition to the Bible and the Talmud, there are many other important Jewish writings. The first of these, the Midrash ("study" or

---

21. Ibid., 84–86.

22. Jacob Neusner, *The Mishnah: A New Translation* (New Haven, CT: Yale University Press, 1988), viii.

23. De Lange, *Introduction to Judaism*, 54–55.

24. George Robinson, *Essential Judaism: A Complete Guide to Beliefs, Customs and Rituals* (New York: Atria, 2000), 344–46.

"investigation"), is a collection of texts that chiefly interpret the Bible. It includes rabbinic discussions of the Bible during the first several centuries AD. The midrashim are often classified into legal commentary (*halakha*) and nonlegal commentary (*haggadah*). In the beginning of this chapter, I referred to a midrash on the book of Genesis. The midrashim are enjoyable to read and include sometimes fanciful yet always intriguing interpretations of the Hebrew Scriptures. Another important genre of Jewish writings is prayer or liturgical books called *siddurim*. A *siddur* is not only what you might read from if you attend a synagogue service, but also what many Jews use for prayer at the Western Wall in Jerusalem.

Finally, the last Jewish writing I want to mention is the Zohar ("radiance"). It is the most significant of the texts associated with the Jewish mystical tradition called Kabbalah ("receiving"). Commonly regarded as being written in the thirteenth century AD in Spain, the Zohar is concerned with different mystical and esoteric ways to study Torah.[25] It is one of the more interesting Jewish writings—as the initial section of the book reveals:

> There was a man who lived in the mountains. He knew nothing about those who lived in the city. He sowed wheat and ate the kernels raw. One day he entered the city. They brought him good bread. He said, "What is this for?" They said, "Bread to eat!" He ate, and it tasted very good. He said, "What is it made of?" They said, "Wheat." Later they brought him cakes kneaded in oil. He tasted them and said, "What are these made of?" They said, "Wheat." Finally they brought him royal pastry made with honey and oil. He said, "And what are these made of?" They said, "Wheat." He said, "I am the master of all these, for I eat the essence of all these: wheat!" Because of that view, he knew nothing of the delights of the world; they were lost to him. So it is with one who grasps the principle and does not know all those delectable delights deriving, diverging from that principle.[26]

This intriguing parable is about getting to the more advanced levels of Torah and not assuming that because you know something at the basic level, you know it at the deeper level as well.

Part 4: Beliefs

Judaism is one of the most difficult religions for my students to understand. The main reason for this has to do with the students'

In Hebrew, words are made plural by adding the letters *im* or *ot* at the end of the word. For instance, *siddur* (prayer book) becomes *siddurim*; while *mitzvah* (commandment) becomes *mitzvot*.

---

25. De Lange, *Introduction to Judaism*, 60.

26. Daniel Matt, trans., *Zohar: Annotated and Explained* (Woodstock, VT: SkyLight Books, 2005), 2.

assumption that they know more about Judaism than they actually do. While we Christians do share common Scriptures with Judaism and therefore hold many views that are similar, there are also sharp contrasts. So the first lesson we must learn about this religion is that while it is an outgrowth of the Hebrew Bible, contemporary Judaism is not equivalent to the Old Testament.

Indeed, my students are often shocked when I inform them that many Jews today do not even believe in God's existence! It is common for Jews to understand and identify themselves primarily as culturally Jewish rather than religiously so. As one Jewish scholar writes succinctly, "religion is . . . secondary to Jewish identity."[27] What's more, unlike its offspring, Christianity and Islam, Judaism is not a proselytizing religion. The truth is that rabbis generally discourage conversions to the Jewish religion. There is a lengthy tradition admonishing rabbis to send potential converts away three times before allowing their conversion.[28]

Samson Raphael Hirsch (1808–88), the leading rabbi of nineteenth-century German Orthodoxy, went so far as to write that "Judaism is the one religion which does *not* say, 'Outside me there is no salvation.'" Instead, he explained, the upright of all people groups are traveling toward the "same blessed destination."[29] It is not surprising, therefore, that of all religious groups in the world, the Jewish people are the "most likely religious group to describe their outlook as secular or somewhat secular, including 14 percent who could be classified as atheists and agnostics."[30] More than half the Jews in the world do not attend synagogues on any regular basis.[31]

I once had a conversation with an Orthodox Jewish man in Jerusalem. My friend asked the man what would be required for him to convert to Judaism. The man replied bluntly, "You don't have to convert to Judaism. All God requires of you, a Gentile, is to follow the seven laws of Noah. Conversion would be of no value." The man was alluding to the common belief that only the Jewish people are expected to observe the 613 commandments of God. The Gentiles, by contrast, are required to observe only seven basic laws. If we observe these basic laws, we will be afforded a portion of the world to come.

---

27. De Lange, *Introduction to Judaism*, 1.
28. Stephen Prothero, *God Is Not One: The Eight Rival Religions That Run the World—and Why Their Differences Matter* (New York: HarperCollins, 2010), 251.
29. Gwilym Beckerlegge, ed., *The World Religions Reader*, 2nd ed. (London: Routledge, 2001), 47.
30. Cherry, *Introduction to Judaism*, 2:35.
31. Prothero, *God Is Not One*, 267.

Noahic Laws for Goyim (Non-Jews)
1. No murder
2. No sexual immorality
3. No idolatry
4. No eating animals from torn limbs
5. No cursing God
6. No theft
7. Setting up a system of law

This concept comes partly from the Talmudic passage that states: "The Holy One, blessed be He, offered the Torah to every nation and every tongue, but none accepted it until He came to Israel who received it" (Talmud [Avodah Zarah 2b]). Because only the Jewish people accepted the Torah—after every other people group rejected God's offer—only they are expected to keep its commandments or *mitzvot*. The 613 commandments that the Jews are expected to keep are often divided into 365 positive commandments (equaling the days of the solar year) and 248 negative ones (equaling the supposed number of bodily organs). This classification came from Rabbi Simlai in the third century AD, although several rabbis since then have divided the commandments slightly differently.[32]

Religious Denominations

Although all forms of Judaism today trace their heritage back to rabbinic Judaism, there is great diversity within all the denominations or movements in contemporary Judaism. Most of these movements appeared in Europe during the Enlightenment when Jews were granted citizenship and admitted to public universities and professions that were historically barred from them. One of the important Jewish thinkers of this period, Moses Mendelsohn (1729–86), affirmed the rights of Jews to live as free citizens and to be afforded the rights and privileges offered in the countries where they lived. The Jewish people, like their Christian counterparts, responded to the changes of modernity in various ways, the result of which created a Jewish identity that differed greatly from the past. The religious movements that emerged during and after

32. Robinson, *Essential Judaism*, 196.

this time came to be known as Reform, Orthodox, Conservative, and Reconstructionist Judaism.[33]

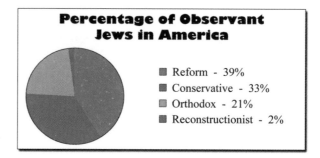

Fig. 4.2. Percentage of observant Jews in America.

Reform Judaism

The first of these movements is Reform Judaism. Although it began in Germany in the eighteenth century, it has thrived in America. One of its key documents, the Pittsburgh Platform, was the result of a conference attended by many rabbis in Pittsburgh in 1885. An excerpt from the document represents some of its radical views on Jewish customs:

> We hold that all . . . Mosaic and rabbinical laws as regulate diet, priestly purity, and dress originated in ages and under the influence of ideas entirely foreign to our present mental and spiritual state. They fail to impress the modern Jew with a spirit of priestly holiness; their observance in our days is apt rather to obstruct than to further modern spiritual elevation.[34]

Fig. 4.3. Map of the world in the nineteenth century AD, when modern Judaism was developing in Europe and in America.

33. The percentages of the religious denominations below come from Prothero, *God Is Not One*, 267.
34. "The Pittsburgh Platform," in Robinson, *Essential Judaism*, 506.

As can be seen, Reform Judaism advocates a radical program of reform and modernization of the Jewish religion into contemporary culture. In this way, there are many similarities between Reform Judaism and liberal Protestantism. Both emerged at the same time in the same area for the same reasons. They were both responses to traditional expressions of their religions and the rapid changes taking place in society. These movements rejected the notion that God had inspired the Bible, affirmed complete gender equality, emphasized ethics and social justice, and abandoned those practices that were seen as antithetical to adaptation and assimilation into contemporary culture. At the same time, they shared many common values with their mother religions and did not want to wholly sever ties with them. Instead, they wanted to modernize and contemporize, and propel their religions into the modern world in ways that aligned with critical scholarship, science, and advances in technology.

Orthodox Judaism

The second religious Jewish movement is (Modern) Orthodoxy. It is the most traditional of the various forms of Judaism and is a continuation of the Judaism practiced by most Jews before the Enlightenment. Orthodox Jews believe that the *halakha* or Jewish laws and customs are completely binding. They regard them as given by God. Although they highly value the study of Torah, Orthodox Jews do not by any means reject secular learning and education. Instead, they seek to hallow secular learning, not flee from it. As for actual practices, Hebrew is spoken in Orthodox services, men and women are divided during worship, people are not allowed to drive their cars on Shabbat (or Sabbath), and men and women must wear head coverings and dress modestly.

In addition to Orthodox Judaism, there is a related group called the ultra-Orthodox or the Haredi. The ultra-Orthodox are the most conservative and traditional of the Jewish religious groups. Unlike the Modern Orthodox, however, they eschew secular learning for themselves (understanding secular learning to be the domain of non-Jews) and focus on studying Torah. They believe it binding on their families to populate the earth—which is the first of the biblical commandments (Gen. 1:28)—and have four times as many children as their Jewish counterparts.[35] I once walked through Mea Shearim, the famous Haredi neighborhood in Jerusalem, where the men and boys were distinctly dressed in white

The word *halakha* ("path") refers to the entire body of Jewish law. This includes the Hebrew Bible, rabbinic interpretations, and other traditions and customs. All religious forms of Judaism are centered on determining how to interpret, observe, and adapt the *halakha*.

35. Benjamin Blech, *The Complete Idiot's Guide to Understanding Judaism*, 2nd ed. (New York: Alpha, 2003), 315.

and black with black hats, and where large posters warned outsiders of entering with immodest clothing.

Conservative Judaism

"Reform [Judaism] declared that Judaism has changed throughout time and that Jewish law is no longer binding. Orthodoxy denies both propositions. . . . Conservative Judaism agrees with Orthodoxy in maintaining the authority of Jewish law and with Reform that Judaism has grown and evolved through time." —Rabbi Robert Gordis

Blech, *The Complete Idiot's Guide to Understanding Judaism,* 321.

The Conservative movement is the response to Reform and Orthodox Judaism. It began in nineteenth-century Europe, but has flourished in the United States. It is "conservative" from the perspective of the Reform rather than the Orthodox. Stated positively, it is "conservative" in the sense that it seeks to conserve and preserve the *halakha* or Jewish laws, but is willing to make modifications when necessary. Like Reform Judaism, the Conservative movement believes that the Jewish religion must be adapted to contemporary culture; like the Orthodox, it believes that the commandments are central. This means that Conservative Judaism is caught between two important yet competing stories of Judaism: the Reform on the left and the Orthodoxy on the right.

One good example of how Conservative Judaism straddles the fence between its two sister denominations centers on the topic of driving to the synagogue during Shabbat. In Exodus 35:3 the Jews are commanded: "You shall kindle no fire in all your dwelling places on the Sabbath day." Practically speaking, this means that Orthodox members of synagogues are not allowed to start their cars on Shabbat (by "kindling" a fire) and thereby driving to the service. Whereas Reform Jews would generally see this commandment as unrealistic in our driving culture (and therefore not necessary to modernize), Conservatives would seek to conserve or preserve this commandment until necessity demanded otherwise. As the interpretation goes, Conservatives decided that it was permissible to drive on Shabbat for the practical reason that many Jews lived too far from the synagogue to walk, so it was better to kindle a fire and attend the service than to literally observe the commandment and miss the service.

Reconstructionist Judaism

The last movement in Judaism is the most recent as well as the smallest. Unlike the other religious movements, it is the only one that was forged in America. The architect of this movement was Rabbi Mordecai Kaplan (1881–1993), who was active in the Conservative movement although he grew up Orthodox. Reconstructionists typically understand Judaism as an "evolving religious civilization," to use Kaplan's words. This means that the emphasis is on preserving the Jewish culture as a civilization. Put bluntly, the Jewish culture is more important than

Jewish belief. Or as one rabbi states, "Reconstructionist Judaism isn't so much concerned with God as it is with Jews."[36] Whereas Conservative Judaism is a middle way between Reform and Orthodox Judaism, Reconstructionist Judaism shares many commonalities between Conservative and Reform Judaism.

Movement	Emphasis
Reform	Ethics
Orthodox	Law
Conservative	Tradition
Reconstructionist	Culture
Secular	Ethnicity
Zionist	Jewish statehood

At the same time, there are key differences. For instance, Reconstructionism can appear just as observant as the Orthodox because many observe the *halakha* even though they do not believe they are binding. Reconstructionists are more likely to observe the dietary laws and follow other traditional customs than the Reform.[37] However, Reconstructionism is perceived to be more "liberal" ethically or theologically than the Reform. Reconstructionism, for example, not only ordains women to the rabbinate (as do the Reform and Conservatives but not traditionally the Orthodox), but also ordains gays and lesbians. What's more, Reconstructionists reject the notion that the Jews are a "chosen people" as well as other traditional Jewish beliefs such as expectation of a future Messiah.[38]

The Unifying Factor

In addition to the four religious movements discussed above, I would be remiss if I did not state again that many Jews do not even believe in God's existence, let alone attend a synagogue or believe that the *halakha* or Jewish laws are binding. They are called "secular Jews," and there is no real stigma attached to this classification. Although this sounds strange to many Christians, it does not to Judaism. Indeed, secular Jews are just as much a part of Judaism as are religious or observant ones.

36. Ibid., 323.
37. Robinson, *Essential Judaism*, 233.
38. Ibid., 62.

Given this great diversity, you may be wondering what it means "to be a Jew." This is a difficult question to answer; each of the religious and secular movements would respond to it in divergent ways. But two things come to mind. The first response is that Judaism—however we define it—is more focused on deeds than on creeds. As one Jewish rabbi states it, "It is not so much what we believe, but rather what we do, that defines us as Jews."[39] Practically speaking, the locus of this question—however we answer it—should concentrate less on defining Jews as *believing* in certain things than on *doing* certain things. Jews emphasize action over belief.

This leads us to a second response, which I mentioned in the beginning of this chapter: Judaism can be defended and defined as a religion, a culture, an ethnicity, or a civilization. It is only after we understand Judaism as an identity *rather than strictly as a system of belief* that we will begin to comprehend what it truly means "to be a Jew." Although Jewish identity traditionally meant being born to a "Jewish" woman, today it means many different things. Reform and Reconstructionist Judaism, for instance, affirm that one can be considered Jewish from the father's side, while Orthodoxy has always affirmed that anybody can become a "Jew by choice" by fully converting to Judaism and following the Jewish laws.

> The Jewish tradition has always been a dance, or perhaps a wrestle, between the old and the new. And it is this give and take that keeps it vital.

Part 5: Worship Practices

The Jewish life is punctuated by regular practices and observances. These range from daily prayers to weekly rituals to yearly festivals. Of all the world religions, Judaism is perhaps most aware of and in tune with sacred space and sacred time. The two principal places where sacred space is most manifest for Jews are the synagogue and the home. The first of these, synagogues, are variously called temples and shuls. The essential structure of the synagogue reflects the physical arrangement of the former Jewish temples. Central to a synagogue is the ark, which houses the Torah scrolls. This is a reminder of the ark of the covenant. The *bimah* or altar, which is another important component to Jewish synagogues, is a platform from which the Torah is read.

There is a long tradition of Jews' having three daily services at synagogues, which reflect the sacrificial system of the temple periods. Synagogues also have weekly Sabbath or Shabbat services, which occur on Friday evenings and Saturday mornings. A typical service includes reading from the Torah, singing or responding orally out of the prayer

---

39. Rabbi Jerome Epstein, "The Ideal Conservative Jew: Eight Behavioral Expectations," in Robinson, *Essential Judaism*, 522.

book, bowing and standing (when the Torah passes by), and saying prayers and blessings. Depending on the denomination, the primary or secondary language (for the liturgy) may be in Hebrew. In Orthodox synagogues, men and women are separated during worship and men are expected to wear *kippot* or hats and women are expected to wear head coverings. Men are also required to wear *tallitot* or prayer shawls. In other Jewish movements, customs vary widely from synagogue to synagogue. If you ever attend a synagogue, my advice to you is to wear modest clothes and to observe whether other people are wearing hats or prayer shawls, and not to be shy about asking how to respect the customs of the synagogue.

Besides public worship, the center of Jewish life is in the home. Many Jewish homes have a *mezuzah* ("doorpost"), which is a case hung next to a door filled with a parchment of the Shema (Deut. 6:4–9). These homes may also have a *menorah* or seven-branched lampstand, the Bible, and perhaps other Jewish books. Two regular rituals practiced in the home are celebrations of Passover and of Sabbath. The Passover meal or *seder* is celebrated annually to remember Israelite emancipation out of Egypt. It is an exciting night observed at the home where everyone is able to participate. The other home ritual is observing Shabbat, which begins on Friday evening and ends Saturday evening. Shabbat is the highlight of the Jewish week, and specific preparations are made—lighting candles, singing, eating certain food, and drinking wine. There are also special ways to end Shabbat on Saturday evening.

Part 6: Point of Contact

A few years ago, I was friends with a Jewish young man from work. We talked about many different things over the course of our time together. Sometimes I would talk to him about religion. When I did so, I always tried to bring our conversation to some story or event in the Old Testament, since I assumed that he—as a Jew—was familiar with these stories and events. One day he told me that he was not at all familiar with the stories and that he did not see them as particularly significant to his Jewish identity.

Because Christians affirm the authority of the Hebrew Bible, many of us believe this is the best place to begin a religious conversation with our Jewish brothers and sisters. This is based on the assumption that Judaism is equivalent to the Hebrew Bible. Yet the truth is that Judaism has developed and progressed over the centuries just as Christianity has. And although I am not discouraging anyone from talking about the

---

Synagogues are generally administered by elected members who make up a council. The rabbi (which is an earned and not a hereditary title) leads the synagogue. Priests and Levites (both hereditary titles) are honored in Orthodoxy, but not usually in other Jewish movements.

"The Sabbath is a day of rest for the sake of life . . . It is not an interlude but the climax of living."
—Abraham Heschel

Abraham Heschel, *The Sabbath* (New York: Farrar, Straus and Giroux, 1951), 14.

Hebrew Bible with Jews, it has been my experience that Jews are more readily interested in other items of discussion.

One of the concerns I have experienced most often in conversations with Jewish individuals has to do with identity. I have spoken with several Jewish people whose primary hindrance to Christianity is the supposition that they cease to be Jewish if they become Christian. This is understandable in many ways, since Christianity has become a "Gentile" religion through and through. Although it emerged out of Judaism in the first century AD, Christianity quickly became an international and ethnically diverse religion. At the same time, Christianity is less about losing one's prior identity and more about gaining another identity, namely, of one who is, in the words of the Jewish apostle Paul, "in Messiah." Stated differently, Jews do not lose their Jewish identity or heritage if they become Christians. On the contrary, as Jesus himself said, "I came that they may have life and have it abundantly" (John 10:10). Jesus also said, "Do not think that I have come to abolish the Law or the Prophets; I have not come to abolish them but to fulfill them" (Matt. 5:17). Jesus' mission in life was not to abolish Jewish identity but rather to complete and amplify it.

This is the case for all people groups—Jewish ones included. When I became a Christian, for instance, I did not lose my identity as an American or as a son or as a brother. Rather, I began to understand that my identities as an American and as a son and as a brother are best understood from the lens of my primary identity as a Christian. My Christian identity illuminated and informed my identity as an American. I forever came to be defined by my identity "in Messiah." I am a Christian before I am anything else. This is the same for Jewish people. Jesus does not demolish one's former identity; he fulfills it.

Discussion Questions

1. How should Christians understand the Jewish religion given that Christianity emerged out of this religion and culture? How should Christians relate to Jews, especially in view of the extreme brutality that many Jews have experienced over the centuries under the authority of a culture that was "Christian"?

2. What is rabbinic Judaism? Why is it so important in the history of Judaism? What events led up to the emergence of this movement, and how has it changed the Jewish religion? What would Jesus have thought about this movement when it emerged in the second half of the first century AD?

3. Discuss the major branches of Judaism. Why are they so different? What is similar about the different branches of Judaism and the different branches of Christianity?

4. Based on the fact that many Jewish people today are not religiously observant and many don't even believe in God, is it possible to be a "Christian atheist"? Why or why not?

Further Readings

De Lange, Nicholas. *An Introduction to Judaism*. 2nd ed. Cambridge: Cambridge University Press, 2010.

Robinson, George. *Essential Judaism: A Complete Guide to Beliefs, Customs and Rituals*. New York: Atria, 2000.

Scheindlin, Raymond. *A Short History of the Jewish People: From Legendary Times to Modern Statehood*. Oxford: Oxford University Press, 2000.

Solomon, Norman. *Judaism: A Very Short Introduction*. Oxford: Oxford University Press, 2000.

Solomon, Norman, trans. *The Talmud: A Selection*. London: Penguin, 2009.

chapter 5

Islam: The Story of Submission

Although Islam is the youngest of the major world religions . . . [it] is the second largest and fastest-growing religion in the world. To speak of the world of Islam today is to refer not only to countries that stretch from North Africa to Southeast Asia but also to Muslim minority communities that exist across the globe. Thus, for example, Islam is the second or third largest religion in Europe and the Americas.

John Esposito

Islam is a religion, a civilization, a state, a social system, as well as a philosophy.

Yahiya Emerick

The [vast] majority of Muslims today live in south or southeast Asia. The universalism of Islam transcends the cultural boundaries of Arab civilization.

Vincent Cornell

Part 1: The Beginning

In the beginning Allah—*the* God of the world—said, "Be!" and a giant object appeared before him like a ball. God ripped apart this ball, which we call heaven and earth, and separated it into two pieces. There was smoke everywhere. Allah said, "Come into being, willingly or not." In submission to this God, all things came into being—willingly. Allah then spread out the earth as flat as the prairie and created mountains that acted as giant pegs to keep the earth in place. God put the stars in orbit and established the necessary conditions for life. God created man out of dried clay from dark mud and placed him "as a drop of fluid" into a garden. From a drop of fluid to a clinging form to a lump of flesh and finally to a flesh-and-bones creature this man came into existence. He was designed to work and toil.

Before creating humans, Allah had created angels that were made of light and have no free will. Allah also created energy-based creatures called jinn that were made of fire. They, like humans, have free will. God commanded the angels and jinn to bow down before Adam, the first man. Iblis, a jinn later known as Satan, refused. "What prevented you from bowing down as I commanded you?" God demanded of Iblis. "I am better than him," the defiant jinn replied: "You created me from fire and him from clay." Many jinn were persuaded by Iblis to disobey God. In anger God banished Iblis from his presence and declared that on the day of judgment he would cast him down into the fires of hell. But in the meantime, God agreed to let Iblis roam the earth and lie in wait for those not following the straight path—the way of submission to Allah. Iblis immediately approached Adam and his wife and tricked them into eating from the tree God had commanded them not to approach. After the man and woman did so, their nakedness was exposed and God banished them from the garden. Although they put leaves on themselves as garments to cover their nakedness, God rejoined that "the garment of God-consciousness is the best of all garments."

After creating heaven and earth in six symbolic days, God established himself on his throne. He did not rest on the seventh day, as God has no need of rest. Instead, Allah sits on his throne, high above his creation, where he directs and determines the outcome of earthly events. God has sent many prophets and messengers on earth to lead people to the straight path and to the performance of good deeds. About fifteen hundred years ago, Allah sent his final prophet and messenger upon the earth. The message this prophet gave is the last revelation until the day of judgment—at which time God will judge humans and jinns and send them to heaven or hell.[1]

So goes the creation account of Islam. Although there are many commonalities between the Qur'anic and biblical accounts, let us examine the differences. The first major difference to note is that Hawwa or

---

1. The following creation story was pieced together from various portions of the Qur'an, specifically: 7:10–27; 9:4; 10:3–4; 13:1–4; 15:19, 26–50; 18:50–53; 20:121–24; 21:30–33; 23:12–15; 41:9–12; 81:25; 51:47–49. All quotations from the Qur'an come from M. A. S. Abdel Haleem, trans., *The Qur'an* (Oxford: Oxford University Press, 2010). Note that the terms *Allah* and *God* will be used interchangeably in this chapter for the Muslim deity.

Eve, who is never explicitly mentioned in the Qur'an by name, is neither made from Adam nor responsible for their transgression before God. If anyone is to blame for Adam and his wife's eating from the forbidden tree, it is Iblis or Adam, but not Eve. The second difference is that Allah—"the Lord of Mercy, the Giver of Mercy" (Qur'an 1:1)[2]—quickly forgave Adam and his wife for their transgression and did not curse them or creation. As a result, there is no concept of original sin in Islam. In other words, none of the descendants of Adam and Eve ever received a sinful disposition. On the contrary, Allah gave free will to humans, who can do good or bad deeds as they choose.

The next difference between the Qur'anic and biblical accounts of creation is that Allah made a creature in addition to humans and angels called jinn. Coming from the Arabic word for *hidden*, jinn are invisible creatures that live in a parallel dimension. Besides humans, jinn are the only creatures that Allah created who have free will. All other creatures and creations—including angels, rocks, and animals—are by nature *Muslims*, that is, beings or things that are completely surrendered or submitted to Allah. Jinn, like humans, can be either good or bad. Good jinn do not interact with humans, but bad jinn—like Iblis—whisper bad thoughts to humans, haunt houses, possess people, and give predictions to fortune-tellers.[3]

The last difference to mention between the Qur'anic and biblical stories of creation is the Muslim emphasis on submission. When I teach on Islam, I distribute a handout to students that was given to me by a Muslim. The document reads boldly that "Jesus is a Muslim." It's a shocking declaration, and it takes students a moment to respond to this statement. One of the reasons I share this with students is to communicate to them that Islam understands itself to be all-encompassing. Although many of us in the Judeo-Christian world think of Islam as a religion that began with Muhammad several hundred years after Christ, Muslims claim that Islam has always existed and that the biblical characters that we claim as our own spiritual descendants, such as Abraham, Moses, and David, were devout Muslims. Indeed, Muslims assert, Jesus himself was a Muslim prophet whose teachings were later corrupted by his followers.

> "We [Muslims] believe in God and in what has been sent down to us and to Abraham, Ishmael, Isaac, Jacob, and the Tribes. We believe in what has been given to Moses, Jesus, and the prophets from their Lord. We do not make a distinction between any of them."
> —3:84

Part 2: Historical Origin

The story of Islam is one of the most impressive in the world. Exactly how a handful of marginalized people in the early part of the seventh

---

2. In this chapter all citations come from the Qur'an unless otherwise noted.

3. Yahiya Emerick, *The Complete Idiot's Guide to Understanding Islam*, 2nd ed. (New York: Alpha, 2004), 24.

century were able to flourish into several thousand within a few years and propel themselves into virtual world dominance over the next centuries and become the second-largest global religion continues to intrigue onlookers. In this section we will trace the history of Islam in several stages: (1) Early Origins, (2) Rightly Guided Caliphate, (3) Dynastic Period, and (4) Modern Islam.

Early Origins

Although Muslims claim that Adam was the first Muslim—which is important to bear in mind when studying Islam—the origins of the Islamic world properly begin with Muhammad. Born into the minor Hashim clan within the much larger and prestigious Quraysh tribe in the year AD 570, Muhammad was orphaned at a young age and eventually taken under the guardianship of his paternal uncle, Abu Talib, who was the head of the Hashim clan.[4] Mecca, the city where Muhammad was born, was of vital religious and economic importance in Arabia because it contained the Kaaba—a cubed shrine that housed hundreds of deities and that brought in countless pilgrims on their way to see and ritually circumambulate (or walk around) it. The Kaaba itself was believed to have been built by Adam and later rebuilt by Abraham and his son Ishmael.[5]

As an adult, Muhammad was known for his integrity and honesty. His nickname was *al-Amin*, "the trustworthy one."[6] By profession Muhammad was a caravan trader. Although originally of a lower socioeconomic status, he married a wealthy widow named Khadijah when he was twenty-five years old. He eventually came to be regarded as a powerful and respected figure in Meccan society. In addition to being an adept businessman, Muhammad had a contemplative side. Once a year he would leave Mecca and spend a month privately in a cave on Mount Hira. There he prayed and meditated. One night in AD 610, when he was forty years old, he experienced something on this cavernous mountain that forever changed his life—and more than a billion people since then.

As Muhammad was asleep, an invisible angel entered the cave and began squeezing the life out of the confused man, and demanded that he

"Muhammad was middle-sized, did not have lank or crisp hair, was not fat, had a white, circular face, wide black eyes and long eyelashes. . . . The upper part of his nose was hooked; he was thick bearded, had smooth cheeks, a strong mouth and his teeth were set apart."
—Annemarie Schimmel

Annemarie Schimmel, *And Muhammad Is His Messenger* (Chapel Hill: University of North Carolina, 1985), 34.

---

4. Fred Donner, "Muhammad and the Caliphate," in *The Oxford History of Islam*, ed. John Esposito (Oxford: Oxford University Press, 1999), 6.

5. Daniel Brown, *A New Introduction to Islam*, 2nd ed. (Oxford: Wiley-Blackwell, 2009), 27.

6. Reza Aslan, *No God but God: The Origins, Evolution, and Future of Islam* (New York: Random House, 2006), 32.

"recite" or "read" from a book the angel carried.[7] Despite protestations by Muhammad that he did not know what to read, the angel—in a cascade of rolling demands—continued commanding him to "read." Finally, the angel released its powerful grip. Then the frightened businessman heard clearly:

> Read! In the name of your Lord who created: He created man from a clinging form. Read! Your Lord is the Most Bountiful One who taught by the pen, who taught man what he did not know. (96:1–4)

So goes the first revelation that Muhammad received, the rest of which would eventually comprise the Qur'an. Upon awakening, Muhammad raced outside the cave and saw the angel Gabriel standing on the horizon (53:1–11). Terrified, Muhammad fled the mountain and returned to his wife, Khadijah. She comforted him. Over the course of the next three years Muhammad privately received more revelations and gradually attracted followers from among his family and friends.[8] Eventually, in about 613, Allah commanded Muhammad to "proclaim openly" what had been revealed to him (15:94).

This was a risky thing to do, for it meant confronting the religious, political, and economic powers in Mecca. Driven by his conviction that "there is no god but God," Muhammad began preaching to the polytheists in Mecca that Allah alone was lord of the world and the only one worthy of worship. The people of means in Mecca—some of whom made a living from the pilgrims and traders visiting the Kaaba—leveled a boycott on Muhammad and his clan for three years that made the young prophet odious in the sight of his people. Shortly thereafter, Muhammad's wife, Khadijah, as well as his protector, Abu Talib, died. He was left powerless and without protection. With no other choice, Muhammad fled Mecca at night to join the handful of people who were waiting for him in a cluster of villages that would later be renamed Medina—some 250 miles north of Mecca. Muslim historian Reza Aslan captures well this scene and the incredible events that soon followed:

> It is a wonder—some would say a miracle—that this same man, who had been forced to sneak out of his home under cover of night to join the seventy or so followers anxiously awaiting him in a foreign land hundreds of miles away, would, in a few short years,

In 621, a year before the *Hijra*, Muslims believe Muhammad made a miraculous one-night journey from Mecca to Jerusalem—at the current-day Dome of the Rock—where he ascended to the seven levels of heaven. There he saw Adam, Jesus and John the Baptist, Joseph, Idris, Aaron, Moses, and Abraham. Though God originally commanded Muhammad's followers to pray fifty times a day, Moses helped Muhammad get that number down to five times a day.

Brown, *A New Introduction to Islam*, 58–60.

---

7. There are contrasting stories of how Muhammad received his first revelation. See Aslan, *No God but God*, 34–35.

8. Brown, *A New Introduction to Islam*, 55.

Medina was
originally
referred to as
Yathrib. It was
changed when
Muhammad
moved there
and came to be
known as *Medi-
nat un Nabi*,
"the city of the
prophet," which
was eventually
shortened to
Medina, "the
city."

return to the city of his birth, not covertly or in darkness, but in the full light of day, with ten thousand men trailing peacefully behind him; and the same people who once tried to murder him in his sleep would instead offer up to him both the sacred city and the keys to the Ka'ba—unconditionally and without a fight, like a consecrated sacrifice.[9]

This secret journey Muhammad took to Medina in AD 622 is known as the *Hijra* ("migration"). It marks the official beginning of the Islamic calendar: year one. Over the next several years Muhammad battled with the Meccans and other tribes but managed to gain continued support and allies. By the time he returned to Mecca in 630, Islam was a mounting religion with distinct rituals, beliefs, practices—and armed men. At this time, Muhammad and his army of men marched (peacefully) to Mecca, took the keys to the Kaaba, forgave the Meccans and invited them into their fold, and ceremonially "cleansed" the shrine. One by one the prophet took the 365 idols in the Kaaba and smashed them to pieces before the astounded crowd—forever ending the practice of polytheism in Mecca and the Middle East at large. (Interestingly, because of his respect for Christianity, Muhammad preserved the statues of Jesus and Mary.)[10]

Rightly Guided Caliphate

"He who honors
Muhammad
must know that
he is dead. But
the one who
honors the God
of Muhammad
must know
that He is living
and immortal."
—Abu Bakr in
632

Within two short years of Muhammad's conquering of Mecca, he died in his home in Medina in 632. Because he—like the Buddha—did not appoint a successor, the Muslim community faced an unprecedented challenge. Who would take charge? Although there would never be another leader who could equal Muhammad as prophet and messenger, strong leadership was essential for the preservation and continuation of the new Muslim community or *Ummah*. There were several candidates capable of succeeding Muhammad who had known him personally and were related to him by marriage. By dawn of the morning after the prophet's death in Medina, the Muslim assembly had chosen a successor.

The first successor or caliph to Muhammad was Abu Bakr (573–634). He was Muhammad's father-in-law as well as his companion during the *Hijra* to Medina in 622. Abu Bakr had also been designated by Muhammad to lead prayers in Medina while Muhammad

Montgomery Watt,
"Islam: The Way
of the Prophet," in
*Eerdmans' Hand-
book to the World's
Religions* (Grand
Rapids: Eerdmans,
1994), 314.

9. Aslan, *No God but God*, 49.
10. See ibid., 106.

was ill before his death.[11] Bakr, as the new caliph of Islam, experienced immediate difficulties. Now that Muhammad was dead, several Arab tribes rescinded their oaths to the newly formed Muslim *Ummah*, and some individuals even claimed that they were prophets.[12] Bakr and his army defeated these tribes and expanded Muslim territory beyond what Muhammad had subdued.

When Abu Bakr died in 634, succession went from Umar (d. 644) to Uthman (d. 656) to Ali (d. 661). Together this succession is known as the Rightly Guided Caliphate, since it was seen as the golden age of Islam when the *Ummah* or community was ruled by Muhammad's religious principles. Like Abu Bakr, these men were each confronted with continual warfare and territorial expansion. Indeed, they were instrumental in setting a trajectory in Islamic history of ongoing conquering and extension of not only Arab but also non-Arab communities. Principal among this conquering and extension of non-Arab communities during the Rightly Guided Caliphate was the defeat of the Sassanid Empire (224–651) in Persia.

Years	Caliph	Highlight	Death
632–34	Abu Bakr	First successor to Muhammad	Natural death
634–44	Umar	Developed Muslim calendar	Assassinated
644–56	Uthman	Codified official Qur'anic version	Assassinated
656–61	Ali	Followers called Shiites	Assassinated

The first major schism experienced among Muslims occurred during this period and revolves around the caliphate of Ali, who was the fourth and last of the caliphs during the Rightly Guided Caliphate. This schism is called the First Civil War, which took place from 656–61—tellingly, the exact years of Ali's reign. For his part, Ali was a significant person in Islamic history. He was not only one of Muhammad's first converts but also his son-in-law. When he was chosen as caliph in 656, he was caught between rival forces and was never free from opposition. This led him to move the capital of the Islamic empire from Medina to Kufa in present-day Iraq. Unable to unite all the Muslim factions vying for power and rule, he was

---

11. Mircea Eliade and Ioan Couliano, *The Eliade Guide to World Religions* (New York: HarperSanFrancisco, 1991), 148.

12. Brown, *A New Introduction to Islam*, 117.

murdered in 661 by a group that had seceded from him called the Kharijites.[13]

Fig. 5.1. Map of the world in the seventh century AD, when Islam was emerging as a world religion.

Dynastic Period

The Rightly Guided Caliphate came to an end at the death of Ali. In its place emerged a new period of Islamic history that lasted from the seventh to the twentieth centuries. This was the transition from a religious community to a political empire. The first dynastic movement in Islam is called the Umayyad Dynasty (661–750). It began with the reign of Muawiya (602–80), who was part of the Quraysh tribe in Mecca and was the opponent of Muhammad and the Muslims until being conquered by them in 630. Eventually he was appointed governor of Syria by his cousin Uthman, who was the third caliph. Muawiya proved successful in this role and gained control of the Muslim community after the murder of Ali—with whom he had regularly fought—despite the fact that Muhammad's grandson and Ali's son, Hassan, had also made a claim to the caliphate. Muawiya moved the capital of the empire from Kufa to Damascus, Syria. There the Muslim empire expanded and enlarged during the next century under hereditary succession. As one author notes about the Umayyad Dynasty:

> During their tenure, the borders of the empire expanded in all directions, from China to France. Islamic learning flourished, and the major traditions of Islamic Law began to be established. Hundreds of books were written every year on every subject imaginable, from gardening to politics. Free public hospitals and schools were set up

13. Adam J. Silverstein, *Islamic History: A Very Short Introduction* (Oxford: Oxford University Press, 2010), 16.

in every city and town, and Muslim scientists and philosophers were busy making new discoveries and organizing the knowledge they had acquired from their subject nations.[14]

Despite the successes of the Umayyad Dynasty, internal and external factions were always close at hand. A Second Civil War (680–92) erupted after Muawiya's death, which portended the temporal reign of this dynasty. In 750 the Abbasid family, which claimed descendancy from the prophet Muhammad's uncle, overthrew the Umayyad Dynasty—marking the beginning of a new era. The Abbasid Dynasty (750–1258) moved the capital from Damascus to Baghdad, which was close to the old capital of the Persian Sassanid Empire. The period of the Abbasid Dynasty was one of wealth and continual advances in science, literature, and mathematics. It was also the time of Muslim missions eastward into India and ultimately China. Eventually, the empire was too unwieldy to maintain, and many regional caliphates emerged that took control of various regions in Europe, North Africa, the Middle East, and Asia.

One of the more important developments in Islamic history at this time was the migration of Turks from Central Asia westward. This resulted in the Great Seljuk Empire (1037–1194), which was a conglomeration of regional empires. It was due to the Seljuk Empire's disconnected realms, in fact, that the Christians were able to retake different regions of it during the Crusades.[15] In the thirteenth century another pivotal figure in the history of Islam arrived on the scene. Later known as Genghis Khan or "Great Emperor" (d. 1227), this Mongolian-born warrior founded the Mongol Empire (1206–1368) and conquered virtually all the territories from Asia to Iraq. In 1258 one of Genghis Khan's grandsons killed the last Abbasid caliph in Baghdad and ravaged the city. And so for the first time in Islamic history, "a significant part of the Islamic world had been subjected to the domination of a non-Muslim power."[16]

Although the Mongols were powerful warriors and were initially impervious to the Muslim religion, they eventually came to accept it and integrated Islam into their culture. As their empire dwindled, regional empires emerged. Two of the most enduring of these Muslim empires were the Mogul (1526–1858) and the Ottoman empires. The Mogul Empire ruled over vast portions of Greater India, which had been reached by Muslim armies as early as the eighth century before being dispossessed by the British in 1858.

14. Emerick, *The Complete Idiot's Guide to Understanding Islam*, 326.
15. Donner, "Muhammad and the Caliphate," 56.
16. Ibid., 59.

Two of the most enduring achievements of the Abbasid Dynasty are the Dome of the Rock and *Arabian Nights*. The Dome is a shrine in Jerusalem built upon the rock believed to have been the site of Abraham's binding of Isaac and of Muhammad's night journey. *Arabian Nights* is a famous collection of Middle Eastern stories and folk tales.

The Crusades were a series of battles fought between Christians and the Great Seljuk Empire in the Holy Land from the eleventh to the thirteenth centuries.

Dynasty	Dates	Capital	Highlights
Rightly Guided	632–61	Medina	Ruled by caliphs who knew Muhammad personally and followed him closely; came to an end after Ali was assassinated
Umayyad	661–750	Damascus	Completed conquest of Persian and eastern (Byzantine) Roman empires; came to an end at Abbasid slave revolt
Abbasid	750–1258	Baghdad	Produced wealth, power, education and progress, and dominant culture; replaced by a series of sultanates after Moguls destroyed the capital in the thirteenth century
Seljuk	1037–1194	Iran	Covered a vast area from Central Asia to the Middle East; served as the target of the First Crusade
Mamluk	1250–1517	Cairo	Made up predominantly of former slaves; dealt the first decisive blow to the Moguls by halting them in Palestine
Safaved	1501–1733	Iran	Developed Twelver school of Shiite Islam; produced beautiful art and architecture; dismantled by surrounding tribes
Mogul	1526–1858	India	Most well known for new trade routes, art, and architecture (Taj Mahal); dismantled after the British gained control over Indian Empire and later divided the empire into India and Pakistan
Ottoman	1300–1922	Istanbul	Reigned over huge area, including Asia and Europe; dismantled during First World War by Turkish and European powers

The Ottoman Empire (1300–1922) reigned over large areas in Eastern Europe, North Africa, and the Middle East. This empire is most well known to Christians because of the conquering of Constantinople in 1453 and its subsequent renaming as Istanbul. After sacking (Christian) Constantinople, the Ottoman Turks also overpowered Muslim kingdoms—first wresting Cairo, Jerusalem, Mecca, and Medina from the Mamluk Sultanate (1250–1517) and then taking Baghdad from the Safaved Dynasty (1501–1733). Islamic historian Adam Silverstein summarizes the story of the Ottoman Empire well:

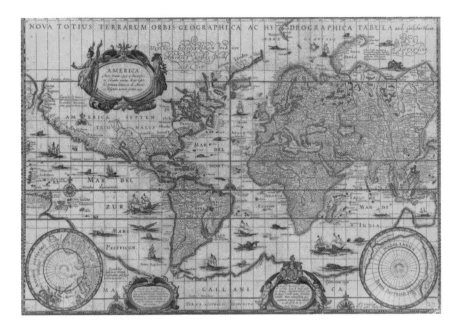

Fig. 5.2. Map of the world in the seventeenth century AD, when (Muslim) Mogul and Ottoman empires were dominant in the East.

By the mid-16th century, the Ottomans had created a strong, central-ized, and cosmopolitan empire that incorporated some of Islam's—and the world's—greatest cities and resources, with footholds in Europe, Asia, and Africa. But being cosmopolitan proved to have both positive and negative results: on the one hand, trade and culture in Ottoman cities were boosted through the [inhabitation of Jews, Christians, and differing Muslims]. . . . On the other hand, by the end of the 19th century, it would be clear that there was very little to unite this patchwork of populations.[17]

Modern Islam

Contemporary Islam is diverse. It includes more than fifty Muslim states—let alone all the non-Islamic states with growing Muslim populations—that vary in language, ethnicity, customs, politics, and economic systems. Most of these states were colonized by Europeans, and many of them are officially countries with less than a century of existence. When the colonial era ended after World War II and countries such as England and France pulled out of their colonial territories, many

"Islam repre-sents a basic unity of belief within a rich cultural diversity. Islamic practice expresses itself in different ways within a vast array of cultures that extend from North Africa to Southeast Asia as well as Europe and America."
—John Esposito

John Esposito, *What Everyone Needs to Know about Islam,* 2nd ed. (Oxford: Oxford University Press, 2011), 4.

17. Silverstein, *Islamic History*, 39.

Muslim states began to emerge.[18] In this way, the twentieth century has been one of the most innovative and explosive centuries in Islamic history.

Group	Response to Modernity
Secularist	Religion is private and should be separate from politics.
Traditionalist	Islamic law and doctrine should guide society.
Revivalist (Fundamentalist)	Society should return to original aims of Islam and purge non-Muslim ways of life from society.
Modernist	It appropriates the best of the West but resists assimilation into Western culture and values.

One of the most pressing issues in Islamic history in the twentieth and twenty-first centuries has to do with modernity. In short, what has been the impact of modernity on Islam?[19] Because of the diversity of Islam, there are many responses to this question. The first is that Islam should progress toward adaptation and modernization. This can be seen in the work of Sayyid Ahmad Khan (1817–98), an educator and politician in India during the time of British occupation. At the height of the Indian Rebellion of 1857 against the British, Sayyid Ahmad encouraged his countrymen to remain loyal to British governance and to embrace India's modernization. Instead of fighting the changes taking place in his homeland, he argued that the well-being of Muslims "lies in leading a quiet life under the benign rule of the British government."[20] He also believed that adaptation of Islam to modern science, reason, and technology was not a rejection of the Muslim religion but rather a "new theology" that propelled it forward and realigned it with its original vision.[21]

A similar aim for Islam was secularization. This is perhaps most apparent with the agenda of the first Turkish president, Mustafa Kemal (1881–1938), known as Ataturk or "Father of the Turks." When he abolished the caliphate and the Ottoman Empire in Turkey in the early 1920s, he immediately "established a thoroughly secular state . . . suppressing or marginalizing religious institutions, and replacing them with European-based

18. S. V. R. Nasr, "European Colonialism and the Emergence of Modern Muslim States," in Esposito, *The Oxford History of Islam*, 552.

19. Brown, *A New Introduction to Islam*, 259.

20. John Donahue and John Esposito, *Islam in Transition: Muslim Perspectives* (Oxford: Oxford University Press, 1982), 40.

21. John Esposito, "Contemporary Islam: Reformation or Revolution?" in Esposito, *The Oxford History of Islam*, 648.

laws and institutions."[22] Although Ataturk was not opposed to religion, he ensured that the new Turkish state separated Islamic law from secular law, and he created a new culture of progress and modernization rather than tradition and conservatism.

On the opposite end of this spectrum were revivalists who reacted strongly and negatively to modernization. Two individuals who embody this response to modernity were Hasan al-Banna (1906–49) and Sayyib Qutb (1906–66). Al-Banna was an Egyptian teacher who founded the Muslim Brotherhood in 1928 and soon moved its headquarters to Cairo. The designated purpose was to promote Muslim piety, institute social policies, and purge secular influences from Islamic societies. The Brotherhood believed that Islam was a comprehensive way of life and that religion and politics should not be separated, as was being done in Turkey. After al-Banna was assassinated by Egyptian police in 1949, the Muslim Brotherhood took on a more extremist and violent posture as it came to be led by Qutb, who became the "ideologue of radical Islam" for many later Muslim extremists or fundamentalists.[23]

Finally, between these two extreme positions are modernists who seek to steer a middle course between secularization and fundamentalism. They seek to learn from the West and to appropriate all the best of science, medicine, technology, and education without compromising their religious beliefs and Muslim heritage. An example of a modernist leader is Abdurrahman Wahid (1940–2009), who was the first democratically elected president of Indonesia.[24] Although a Muslim in a predominantly Muslim state, he insisted on religious pluralism in a country that is influenced and inhabited by Hindus, Buddhists, and Christians. Like many others in that country, Wahid advocated separation of religion and politics.

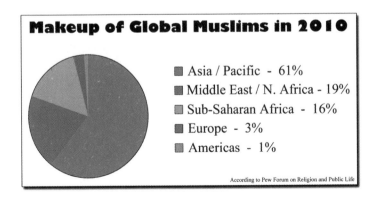

Makeup of Global Muslims in 2010

- Asia / Pacific - 61%
- Middle East / N. Africa - 19%
- Sub-Saharan Africa - 16%
- Europe - 3%
- Americas - 1%

According to Pew Forum on Religion and Public Life

Fig. 5.3. Makeup of global Muslims by region in 2010 according to the Pew Forum on Religion and Public Life.

22. Ibid., 652.
23. Esposito, *What Everyone Needs to Know about Islam*, 196.
24. Ibid., 69.

What does the future hold for Islam? Because Islam is so diverse, the response will vary according to any number of factors, including region, country, education, family background, denominational affiliation, and socioeconomic standing. But one thing most Muslims have in common is that they are at a crucial juncture in their history. Muslim scholar John Esposito responds to this question well:

Qur'anic readings are preceded by the phrase: "I take refuge with God from Satan, the accursed one," and followed by: "God Almighty has spoken truly!"

Malise Ruthven, *Islam: A Very Short Introduction* (Oxford: Oxford University Press, 2000), 21.

> Muslims today are at a critical crossroads. They are faced with making radical social, political, and economic changes that the Western world has had many decades to implement gradually. Amidst increasing globalization, Muslims strive to survive and compete, often with limited resources, and to preserve their identity in a world dominated (culturally as well as politically and economically) by the West. For many, the role of religion is critical in the preservation of their personal and national identities. It provides a sense of continuity between their Islamic heritage and modern life. For some, the temptation is to cling to the authority and security of the past. Others seek to follow new paths, convinced that their faith and a tradition of Islamic reform that has existed throughout the ages can play a critical role in restoring the vitality of Muslim societies.[25]

In the end, Islam—although not as diverse as Christianity—is nevertheless quite varied in its responses to modernity. Muslims, like Christians, will be confronted with innumerable challenges as they seek to live out their beliefs in an ever-changing world.

Part 3: Religious Writings

The Qur'an

Compared with Hinduism or Buddhism, Islam has few religious writings. Besides the sayings of Muhammad, which are important to the history and interpretation of the religion, the Qur'an is the centerpiece of Islamic thought. Its significance within the Islamic tradition is difficult to overestimate. As a contemporary translator of the Qur'an notes:

> The Qur'an is the supreme authority in Islam. It is the fundamental and paramount source of the creed, rituals, ethics, and laws of the Islamic religion. It is the book that "differentiates" between right and

25. Ibid., 66–67.

wrong, so that nowadays, when the Muslim world is dealing with such universal issues as globalization, the environment, combating terrorism and drugs, issues of medical ethics, and feminism, evidence to support the various arguments is sought in the Qur'an. This supreme status stems from the belief that the Qur'an is the word of God, revealed to the Prophet Muhammad via the archangel Gabriel, and intended for all times and places.[26]

It is critical to recognize that the Qur'an is the source not only for theological beliefs and ritual practice in the Islamic world but also for such things as Arabic grammar and language, calligraphy, the arts and sciences, law, philosophy, and politics. As a fifteenth-century Muslim jurist once quipped, "Everything is based on the Qur'an."[27]

Its name literally meaning "reading" or "reciting" in Arabic, the Qur'an is a series of revelations that Muhammad received from Gabriel from 610 until his death in 632. Although some scholars—even Islamic scholars—have argued that "there is no historical justification" for the view that Muhammad was illiterate given that he was a successful merchant, Muslims have traditionally claimed that the prophet was unable to read or write.[28] This interpretation validates Muhammad's revelation from the archangel as a miracle. Like Joseph Smith in the nineteenth century, Muhammad went into a trance as he experienced these revelations over the course of two-plus decades. After receiving a revelation, he memorized it and dictated it to a close friend, who recorded it on parchment or leather scrolls. He also taught the revelation to other close friends to memorize.

The first caliph, Abu Bakr (r. 632–34), is traditionally viewed by Muslims to have been responsible for having the first Qur'an written down after a battle in which many of those who had memorized the Qur'an were killed. The book was arranged, recorded on paper, and placed in the care of one of Muhammad's widows. A decade later the third caliph, Uthman (r. 644–56), noticed that many non-Arab Muslims were making their own versions of the Qur'an. As was the case with rival interpretations and versions of the Buddha's teaching, these Qur'anic versions differed from one another. As a result, Uthman ordered an official version to be written (based on Abu Bakr's copy), and distributed duplicates to the different regions of the empire so that only one version would be used. The faulty versions were to be burned.[29]

"Muslims believe that the Quran, as well as the Torah and Gospels, is based on a tablet written in Arabic that exists in heaven with God. They believe that the teaching of these scriptures, revealed at different times in history, originates from this source. The Quran, recited by Muhammad as it was revealed to him by the angel Gabriel, and later recorded in Arabic, is thus believed to be the direct word of God."
—John Esposito

Esposito, *What Everyone Needs to Know about Islam*, 10.

26. M. A. S. Abdel Haleem, "Introduction," in *The Qur'an*, ix.
27. Ibid.
28. Aslan, *No God but God*, 35.
29. Emerick, *The Complete Idiot's Guide to Understanding Islam*, 239–40. Certain scholars argue that the Qur'an betrays a context much later than seventh-century Arabia and suggest that the

The Qur'an is organized into 114 chapters or *suras* ("rows"). It is roughly the same size as the New Testament. Like Paul's letters in the Christian Bible, the Qur'an is arranged according to length rather than chronology or theme. The only exception is the first *sura*, which is called the Fatiha or "Opening." It serves as the introduction to the Qur'an and is prayed daily by observant Muslims. It reads as follows:

> In the name of God, the Lord of Mercy, the Giver of Mercy! Praise belongs to God, Lord of the Worlds, the Lord of Mercy, the Giver of Mercy, Master of the Day of Judgement. It is You we worship; it is You we ask for help. Guide us to the straight path: the path of those You have blessed, those who incur no anger and who have not gone astray. (1:1–7)

About two-thirds of the Qur'an—eighty-five chapters in total—was delivered to Muhammad in Mecca, while the rest was delivered afterward in Medina.

When I read this chapter to my students, what catches their attention most often are the many references to Allah's mercy. Contrary to what many in popular culture think of Allah, the god of Islam, Muslims believe Allah to be extremely merciful. In fact, the first two references to Allah in the Qur'an are that he is the Lord *and* giver of mercy!

Each of the 114 *suras* is given a special name taken from a theme or word in each chapter. Scholars divide the messages as having an origin in either Mecca or Medina. The Meccan revelations are the oldest parts of the Qur'an, which Gabriel gave to Muhammad before he had made the *Hijra* or migration to Medina. The Meccan *suras* emphasize the unity of God (since the Meccans believed in many gods) and the legitimacy of Muhammad as a prophet (since the Meccans did not originally accept him as such). A Meccan *sura* that illustrates these concepts is Sura 35:

> People, remember God's grace towards you. Is there any creator other than God to give you sustenance from the heavens and earth? There is no god but Him. How can you be so deluded? If they call you [speaking to Muhammad] a liar, many messengers before you were also called liars: it is to God that all things will be returned. People, God's promise is true, so do not let the present life deceive you. (35:3–5)

The Medinan *suras* have a different context from the Meccan ones. Whereas Muslims were a tiny and persecuted minority in Mecca, for instance, they were a powerful and established community in Medina. Revelations at this later time—in Medina—emphasize communal laws and practices, and speak about the "people of the book," that is, Chris-

Qur'an was recorded a century or two after Muhammad's time. See especially John Wansbrough, *Quranic Studies: Sources and Methods of Scriptural Interpretation* (Amherst, NY: Prometheus, 2004).

tians and Jews, with whom the Muslims interacted increasingly after living in Medina.[30]

The content of the Qur'an is varied. It addresses a range of issues surrounding the *Ummah* in Mecca and in Medina. One of the more intriguing aspects of the Qur'an for Christians is its reference to countless biblical persons and events. This is especially the case for Jesus, who is mentioned many times—always positively. The Qur'an recognizes Jesus as a great prophet from God who gave the Gospels to his community. Jesus is regarded as being born of the Virgin Mary (19:20–22) and a miracle worker filled with the Holy Spirit (2:87, 252–53). At the same time, the Qur'an asserts that Jesus was not crucified and that he came only to deliver the message of Allah (3:55). As one *sura* explains:

> This [Qur'an] is knowledge for the Hour: do not doubt it. Follow Me for this is the right path; do not let Satan hinder you, for he is your sworn enemy. When Jesus came with clear signs he said, "I have brought you wisdom; I have come to clear up some of your differences for you. Be mindful of [Allah] and obey me: [Allah] is my Lord and your Lord. Serve Him: this is the straight path." (43:61–65)

Muslims strongly declare that besides being a Muslim prophet sent from Allah, Jesus was not God's Son, since God can have no equals. This is asserted many times in the Qur'an. As one of the last *suras* proclaims, "Say, '[Allah] is God the One, God the eternal. He begot no one nor was He begotten. No one is comparable to Him'" (112).

The Hadith and Sunna

In addition to the Qur'an, one more body of literature is important to the Islamic tradition. Called the Sunna ("trodden path") or the Hadith ("traditions"), these are stories about Muhammad's life that were collected and circulated orally until being written down decades and even centuries after the prophet's death. Sometimes regarded as synonymous, a hadith is technically a narration of the prophet's life—which is sometimes difficult to verify as authentic—while a sunna is a custom or practice of the prophet in that narration.[31] There are multiple versions of the Hadith, since many groups collected and recorded Muhammad's sayings. Six of the most authoritative—according to Sunni Muslims—are those assembled by Imam Bukhari (d. 870), Muslim b. al-Hajjaj (d. 875),

---

30. Abdel Haleem, "Introduction," xvii.
31. Charles Braden, *The Scriptures of Mankind: An Introduction* (New York: Macmillan, 1922), 453.

Abu Dawud (d. 879), al-Tirmidhi (d. 882), Ibn Maja (d. 887), and al-Nasai (d. 915). These are known collectively as The Authentic Six, the first two of which enjoy special privilege.[32]

The Hadith are important to Muslims because of their focus on Muhammad. Indeed, whereas the Qur'an contains the words of God and no one else—Muhammad is rarely mentioned in the book and he did not write it or add anything to it—the Hadith is focused on the stories of the prophet's life. According to pious Muslims, Muhammad lived a virtually perfect life, and his words, actions, habits, and customs should be imitated by Muslims today.[33] Stated differently, the Hadith is the Qur'an in action. The reasoning for this is straightforward: since Allah chose Muhammad to be the recipient of his message, he must know better than anyone else how to live out the message he received. In this way, the Hadith and the Sunna are the primary sources for the correct interpretation of the Qur'an. This includes formal interpretations about doctrine and practice as well as informal anecdotes about how to comb one's hair or brush one's teeth. Below are examples taken from the Hadith:

The Shariah (or Islamic law) is based on the Qur'an and the Sunna. Islamic scholars of law are called the ulama, a very important group in the Islamic tradition.

> Every child conforms to the true religion [Islam]: It is his parents who make him a Jew [or] a Christian.
>
> You should worship God as if you see Him. If you do not see Him, He still sees you.
>
> You will recognize the faithful in their having mercy upon each other and in their love for one another.
>
> God has no mercy on him who is not merciful to others.
>
> Your body has a right over you, your soul has a right over you, and your wife has a right over you.
>
> Never did God allow anything more hateful than divorce. With God, the most detestable of all things allowed is divorce.
>
> No one eats better food than that which he eats out of the work of his own hand. God did not raise a prophet who did not also pasture goats. Yes! I used to pasture them for the people of Mecca.[34]

Part 4: Beliefs

There are six primary articles of belief in Islam. These include belief in (1) God, (2) angels, (3) scriptures, (4) prophets, (5) predestination, and (6) heaven and hell and a divine judgment. At face value, these beliefs are

---

32. Ibid., 455; Esposito, *What Everyone Needs to Know about Islam*, 13.
33. Brown, *A New Introduction to Islam*, 89.
34. Gwilym Beckerlegge, ed., *The World Religions Reader* (London: Routledge, 2001), 167–69.

similar to those found in Christianity, which is Islam's closest relative as well as the religion that puts most emphasis on belief. Differences begin to emerge in these two religions, however, when we move from generalities about believing in God and in the Holy Scriptures to believing in Jesus as God's Son or in the New Testament as the inspired Word of God.

Fig. 5.4. The name of Allah or "God" in Arabic.

The first article of faith in Islam is belief in Allah. Although alluded to above, it is important to underscore that Muslims do not believe in just any God. Rather, they believe in "*the* God," which is the literal meaning of the word *Allah* in Arabic. As one author points out, "To proclaim *Allah* in Arabic is to deny the possibility of any co-existing deities, which is why the pagan Arabs avoided using the term."[35] Muslims, in fact, are adamant about the oneness of God. Practically speaking, this means that God's existence excludes any possible existence of another god—whether Jesus or Krishna or any other being. (In fact, to ascribe divinity to Jesus is a major and unforgivable sin in Islam known as *shirk* or "sharing.") At the same time, Muslims believe that Allah is the same God revealed to Jews and Christians, although both groups eventually distorted the true message they received. A good example of the qualities and attributes of Allah is found in the following verse, taken from the longest chapter in the Qur'an, called "The Cow":

> God: there is no god but Him, the Ever Living, the Ever Watchful. Neither slumber nor sleep overtakes Him. All that is in the heavens and in the earth belongs to Him. Who is there that can intercede with Him except by His leave? He knows what is before them and what is behind them, but they do not comprehend any of His knowledge except what He wills. His throne extends over the heavens and the earth; it does not weary Him to preserve them both. He is the Most High, the Tremendous. (2:255)

35. Raana Bokhari and Mohammad Seddon, *The Complete Illustrated Guide to Islam: A Comprehensive Guide to the History, Philosophy, and Practice of Islam around the World with More than 500 Beautiful Illustrations* (Leicester, England: Hermes House, 2009), 116.

The second article of faith in Islam is belief in the angels. Like Jews and Christians, Muslims believe that angels perform different functions for God—including protecting and relaying God's message to human beings. Muslims assert that angels are made from light and can materialize in any way that is necessary. But unlike humans and jinn, they do not have free will. Thus, all angels are good and completely submissive to God's will. According to many Muslims, each person is attended to by two angels that record the person's daily actions, which will be the source of that person's judgment on the last day.[36]

Messenger	Message
Moses	Torah
David	Psalms
Jesus	Gospels
Muhammad	Qur'an

The third and fourth articles are belief in the prophets and in the messages these prophets gave as recorded in the scriptures. However, Muhammad is God's final prophet and messenger. His prophecy confirmed and completed all revealed messages from Adam's day to the day of judgment.[37] Whereas the term *prophet* refers to Muhammad's role of preaching God's word to the people, the word *messenger* refers to the written message he received from Gabriel as found in the Qur'an. In the Judeo-Christian tradition, it is exceptional for someone to be regarded as both a prophet and a messenger. For the most part, this privileges Moses in the Jewish tradition and Jesus in the Christian tradition. Muslims believe that God gave truthful messages to them and made covenants with their people. However, Muslims also believe that Jews and Christians altered and distorted the Judeo-Christian writings as they have come down to us in the Bible (5:12–14). The Qur'an, by contrast—the final revelation of God—contains the truthful accounts of the messages of Moses and Jesus. As the Qur'an asserts, "We sent to you [Muhammad] the scripture with the truth, confirming the scriptures that came before it, and with final authority over them" (5:48). Just as Muslims sometimes appeal to the doctrine of abrogation—by which later *suras* in the Qur'an abrogate or rescind former revelations—so Muhammad's revelations

Muslims believe that Gabriel is the angel who revealed God's message to Muhammad, while Michael is the angel who controls the weather.

36. Esposito, *What Everyone Needs to Know about Islam*, 28.
37. Ibid., 19.

to the people in the seventh century are the final authority relative to revelations given by former prophets.

The last two articles of belief in Islam are predestination and the day of judgment. Below is a section of the Qur'an that encompasses both of these concepts:

> I [Allah] created jinn and mankind only to worship Me: I want no provision from them, nor do I want them to feed Me—God is the Provider, the Lord of Power, the Ever Mighty. The evildoers, like their predecessors, will have a share of torment—they need not ask Me to hasten it—and woe betide the disbelievers on their promised Day. (51:56–60)

Christian Doctrine	Muslim View
Original sin	Since Adam and Eve were forgiven, no taint of sin was passed on to descendants.
Trinity	God is one and has absolutely no partners.
Atonement	Jesus did not die on the cross, nor is there any need for him to do, so since there is no original sin.
Priesthood	There is no priesthood in Sunni Islam, although this concept does exist in Shia Islam.

According to Islam, God is the master and people are his servants. Stated differently, Allah is the submitter and all of Allah's creation are the submitted (ones). Although human beings and jinn (or genies) were originally created by Allah to give him worship, "there is no compulsion in religion" (2:256), so humans and jinn are free to do good deeds or bad as they desire. In this way, there is a paradox in Islam, given that God determines or predestines all things while human beings, in particular, exercise free will. On the last day, Muslims believe, Jesus will return to earth and defeat an antichrist figure known as al-Dajjal ("False Messiah"). On earth, Jesus will reign in righteousness for forty years and marry before judging the living and the dead.[38] On the day of judgment, everyone will line up before Jesus, and he will determine whether one is resurrected to heaven or to hell. Those who did good deeds and submitted to Allah will experience a "Garden of Bliss" (10:9) in the life to come. Those who did bad deeds and did not submit to Allah will be the "losers in the Hereafter" (3:85), eternally experiencing "agonizing torment" (10:4) in hell (23:102–4).

38. Ibid., 28–29.

Part 5: Worship Practices

The practices of Islam are best summarized in what are called the five pillars of the faith. These five pillars serve as the foundation of Islamic practice. The first is the most basic, which is called the declaration of faith: Muslims confess that there is only one God, Allah—*the* God—and that Muhammad is his final prophet and messenger. This is the primary confession of Muslims, the first step that one must take on the road to converting to Islam. It is tantamount to affirming one's belief in the Trinity at baptism in the Christian faith or taking refuge in the Three Jewels in Buddhism. I was once in Casablanca, Morocco, visiting a beautiful mosque with the tallest minaret[39] in the world. What caught my attention as I stood gazing upon the intricate design of the mosque was oneness or unity—and for good reason. The oneness of God is a crucial tenet in Islam. It is found in countless passages in the Qur'an, such as the following: "God: there is no god but Him" (2:255). In fact, whereas the unforgivable sin in Christianity is to blaspheme the Holy Spirit (Mark 3:28–29), the unforgivable sin in Islam is to reject the oneness of God and to ascribe a partner—such as Jesus—to him:

Fig. 5.5.
The Hassan II Mosque in Casablanca, Morocco, which boasts the world's tallest minaret.

39. A minaret is a tall spire with a small opening that is attached to a mosque for the call to prayer. Its distinct architectural design is visible in many Muslim countries.

Five Pillars	Description
Confession	Belief in Allah and final prophet Muhammad
Prayer	Five prayers a day facing Kaaba in Mecca
Almsgiving	Giving 2.5 percent of wealth to the needy
Fasting	Fasting in the month of Ramadan
Pilgrimage	Making a pilgrimage to Mecca once in one's lifetime

God does not forgive the joining of partner with Him: anything less than that He forgives to whoever He will, but anyone who joins partners with God has fabricated a tremendous sin. (4:48)

The second pillar in Islam is prayer. Muslims pray (or worship) five times a day at different intervals (set by a calendar) from dawn to dusk. I distinctly remember having lunch one day in the ancient city of Jericho in Palestine. As I was eating falafel and hummus, the muezzin (a person standing atop the minaret in a nearby mosque) called for prayer.[40] The owner of the restaurant obediently pulled out his prayer mat and began praying in the middle of the restaurant. This man's piety underscores the importance of prayer in the Muslim world. While it can be performed alone—any place in the world that is considered clean—it is best done with fellow believers.

Observing Muslims in prayer is striking. Muslims—separated by gender—stand shoulder to shoulder in distinct rows facing Mecca. They follow a strict yet simple ritual of standing, bowing, kneeling, touching the ground with their foreheads (at the exact moment they are to say that God is the highest), and sitting. The ideal place for Muslims to pray is at a mosque. Although there are set times throughout the day to pray there, the busiest time each week is Friday afternoon. Called *Jumuah* ("Friday prayer"), Friday afternoon prayer at the mosque is based on the following Medinan *sura*:

Believers! When the call to prayer is made on the day of congregation, hurry towards the reminder of God and leave off your trading—that

Muslims believe that Friday is the day "on which God created Adam, the day Adam was sent to earth from heaven, the day he died, the day when the Final Judgement will come and the day on which there is an hour, toward the end, just before sunset, when all prayers are answered. Islam teaches that all prayers are witnessed by the angels, but that on Friday, the angels record all those who go to the mosque and pray. As a reward, they are forgiven all sins committed between that Friday and the next."
—Raana Bokhari and Mohammad Seddon

Bokhari and Seddon, *The Complete Illustrated Guide to Islam*, 162.

40. The muezzin calls out the following in Arabic for prayer: "God is most great, God is most great, God is most great, God is most great. I witness that there is no god but God; I witness that there is no god but God. I witness that Muhammad is the messenger of God. I witness that Muhammad is the messenger of God. Come to prayer; come to prayer! Come to prosperity; come to prosperity! God is most great. God is most great. There is no god but God." See Esposito, *What Everyone Needs to Know about Islam*, 19.

is better for you, if only you knew—then when the prayer has ended, disperse in the land and seek out God's bounty. (62:9–10)

Every time I attend a Friday prayer service at a mosque, the procedure has been the same. Just as Jews are encouraged to make haste to worship God on Shabbat—this is most apparent on Friday afternoons at the Western Wall in Jerusalem—so Muslims hurry into the mosque on Friday afternoon, say prayers, socialize with each other, and then return to work or other daily activities.

The third practice of Islam is obligatory almsgiving or *Zakat* ("purification"). Islam teaches that wealth is a blessing from Allah and that those blessed must share their blessing with others. This has traditionally been interpreted to signify that Muslims give 2.5 percent of their wealth to the needy. Although Muslim governments historically collected this tax, nowadays people distribute their wealth based on individual conscience.[41] The recipients of this required tax or almsgiving are stipulated in the following Medinan *sura*:

> Alms are meant only for the poor, the needy, those who administer them, those whose hearts need winning over, to free slaves and help those in debt, for God's cause, and for travelers in need. This is ordained by God; God is all knowing and wise. (9:60)

The fourth ritual practice in Islam is fasting during Ramadan, which is the ninth month in the Islamic calendar. Ramadan is important to Muslims because it was believed to have been the month of the first message Muhammad received from Gabriel. During Ramadan all Muslims who are physically able abstain from food, drink, and sexual activity during daylight hours for the purpose of reflecting on our human frailty and remembering the less fortunate. Muslims eat and drink before dawn, and after sundown they prepare a more elaborate communal meal, which contains special foods that are served only during this time.

I was once invited to a Ramadan feast. Although we in the Christian tradition tend to look upon fasting as a solemn occasion, the mood at this feast—despite the fact that Muslim believers had been fasting all day—was joyous and celebratory. It was more like an Easter Sunday meal than an Ash Wednesday service. Toward the end of Ramadan, Muslims celebrate what is called the Night of Power. This is the anniversary of the night Muhammad received his first revelation of the Qur'an from Gabriel. The monthlong fast of Ramadan ends with the Eid festivities

"[Ramadan] is a month of intense spiritual renewal and reflection for Muslims, when they call upon God and re-establish their covenant with him. The nights of Ramadan are marked by an extra prayer . . . where the whole Quran is recited over the month."
—Raana Bokhari and Moham-mad Seddon

Bokhari and Seddon, *The Complete Illustrated Guide to Islam*, 156.

41. Ruthven, *Islam*, 141.

when Muslims pay a special tax to the needy and exchange presents with one another. This feast, formally called Eid al-Fitr ("the Feast of the Breaking of the Fast"), is similar to the Jewish celebration of Hanukkah or the Christian celebration of Christmas.

The final practice in Islam is *Hajj* or "pilgrimage." It is a requirement of each physically healthy and financially able Muslim to make a pilgrimage to Mecca once in his or her lifetime. The prescription is based on the following Medinan *sura*:

> We showed Abraham the site of the House [Kaaba], saying, "Do not assign partners to Me. Purify My House for those who circle around it, those who stand to pray, and those who bow and prostrate themselves. Proclaim the Pilgrimage to all people. They will come to you on foot and on every kind of lean camel, emerging from every deep mountain pass to attain benefits and mention God's name, on specified days, over the livestock He has provided for them. Feed yourselves and the desperately poor from them. Then let the pilgrims perform their acts of cleansing, fulfill their vows, and circle around the Ancient house." All this [is ordained by God]: anyone who honours the sacred ordinances of God will have good rewards from his Lord. (22:26–30)

There is sometimes recognized a sixth pillar of Islam called jihad ("struggle"). Often seen as controversial by non-Muslims, this wide-ranging term can refer to struggle against one's ego, evil, injustice, or oppression. Although this mostly includes spiritual warfare, it sometimes includes armed struggle and violence.

Fig. 5.6. Muslims circumambulating the Kaaba in Mecca, Saudi Arabia, during the *Hajj*.

The *Hajj* is performed during the last month of the Islamic calendar and consists of observing set rituals. For instance, men and women wear simple clothing to symbolize their equality before God, circle the Kaaba seven times to signal their entry into the divine presence, pray at specific times and locations, and drink water from the well believed to have been provided for Hagar and Ishmael. Some pilgrims also make the trek to Medina, also in current-day Saudi Arabia, in order to pay respect to Muhammad, who is buried there in the Mosque of the Prophet, which is both the second holiest site in the Islamic world and the oldest mosque in the world.[42]

Part 6: Point of Contact

Given the ongoing attention that Islam has received in the news especially in the last decade, many Westerners are now aware of the basic beliefs of Islam and even some of its history. Some Westerners are even familiar with portions of the Qur'an and specific terms from the Islamic religion. In this section I would like to explain the origin of two key terms—Sunnis and Shias—and suggest how the differences between these two Muslim groups or sects may serve as a point of entry into a conversation with Muslims.

Sunnis	Shias
• Succession of leadership based on character and not heredity	• Succession of leadership based on heredity
• Constitutes 85 percent of Muslims	• Constitutes 15 percent of Muslims
• Have their own Hadith or traditions of Muhammad distinct from the Shia	• Mainly in Iran, Iraq, Yemen, and Lebanon
	• Divided into further divisions based on number of imams after Muhammad through Ali: Fivers, Seveners, Twelvers

Because Muhammad left no male heirs, some in the *Ummah* argued that rightful succession of the Muslim community belonged to Ali—who was Muhammad's closest relative, the husband of his daughter Fatima, and father of Muhammad's grandsons. This group would eventually come to be known as the Shia (singular: Shiite), or the Party of Ali, which today is the second-largest branch within Islam—about

42. Ibid., 158–59.

15 percent of Muslims worldwide.[43] The other major group in Islam, the Sunni, constitutes the remaining 85 percent of the Muslim community. The Sunnis believe that succession of the Muslim community rightly went to Abu Bakr, the first caliph, and that succession was to be passed down to the most qualified person—not the one who was most closely related to the prophet Muhammad. Although these two groups agree on the essentials of the faith, Sunnis and Shia have developed distinct customs and even beliefs.

One key difference between the two is the high regard the Shia preserve for the imam. In Sunni Islam an imam ("one who stands before") is the leader of a mosque but is not considered clergy. There is no concept of clergy in this major branch of Islam. In contrast with the Sunnis, who concentrate religious authority on the *Ummah* and the *ulama* (Muslim legal scholars), the Shia—not wholly unlike Roman Catholics in their conviction about the pope—believe that the imam is not only clergy but also religiously inspired and infallible in his legal and theological declarations.[44] The Shia also affirm that imams were historically descendants of Fatima and Ali, though the direct line of succession ended centuries ago. Among these descendants the Shia are divided into three main groups: the Fivers, Seveners, and Twelvers. These sects get their names based on the number of perceived rightful imams after Muhammad: five, seven, and twelve.

Among the Shia the Twelvers are the overwhelming majority. They are roughly equivalent to the Sunni in relation to the total percentage of Muslims. The Twelvers believe that the twelfth imam—known as the Hidden Imam—went into occultation or hiding in 941 and will return as the Messiah or *Mahdi* ("the Guided One") on the day of judgment. He will establish the right practice of Islam and lead a battle of good forces against evil.[45] In fact, all Muslims—not just the Shia—believe that the *Mahdi* or Messiah will return on the day of judgment.

Some of the best conversations I have had with Muslims over the years have been those concerning the day of judgment and the Messiah. Although Muslims and Christians differ on any number of important beliefs and practices, one thing we hold in common is our conviction that the world is not as it should be. Few would deny the level of evil, oppression, and injustice that is perpetrated on a daily basis. We all long for the day when the world will be set to rights. For Muslims, just as for

43. Esposito, *What Everyone Needs to Know about Islam*, 49.
44. Ibid., 43.
45. Bokhari and Seddon, *The Complete Illustrated Guide to Islam*, 236–37.

Christians, that day will occur when the Messiah appears and does away with the forces of darkness.

In one conversation with a Muslim man, I told him that Christians believe that the world is not right based on sin. I then asked him why Muslims believe that the world is in need of a Messiah if there is no concept of original sin. This led to an interesting discussion. Because I know that for a Christian to speak directly about Jesus to a Muslim can be off-putting, I did not mention his name or draw any parallels between Jesus' role in the end times in both Islam and Christianity.

This conversation, which led to more conversations, reinforced to me that it is sometimes better to speak about what we as Christians have in common with other religions before talking about what we do not have in common. As I spoke with this man about some of the similarities in our beliefs about the end times, we gradually discovered that we shared other commonalities and we were able to speak on common terms. Although there is a time and a place both to speak freely about Jesus and to emphasize the differences between Christianity and Islam, it has been my experience that it is best to be cautious when speaking about our faith with Muslim believers rather than being too hasty.

Discussion Questions

1. How have the events of 9/11 changed the way in which many Westerners see Islam? Do you think that Islam is an extremist or violent religion? How do you reconcile this with the fact that Muslims understand Allah to be all-merciful? Discuss these questions in connection with the first chapter of the Qur'an.

2. If you lived in a predominantly Muslim state, what would be your greatest fear? Is there anything about the Muslim religion that you would appreciate as a Christian? What can Christians learn from Islam?

3. Islam has five major practices that are essential to the religion. Discuss some similarities between these major practices and what you would consider to be the five major practices of Christianity.

4. What are some of the key differences between the nature of God in Islam and Christianity in terms of God's attributes, qualities, and personality?

5. What are some potential obstacles you might encounter when talking to Muslims about Jesus? How would you share your faith with a Muslim?

Further Readings

Abdel Haleem, M. A. S., trans. *The Qur'an*. Oxford: Oxford University Press, 2010.

Aslan, Reza. *No God but God: The Origins, Evolution, and Future of Islam*. New York: Random House, 2006.

Brown, Daniel. *A New Introduction to Islam*. 2nd ed. Oxford: Wiley-Blackwell, 2009.

Esposito, John. *What Everyone Needs to Know about Islam*. 2nd ed. Oxford: Oxford University Press, 2011.

Ruthven, Malise. *Islam: A Very Short Introduction*. Oxford: Oxford University Press, 2000.

PART 2

Christian Responses to These Stories

The second part of the book will take us on a tour of Christian responses to other religions. Truth be told, the biblical authors faced some of the same situations that we face today. In the Old Testament the Israelites moved in and out of different religious cultures, and in the New Testament the apostles likewise traveled from place to place. This polytheistic culture in which the biblical community lived exposed them to various expressions of religion. Although the Bible nowhere offers a comprehensive view of nonbiblical religions, it does address some issues that are instructive for current-day Christians.

In addition to biblical responses to other religions, there is a growing literature among Christian theologians who are responding to world religions. We will survey some of these important approaches, and they will allow us to assess and integrate what we have learned in the previous sections into our thinking about other religions. Although there is no classification among Christians that brings about complete consensus on the matter, the various approaches that Christians have adopted over the years will prove useful as we address and engage non-Christian religions.

chapter 6

Biblical Responses to Other Religions

God has revealed himself fully and definitely in the person of Jesus Christ and has through his work made available to humankind an all-sufficient redemption. The truth of creation is indeed reflected in all world religions, but the saving Gospel of reconciliation and redemption is to be found only in Christianity. There are many roads by which man seeks to come to God, but there is only one road by which God comes to man, namely, Jesus Christ.

Donald Bloesch

On the complex question of religious pluralism, confident optimism in the character of God and theological modesty about our conclusions will serve us well as we proclaim that Jesus Christ is the way, the truth, and the life (John 14:6). We must try to steer a path between saying too much, which could lead to a needlessly harsh position that drives people into radically pluralistic viewpoints, and saying too little, which could to our own peril slide into religious relativism. In the words of John Calvin . . . we should leave alone what God has left hidden, but not neglect what he has brought into the open.

Daniel Clendenin

GOD WANTS PEOPLE from all nations to know and worship him (Rev. 5:9). That is the overarching theme of Scripture. This story of God's vision for the world is evident from the earliest pages in Genesis to the final scenes in Revelation. From beginning to end, the biblical story is told from the perspective that "God so loved the world" (John 3:16) that he has graciously provided the means by which people can become right with him. Whereas the Old Testament has a centralized vision of all nations pouring into Jerusalem to worship Yahweh God on Mount Zion (Isa. 2:1–4), the New Testament centers on Jesus as the personal fulfillment of God's promises to Israel and the world (2 Cor. 1:19–20). The biblical vision is for all people groups to worship God "in spirit and truth" (John 4:24) and for "every knee . . . in heaven and on earth and under the earth" to bow down at the name of Jesus (Phil. 2:10).

Despite the Bible's grand vision for all people groups to come to the knowledge of the truth, it is still quite apparent in Scripture that many people ignore, squelch, or outright reject God's plan of salvation and restoration. Indeed, as the apostle Paul explains in his letter to the Romans, those who deny Jesus' central role in cosmic and earthly history "suppress the truth" (1:18) even though God has made it clear throughout creation that he indeed exists and that all things find fulfillment in him.

As we discuss the Bible's relationship with and response to other religions, it will be apparent that the Bible nowhere presents a comprehensive theology of other religions. Scripture engages other religions and at times makes references to them, but other religions are not a major focus of the Old or New Testament. When the Bible does mention them, it is always in the context that these other religions are not salvific. In other words, they do not provide salvation. In the Old Testament, for instance, this means that a person must enter into a covenant relationship with God to inherit his eternal promises, while in the New Testament this means that a person must enter into a saving relationship with Jesus. Apart from these basic assumptions, discussion about the biblical responses to other religions is varied and requires us to interpret a range of passages addressing this topic.

The Old Testament and Other "Gods"

The story of the book of Genesis depicts a God who is simultaneously lord over heaven and earth. Although different people groups existed who in turn engendered distinct nations, all people were made in the image of this God and therefore share a common origin and purpose. Early on in the biblical narrative this cosmic God chose one man, Abraham, to be the harbinger of universal blessing (Gen. 12:1–3). From this one man God brought forth an entire nation, Israel, to be the recipient of his covenant love so that the nation would display this covenant love to the world (Isa. 42:6). In this way, God's election of Israel was set within the context of a universal history of humankind—the one, Israel, was chosen to be a conduit of God's blessing to the many, the world (Gen. 17:4).

In fact, God's purpose for Israel was not only to be the recipient and conduit of divine blessing but also to be the means by which God revealed his sovereignty over the world. This is seen most clearly during the exodus, which is regarded by many to be the paradigmatic event in the Old Testament. It occurred after Israel had languished in slavery for hundreds of years in Egypt. What is striking about the exodus is not only that God exercised his authority over pagan Egypt but also that God wielded his power over the Egyptian gods. Indeed, the culmination of God's judgment on Egypt was ultimately directed against its "gods."

> For I will pass through the land of Egypt that night, and I will strike all the firstborn in the land of Egypt, both man and beast; *and on all the gods of Egypt I will execute judgments: I am the Lord.* (Ex. 12:12)[1]

As commentator Philip Ryken notes, "With this final plague God accomplished his objective—namely, to demonstrate his lordship over the Egyptians by defeating *all* their gods, together with the demonic powers they represented."[2] In fact, we may surmise from an earlier section in Exodus that the "gods" the Lord[3] God battled with were powerful entities that were likely the source of the Egyptian magicians' ability to conjure up and imitate Moses' first sign in front of Pharaoh (7:22).

As we consider this passage above, we realize that the theme of the Lord God's sovereignty over other "gods" is quite prominent in the book of Exodus. In addition to Exodus 12:12, many passages in Exodus allude to this theme, including some of the following:

> "Who is like you, O Lord, *among the gods*?" (Ex. 15:11)

> "You shall have *no other gods* before me." (Ex. 20:3)

> "Whoever sacrifices *to any god*, other than the Lord alone, shall be devoted to destruction." (Ex. 22:20)

Taking our cue from Philip Ryken, the immediate context of the book of Exodus is the Lord God's desire to demonstrate his sovereignty

"Genesis 1–11 assumes that human beings are created in God's image and aware of God. Their disobedience and their loss of an immediate relationship with God did not remove the image or the awareness."
—John Goldingay and Christopher Wright

John Goldingay and Christopher Wright, "Yahweh Our God Yahweh One: The Oneness of God in the Old Testament," in Andrew D. Clarke and Bruce W. Winter, *One God, One Lord: Christianity in a World of Religious Pluralism* (Grand Rapids: Baker, 1992), 44.

---

1. In these passages and several below, I italicize the key parts of the verses.

2. Philip Ryken, *Exodus: Saved for God's Glory* (Wheaton, IL: Crossway, 2005), 213.

3. In this chapter I use the terms *the Lord* and *Yahweh* synonymously. Incidentally, most modern Bible versions translate *Yahweh* as "the Lord."

over the nations by casting judgment over the "gods" of Egypt. Specifically, the first passage above from Exodus is found in the Song of Moses. It celebrates Yahweh God's triumph over the Egyptian gods and his deliverance of Israel from bondage. The next passage makes complete sense within the chronology of Exodus. Because the Israelites had lived in Egypt for hundreds of years, they were still tempted to acknowledge and even worship the rival gods of Egypt. Accordingly, the first two of the Ten Commandments were intended to eliminate worship of any god other than Yahweh. Indeed, it was the LORD God alone, the preface to the Ten Commandments emphasizes, who brought Egypt out of slavery—not any other god (20:2). Finally, despite the tangible victory that Yahweh God won over the Egyptian gods and his clear prohibition against worshiping any others, many Israelites continued to worship other gods from the time of the exodus to the time of the exile several hundred years later. As 2 Kings explains:

> And [the exile] occurred because the people of Israel had sinned against the LORD their God, who had brought them up out of the land of Egypt from under the hand of Pharaoh king of Egypt, and had *feared other gods* . . . . They built for themselves high places in all their towns, from watchtower to fortified city. They set up for themselves pillars and Asherim on every high hill and under every green tree, and there they made offerings on all the high places. . . . And they did wicked things, provoking the LORD to anger, and *they served idols*, of which the LORD had said to them, "You shall not do this." (2 Kings 17:7–12)

This passage indicates a continued pattern throughout the Hebrew Bible that worship of other gods persisted within the nation of Israel. Granted, the "gods" that the Israelites may have worshiped evolved from known Egyptian deities such as Hapi (a god of fertility and flooding) and Heqet (a frog goddess) to the Semitic deities such as Asherah (a mother goddess) and Baal (a storm god); nonetheless, the Israelites continued worshiping gods other than their own covenant God who had rescued them from slavery.

Other "Gods" in the Rest of the Old Testament

All this worship of other "gods" raises an important question: Are these "gods" real beings or just idols? In other words, when the covenant God of Israel commanded the Israelites to have no other "gods" before him, did this imply the existence of real gods besides Yahweh

God, or did this suggest only that the Israelites would be inclined to make an image of the invisible God? Before we answer these questions, let's broaden our context by looking at a few more Old Testament passages that could suggest the view that "gods" in the Old Testament were real beings:

> They made [the LORD God] jealous with *strange gods*; with abominations they provoked Him to anger. They sacrificed *to demons who were not God, to gods whom they have not known.* (Deut. 32:16–17 NASB)

> They served *other gods.* (Josh. 24:2)

> The king said to her, "Do not be afraid. What do you see?" And the woman said to Saul, "*I see a god* coming up out of the earth." (1 Sam. 28:13)

> [Solomon] said, "O LORD, God of Israel, *there is no God like you*, in heaven above or on earth beneath, keeping covenant and showing steadfast love to your servants who walk before you with all their heart." (1 Kings 8:23)

> [Solomon has] forsaken me and worshiped Ashtoreth the *goddess* of the Sidonians, Chemosh the *god* of Moab, and Milcom the *god* of the Ammonites. (1 Kings 11:33)

> There is none like you *among the gods*, O Lord. (Ps. 86:8)

> They mixed with the nations and learned to do as they did. They served *their idols*, which became a snare to them. They sacrificed their sons and their daughters *to the demons.* (Ps. 106:35–37)

> I know that . . . our Lord is *above all gods.* (Ps. 135:5)

> On that day the LORD *will punish the host of heaven, in heaven*, and the kings of the earth, on the earth. (Isa. 24:21)

> Thus says the LORD, the King of Israel and his Redeemer, the LORD of hosts: "I am the first and I am the last; besides me there is no god. Who is like me? Let him proclaim it. Let him declare and set it before me, since I appointed an ancient people. Let them declare what is to come, and what will happen. Fear not, nor be afraid; have I not told you from of old and declared it? And you are my witnesses! *Is there a God besides me?* There is no Rock; I know not any." All who fashion idols are nothing,

and the things they delight in do not profit. Their witnesses neither see nor know, that they may be put to shame. (Isa. 44:6–9)

I will declare my judgments against them, for all their evil in forsaking me. They have *made offerings to other gods*. (Jer. 1:16)

The gods who did not make the heavens and the earth shall perish from the earth and from under the heavens. Jer. 10:11)

Do not go after *other gods* to serve and worship them. (Jer. 25:6)

The LORD will . . . famish *all the gods of the earth*. (Zeph. 2:11)

"Gods" as Real Beings?

There are two general responses to the question above among evangelical Christians as to how we interpret the many references to "gods" in the Old Testament. The first is that these "gods" are real beings that exist just like the God of the Bible exists. Granted, these gods are inferior to their Creator Yahweh God, but they nonetheless have some type of existence. As one Old Testament scholar explains:

> The Old Testament speaks freely, without any hesitation or embarrassment, about the existence of gods other than the God of Israel. . . . To be sure, the supremacy of Israel's God over all other gods is everywhere asserted. But the assertion always drives home the dominion of Yahweh over other gods, not the denial of their existence.[4]

Perhaps the most prominent evangelical today who advances this view is theologian Gerald McDermott. McDermott argues that the "gods" in the Old Testament are best interpreted as angels who—like Satan—turned away from their Creator God and appropriated to themselves worship that rightly belonged to Yahweh God.[5]

Advocates of this position assert that post-Enlightenment Christians, under the influence of rationalism and deism, have been trained to relegate any mention of "spirits" or "gods" to mythology rather than reality.[6] The remedy to this mind-set, it is argued, is found in learning

---

4. Ulrich Mauser, "One God Alone: A Pillar of Biblical Theology," *Princeton Seminary Bulletin* 12, 3 (1991): 259.
5. Gerald McDermott, *God's Rivals: Why Has God Allowed Different Religions? Insights from the Bible and the Early Church* (Downers Grove, IL: InterVarsity Press, 2007), 46, 53, 58.
6. Ibid., 50.

from Christian theologians who were active before the Enlightenment, many of whom believed that the "gods" mentioned in the Bible were spiritual beings. A pre-Enlightenment Christian who represents this position is the second-century apologist (or "defender of the faith") Justin Martyr:

> God, when He had made the whole world, and subjected things earthly to man, and arranged the heavenly elements for the increase of fruits and rotation of the seasons, and appointed this divine law . . . committed the care of men and of all things under heaven to angels whom He appointed over them. But the angels transgressed this appointment [see Genesis 6:1–4; 1 Enoch 6–36; 2 Peter 2:4; Jude 6] and were captivated by love of women, and begat children who are those that are called demons; and besides, they afterwards subdued the human race to themselves, partly by magical writings, and partly by fears and the punishments they occasioned, and partly by teaching them to offer sacrifices, and incense, and libations, of which things they stood in need after they were enslaved by lustful passions.[7]

Like Justin, proponents of this interpretive school emphasize passages in Deuteronomy (29:25–26; 32:8–9, 16–17) where, it is interpreted, God allocated to "gods" or "fallen angels" or "demons"—which are all virtually synonymous—certain regions of the world to govern justly. However, these beings ended up rejecting that role and demanding worship from the people they ruled. Advocates of this position also appeal to Psalm 82, where these "gods" or angels are judged by Yahweh God for ruling improperly:

> God has taken his place in the divine council; *in the midst of the gods* he holds judgment: "How long will you judge unjustly and show partiality to the wicked? Give justice to the weak and the fatherless; maintain the right of the afflicted and the destitute. Rescue the weak and the needy; deliver them from the hand of the wicked." They have neither knowledge nor understanding, they walk about in darkness; all the foundations of the earth are shaken. I said, *"You are gods, sons of the Most High, all of you*; nevertheless, like men you shall die, and fall like any prince." Arise, O God, judge the earth; for you shall inherit all the nations! (Ps. 82)

In the end, the interpretive school above believes that the "gods" in the Old Testament are rebellious angels who demanded worship for themselves over the different nations they ruled.

---

7. Justin Martyr, "Second Apology" 5, in *St. Justin Martyr: The First and Second Apologies*, trans. Leslie Barnard (Mahwah, NJ: Paulist Press, 1997), 78.

"Gods" as Mere Idols?

The second response to the question about how to understand what is meant by the word *gods* is that they are images or idols that people worshiped but have no real existence. Missiologist George Braswell favors this view. He believes that mention of other gods refers to empty idols and not to the actual existence of a being:

> How do the gods of other nations like Ashur and Baal originate? . . . They are idols made with human hands. People fell into vain imaginings, and images were made. The Hebrew idea of utter transcendence of God conflicted with all images and stones.[8]

Advocates of this position often appeal to passages such as Isaiah 44. Indeed, this section of Isaiah is trenchant in its attack on idol worship. From a context in which Israel lived among the shadows of temples dedicated to Marduk (a powerful Babylonian deity), the prophet Isaiah took pains to express that "besides [the LORD God] there is no god" (Isa. 44:6). Much of the remaining part of the chapter mocks even the notion of idol worship given the absurdity, it is viewed, of fashioning one's own god out of a tree. As one commentator on the passage in Isaiah expresses it:

> A god carved and gold-plated by artisans and borne on the shoulders of porters is a god neither capable of delivering a people from bondage nor worthy of that people's devotion.[9]

"The gods of the nations are regarded as simply impotent. Worship of them is not so much culpable as futile. They cannot save."
—John Goldingay and Christopher Wright

Goldingay and Wright, "Yahweh Our God Yahweh One," 52.

Another passage that advocates the position that "gods" are mere man-made idols rather than actual beings comes from the prophet Elijah's taunting of the prophets of Baal:

> "[Y]ou call upon the name of your god, and I will call upon the name of the LORD, and the God who answers by fire, he is God." And all the people answered, "It is well spoken." Then Elijah said to the prophets of Baal, "Choose for yourselves one bull and prepare it first, for you are many, and call upon the name of your god, but put no fire to it." And they took the bull that was given them, and they prepared it and called upon the name of Baal from morning until noon, saying, "O Baal, answer us!" But there was no voice,

8. George Braswell, *Understanding World Religions* (Nashville: Broadman and Holman, 1994), 176.

9. Paul Hanson, *Isaiah 40–66* (Louisville, KY: John Knox Press, 1995), 89.

and no one answered. And they limped around the altar that they had made. And at noon Elijah mocked them, saying, "Cry aloud, for he is a god. Either he is musing, or he is relieving himself, or he is on a journey, or perhaps he is asleep and must be awakened." And they cried aloud and cut themselves after their custom with swords and lances, until the blood gushed out upon them. And as midday passed, they raved on until the time of the offering of the oblation, but there was no voice. No one answered; no one paid attention. (1 Kings 18:24–29)

Given the great storytelling of this passage, one can easily imagine Elijah teasing the pitiable prophets of Baal and making a spectacle of their god's inability to light the fire prepared for him or in any way to demonstrate his power, let alone his existence. As one Old Testament scholar writes:

The point of the narrative is not just that Yahweh is the God of Israel, but that Yahweh is God, period. . . . [Baal] is a nonentity. . . . What seems at first to be a battle between two competing gods turns out to be a contest between God and an empty delusion.[10]

In the two passages above from Isaiah and 2 Kings, the "gods" of the other nations appear to be not just ineffective but also imaginary.

The New Testament and Other Religions

As we move from the Old to the New Testament, the worship of beings other than God continues to be a persistent theme. While political, economic, and sociological shifts characterized the world of the Old and New Testaments, the culture remained consistently polytheistic. Yet despite the similar context between the Old and the New Testaments, as biblical scholar Gregory Beale articulates, the New Testament authors did not typically "make reference to specific pagan religions, philosophies, and their belief systems."[11] What they did instead was to assume and make reference to demonic activity. Below are just a few passages that support this perspective:

Then Jesus was led up by the Spirit into the wilderness *to be tempted by the devil.* (Matt. 4:1)

10. Richard Nelson, *First and Second Kings* (Atlanta: John Knox Press, 1987), 120–21.
11. Gregory Beale, "Other Religions in New Testament Theology," in *Biblical Faith and Other Religions: An Evangelical Assessment*, ed. David Baker (Grand Rapids: Kregel, 2004), 79.

But if it is *by the finger of God that I cast out demons*, then the kingdom of God has come upon you. (Luke 11:20)

The ruler of this world is coming. (John 14:30)

For unclean spirits, crying out with a loud voice, *came out of many who had them*, and many who were paralyzed or lame were healed. (Acts 8:7)

And when the crowds saw what Paul had done, they lifted up their voices, saying in Lycaonian, "*The gods have come down to us in the likeness of men!*" Barnabas they called Zeus, and Paul, Hermes, because he was the chief speaker. And the priest of Zeus, whose temple was at the entrance to the city, brought oxen and garlands to the gates and wanted to offer sacrifice with the crowds. But when the apostles Barnabas and Paul heard of it, they tore their garments and rushed out into the crowd, crying out, "Men, why are you doing these things? We also are men, of like nature with you, and we bring you good news, that you should turn from these vain things to a living God, who made the heaven and the earth and the sea and all that is in them. In past generations he allowed all the nations to walk in their own ways. Yet he did not leave himself without witness, for he did good by giving you rains from heaven and fruitful seasons, satisfying your hearts with food and gladness." Even with these words they scarcely restrained the people from offering sacrifice to them. (Acts 14:11–18)

And even if our gospel is veiled, it is veiled to those who are perishing. In their case *the god of this world has blinded the minds of the unbelievers*, to keep them from seeing the light of the gospel of the glory of Christ, who is the image of God. (2 Cor. 4:3–4)

And no wonder, for even *Satan disguises himself as an angel of light*. So it is no surprise if his servants, also, disguise themselves as servants of righteousness. Their end will correspond to their deeds. (2 Cor. 11:14–15)

And you were dead in the trespasses and sins in which you once walked, following the course of this world, *following the prince of the power of the air, the spirit that is now at work in the sons of disobedience*. (Eph. 2:1–2)

We know that we are from God, and *the whole world lies in the power of the evil one*. (1 John 5:19)

And the angels who did not stay within their own position of authority, but left their proper dwelling, he has kept in eternal chains under gloomy darkness until the judgment of the great day. (Jude 6)

It is clear from these passages that the demonic realm was an assumed reality throughout the New Testament. But the question remains: What is the relationship between the demonic realm and other religions?

Paul and Other Religions

The apostle Paul is the New Testament author who teaches in the most depth on the relationship between demonic activity and other religions. Paul's most sustained discussion of these topics is found in 1 Corinthians 8 and 10.[12] In these sections Paul addresses the problem of partaking of food sacrificed to idols. There are two passages important to our discussion here. The first occurs in the opening section of Paul's teaching about idols:

> Therefore, as to the eating of food offered to idols, we know that "an idol has no real existence," and that "there is no God but one." For although there may be so-called gods in heaven or on earth—as indeed there are many "gods" and many "lords"—yet for us there is one God, the Father, from whom are all things and for whom we exist, and one Lord, Jesus Christ, through whom are all things and through whom we exist. (1 Cor. 8:4–6)

Paul's quotation of these two slogans—"an idol has no real existence" and "there is no God but one"—came from the letter that Paul had received from the Corinthian church. Although the apostle agreed with the Corinthian church theologically, he did not support their application of these slogans. Whereas the Corinthians reasoned that idols were not real deities and therefore it did not matter if a person ate food sacrificed to them, Paul impressed on the Corinthians that because so many people in that culture believed in the real existence of these idols—including Christians who were formerly associated with these religions and cults—it was essential not to be associated with them.

This is the origin of Paul's declaration that there are "many 'gods' and many 'lords'" (8:5). As New Testament scholar Richard Hays explains, this verse "simply acknowledges the empirical fact that the world is teeming with representations of such entities and with their worshipers."[13] Although the idols did not correspond to real "gods"—since God is the only existent God—the temples and statues dedicated to other gods in

---

12. Paul's engagement with other religions in Athens in Acts 17 is another important passage in this discussion, but I will not address it here because I speak about it in the introduction and in the conclusion.

13. Richard Hays, *First Corinthians* (Louisville, KY: John Knox Press, 1997), 138.

cities like Corinth were ubiquitous, and those who worshiped in them believed that the gods they solicited and adored were really existent. As a result, context demanded a more nuanced approach to the topic of Christians' eating food sacrificed to idols than the Corinthians had originally thought.

The other central passage in Paul's explanation of idols comes two chapters later:

> What do I imply then? That food sacrificed to idols is anything, or that an idol is anything? No, I imply that what pagans sacrifice they offer to demons and not to God. I do not want you to be participants with demons. You cannot drink the cup of the Lord and the cup of demons. (10:19–21a)

"Demons . . . are angels created by God and thus were originally good; but they sinned and thus became evil. Just when this rebellion took place we do not know, but it must have occurred between the time when God completed the creation and pronounced it all 'very good,' and the temptation and fall of the humans."
—Millard Erickson

Millard Erickson, *Christian Theology,* 2nd ed. (Grand Rapids: Baker, 1998), 472.

While denying that pagan idols exist in and of themselves, the apostle nonetheless "affirms the existence of a world of spiritual powers hostile to God."[14] Paul perceives, as one New Testament scholar warns, "the presence of Satan and his cohorts . . . behind these idols."[15] In fact, Paul's unambiguous statement on the matter—"what pagans sacrifice they offer to demons" (10:20)—is a quotation from the book of Deuteronomy, where the Israelites were judged for sacrificing to "demons" in their worship of other gods (32:16–17). Indeed, New Testament historian Craig Blomberg writes succinctly, Paul "knows from the Law that demons—fallen angels—are the true objects of pagan rituals, however unwittingly they may be worshiped."[16]

Given the two passages and interpretations above, we may return to our original question: What is the relationship between the demonic realm in the New Testament and other religions? Perhaps New Testament scholar Clinton Arnold puts it best:

> One of the central features of Paul's argument [in 1 Corinthians 8 and 10] is that there is a demonic character to non-Christian religions. He agreed with the informed Corinthians in principle that an idol has no real, independent existence (8:4). For the Christian, he concurred, there is no God but the one true God. . . . Nevertheless, Paul went on to affirm some kind of real existence for these gods, noting, "indeed there are many 'gods' and many 'lords'" (8:5). In one sense he did believe in the existence of other "gods" and "lords," but in a qualitatively different way than those who worshiped these beings. Paul [later contended]

14. Ibid., 169.
15. Simon Kistemaker, *Exposition of the First Epistle to the Corinthians* (Grand Rapids: Baker, 1993), 347.
16. Craig Blomberg, *1 Corinthians* (Grand Rapids: Zondervan, 1994), 194.

that the images represent demons (10:20–21) and not true divinities; they are not to be thought of on the same level as the one God. In another sense, however, they are real gods and lords in that they are subjectively believed to be such by those who worship them; they are "real" to their worshipers.[17]

Though intricate—as many of Paul's letters tend to be—the apostle's explanation assumes a correlation between other religions and demonic activity. At the same time, Paul nowhere presents a comprehensive theology of other religions or of demonic activity, so we cannot conclude with certainty exactly how these two are associated.

Humankind's Inclination to Fabricate Religion

Although there is no consensus among evangelical Christians as to the exact relationship between other religions and demonic activity, it is clear from Scripture that there is a direct relationship between other religions and the human inclination to construct or fabricate religious systems. Indeed, as we reflect on other religions in the Bible as a whole, there are two factors to keep in mind: Human beings are made in God's image, and God's creation is apparent to all. As an article in the *ESV Study Bible* explains:

> Similarities [between Christianity and other religions] are not surprising and can be understood in light of the biblical teaching that all people, including adherents of other religions, have been created by God in his image (Gen. 1:26–27; 5:1) and that God has revealed himself in a general manner to all peoples through the created order. (Ps. 19:1–4; Acts 14:15–17; 17:22–32; Rom. 1:18–32; 2:14–15)[18]

As for the first factor, the Bible teaches that humans are made in the image of God (Gen. 1:27). As image-bearers, all humans have a sense of the divine in them. This is because as image-bearers we are, as theologian Louis Berkhof states candidly, "God-related."[19] Because humans are made in God's image and because God is Spirit, it is natural to expect a spiritual element to find expression in human beings.[20] As the apostle Paul writes

---

17. Clinton Arnold, *Powers of Darkness: Principalities and Powers in Paul's Letters* (Downers Grove, IL: InterVarsity Press, 1992), 94–95.

18. "The Bible and World Religions," in *ESV Study Bible* (Wheaton, IL: Crossway, 2007), 2628.

19. Louis Berkhof, *Systematic Theology: A New Combined Edition* (Grand Rapids: Baker, 1996), 2:202.

20. Ibid.

concerning the Gentiles in his letter to the Roman church: "For when Gentiles, who do not have the law, by nature do what the law requires, they are a law to themselves, even though they do not have the law" (Rom. 2:14).

The other important biblical teaching to keep in mind is that God has designed creation in such a way that human beings are aware of God's general revelation. Once again, as the apostle Paul writes about the Gentiles who formerly did not have a covenant relationship with the LORD, "[God's] invisible attributes, namely, his eternal power and divine nature, have been clearly perceived, ever since the creation of the world, in the things that have been made" (1:20). Although God had made a covenant with the nation of Israel in the Old Testament and revealed himself specifically to them, God also revealed himself more generally to other nations and people groups. Theologian John Calvin says it this way:

> That there exists in the human mind, and indeed by natural instinct, some sense of Deity, we hold to be beyond dispute, since God himself, to prevent anyone from pretending ignorance, has [endowed all people] with some idea of his Godhead, the memory of which he constantly renews and occasionally enlarges.[21]

As we reflect on these two teachings from Scripture, the correlation between these truths and other religions can be stated as follows: Because we are made in God's image and because God's general revelation is available to all humans, it is natural for human beings to create religious systems or structures that attempt to appropriate—however incompletely and inadequately—this divine reality. In fact, John Calvin explains, the practice of idolatry "is ample evidence" not only of God's very existence but also of humankind's inclination to create and fashion something to worship or ascribe adoration to other than the one true God.[22] A quotation from New Testament scholar D. A. Carson supports this viewpoint:

> The least that "image of God" language suggests, in addition to human personhood, is that human beings are . . . accorded an astonishing dignity; that human beings are moral creatures with special privileges and responsibilities; that there is implanted within us a profound capacity for knowing God intimately, however much we

"Since the perfection of blessedness consists in the knowledge of God, he has been pleased, in order that none might be excluded from the means of obtaining [happiness], not only to deposit in our minds that seed of religion . . . but so to manifest his perfections in the whole structure of the universe, and daily place himself in our view, that we cannot open our eyes without being compelled to behold him."
—John Calvin

John Calvin, *Institutes of the Christian Religion*, trans. Henry Beveridge (Grand Rapids: Eerdmans, 1995), 1.5.51.

21. Calvin, *Institutes*, 1.3.43.
22. Ibid., 1.3.43–45.

have suppressed and distorted that capacity; that we have a hunger for creating things.[23]

Taking our cue from Calvin and Carson, we see that the very center of human existence is to create and to attempt to respond to the divine seed within each of us. In this regard, some Christians believe that other religions are less animated by and associated with the demonic realm and more indicative of the human inclination to worship something greater than oneself. Whatever the exact relationship between the demonic and other religions, it is nonetheless clear that there is a direct relationship between human beings—who are made in God's image—and their proclivity to connect with the divine by means of religious structures or practices.

Conclusion

Our discussion of the biblical response to other religions has served as an overview of this topic rather than a detailed summary. We have surveyed different parts of the Old and New Testaments in order to understand the nature of other religions. By means of conclusion, I would like to highlight the following statements that have arisen—both directly and indirectly—from this study.

First, religions do not save. Rather, God saves. As important as biblically prescribed religious systems are, they are incapable of bringing about individual or corporate salvation. Ideally these systems or structures point to God and his salvation, but they do not in and of themselves provide salvation. Indeed, the LORD God warns of religious structures devoid of a right relationship with him: "Even though you offer me your burnt offerings and grain offerings, I will not accept them; and the peace offerings of your fattened animals, I will not look upon them" (Amos 5:22). Although the following quote is set in an Old Testament context, it equally applies to the New Testament:

> The whole point of much of the mockery of other gods [by biblical prophets] . . . is that when the crunch comes, they are ridiculously powerless to save. Worse, they are an encumbrance to their worshippers. It is Yahweh alone who saves. The question, therefore, of whether there is salvation in other religions, is in the Old Testament terms a

23. D. A. Carson, *The Gagging of God: Christianity Confronts Pluralism* (Grand Rapids: Zondervan, 1996), 205.

"All the ritu-
als, prayers,
sacrifices, and
worship offered
to the gods of
other nations
were not really
offered to
'gods' at all.
They were
accorded to
angelic impos-
ters usurping
the rightful
place of the
one true God."
—Clinton
Arnold

Clinton Arnold,
*Three Crucial Ques-
tions about Spiritual
Warfare* (Grand
Rapids: Baker,
1997), 152.

non-question. There is salvation in *no* religions because religions don't save. Not even Israel's *religion* saved them. It was at best a response to Yahweh, the living God who had saved them. When the nations come over to Israel, in the prophet's vision, it will not be to say, "Now we realize that your religion is the best one," but to acknowledge, "In Yahweh alone is salvation." (Isa. 45:14, 24)[24]

Again, only God saves. Religions are mere symbols that, at best, point to God's salvation, but they are not able to reproduce what only God can do. Needless to say, therefore, other religions cannot bring about salvation.

Second, the Bible teaches that there is only one God. This is a major theme throughout both the Old and New Testaments. Indeed, one of the most important confessional statements in the Old Testament is the Shema, which begins majestically: "Hear, O Israel: the LORD our God, the LORD is one" (Deut. 6:4). This theological view is advanced throughout the rest of Scripture, including various parts of the New Testament. For instance, the apostle Paul writes, "There is one God, and there is one mediator between God and men, the man Christ Jesus" (1 Tim. 2:5). In this regard, whatever or whoever the "gods" of the Bible are, they are not real gods, since there is only the one true God.

Finally, the Bible can be interpreted differently when it comes to understanding the identity of the beings worshiped in other religions and the power behind them. Among evangelical believers there are two main positions. The first position interprets the "gods" of the Old Testament as fallen angels or demons who divert worship from the true God to themselves. Although the Old Testament often refers to them as "gods," they are not divinities but are rather malicious beings who, like Satan, formerly rebelled against God's authority. What's more, although they are powerful beings, they were created by God and are likewise under the authority of Jesus (Heb. 1:4, 6). The second position understands these "gods" to be artificial names that idol-worshipers created themselves. Instead of being fallen angels who animate or empower false religious structures, these idols are empty, powerless, and downright nonexistent. Whichever of these positions one adopts, however, the Bible makes clear that worship of the one true God is the ultimate vision for the future. As the host of heaven sang the hymn of Moses in anticipation of the fulfillment of God's plan of redemption:

24. Goldingay and Wright, "Yahweh Our God Yahweh One," in *One God, One Lord*, 52.

Who will not fear, O Lord, and glorify your name? For you alone are holy. All nations will come and worship you, for your righteous acts have been revealed. (Rev. 15:4)

The vision for the future is for all people groups and nations to worship the one true God in spirit and in truth and for Jesus Christ to be lifted up as the sacrificial Lamb who died to bring about the salvation and restoration of the world.

Discussion Questions

1. Why do you think the Bible does not address other religions comprehensively, given that both Jews and Christians have always lived in polytheistic cultures?
2. What biblical passages would you cite if you got into a conversation with someone about other religions? Why would you choose those passages over others? What are some differences and similarities between the ways in which the Old and the New Testaments address other religions?
3. Some Christians believe that the "gods" mentioned in the Old Testament refer to fallen angels created by God who have rebelled against his authority and have sought worship for themselves. Some also believe these fallen angels are the ones who animate and stand behind the worship of other religions. How would you respond to these views? What support is there in the Bible for these views?
4. Read 1 Corinthians 8–10. Identity the major issue that Paul is addressing. What are his conclusions and key points? Given that you do not live in a context like the one Paul is describing, how should Christians understand these passages today?
5. How do you account for the many different and competing religions in existence today and over the centuries? Are these religions just the invention of humankind, or is there a demonic aspect to them? Are the people who practice other religions connecting to a power greater than themselves?

Further Readings

Arnold, Clinton. *Three Crucial Questions about Spiritual Warfare*. Grand Rapids: Baker, 1997.

Baker, David, ed. *Biblical Faith and Other Religions: An Evangelical Assessment*. Grand Rapids: Kregel, 2004.

Calvin, John. *Institutes of the Christian Religion*. Trans. Henry Beveridge. Grand Rapids: Eerdmans, 1995.

Clarke, Andrew D., and Bruce W. Winter. *One God, One Lord: Christianity in a World of Religious Pluralism*. Grand Rapids: Baker, 1992.

McDermott, Gerald. *God's Rivals: Why Has God Allowed Different Religions? Insights from the Bible and the Early Church*. Downers Grove, IL: InterVarsity Press, 2007.

Theological Responses to Other Religions

> A theology of religions offers an interpretation for Christians of the meaning of non-Christian religions and their role, if any, in the salvation of the world. There is nothing new about this issue within Christian theology. Christians have been confronted with the need to make sense out of non-Christian religions since the very earliest days of the Christian movement. Today, however, this ancient task has taken on a new urgency.
>
> *James Fredericks*

> Affirming the finality of Christ does not relieve us of the responsibility to explain the relationship between Christianity and other religions.
>
> *Harvie Conn*

DIVERSITY IS ONE of the key features of religion in the twenty-first century. We do not live in a world where we will be around only people who think, act, and live as we do. On the contrary, depending on where we live, there is a good chance that one of our neighbors, a coworker, an acquaintance, or even a family member or close friend practices a religion that is quite distinct from Christianity. Despite the mounting religious diversity in the world today, this is nothing new to Christianity. As theologian James Fredericks asserts in the quote above, Christianity has been confronted with other religions since its emergence in the first century.

Christians have devised a number of approaches over the years to understand the relation between Christianity and other religions as well as Jesus' presence, if any, in non-Christian religions. These approaches

Inclusivists believe that salvation is through Jesus Christ, but Christ's saving grace reaches people who are not Christians.

are (1) inclusivism, (2) exclusivism, (3) pluralism, (4) universalism, and (5) particularism.[1] Although these approaches are not necessarily mutually exclusive—some are actually combined—many of them are quite distinct. What is more, there is a diversity of thought in each category so that two advocates of the same position may disagree on a host of tangential issues. In this chapter, we will explore each of these approaches. We will do so by examining the biblical passages utilized in support of each position as well as by exploring how representatives of each position argue on behalf of their respective theological approaches.

Inclusivism

Inclusivism holds that salvation is only in the name of Jesus Christ, but that Jesus can and does save people outside of the Christian religion. Or, as one scholar states it, inclusivism "affirms the salvific presence of God in non-Christian religions while still maintaining that Christ is the definitive and authoritative revelation of God."[2] This approach agrees with the exclusivist position (discussed below) that Jesus alone saves. However, inclusivists differ from exclusivists in their belief that Jesus Christ is at work in the lives of non-Christians, including non-Christian religions.

As Fredericks contends, "Salvation outside the institutional borders of Christianity is a distinct possibility."[3] In fact, according to most inclusivists, such salvation is a reality. Whereas some inclusivists believe that non-Christian religions are used by God to point people to Jesus, others emphasize that God sometimes meets with individuals or groups who have never heard the gospel preached to them. Still other inclusivists believe that God judges individuals based only on the amount of revelation they have received—whether full revelation through the preaching of the gospel of Jesus Christ or partial revelation by means of the testimony of nature. As the inclusivist theologian Clark Pinnock explains:

> Christ . . . is the Savior of all people, but they do not all come to him at once historically. God's people . . . exist everywhere in the world, not

1. Although certain scholars have questioned the preciseness of some of the categories listed above, particularly inclusivism and exclusivism, we will use them heuristically to help us reflect on the relation between Christianity and other religions. For further discussion of these terms, see Harold Netland, "Inclusivism and Exclusivism," in *The Routledge Companion to Philosophy of Religion*, ed. Chad Meister and Paul Copan (London: Routledge, 2007), 226–36.

2. Gavin D'Costa, *Theology and Religious Pluralism: The Challenge of Other Religions* (New York: Basil Blackwell, 1986), 81.

3. James Fredericks, *Faith among Faiths: Christian Theology and Non-Christian Religions* (Mahwah, NJ: Paulist Press, 1999), 15.

just in churches. People have to be given time to find their way home. Not all of those who will eventually come have yet found Jesus or entered into the communion of Christ's church. The Spirit is working on the inside *and* on the outside of the churches, pursuing his assignment from the Father to make all things new. Christians do not have a monopoly on the Spirit.[4]

Inclusivists appeal to many biblical passages in support of their position. Paul's interaction with the philosophers in Athens is one example:

> So Paul, standing in the midst of the Areopagus, said: "Men of Athens, I perceive that in every way you are very religious. For as I passed along and observed the objects of your worship, I found also an altar with this inscription, 'To the unknown god.' What therefore you worship as unknown, this I proclaim to you." (Acts 17:22–23)

Based on this passage, inclusivists argue that Jesus Christ was somehow active in the religious structure of the Athenians' worship of an unknown god. Although that unknown god was unable to save the Athenian worshipers, Jesus was able to utilize that insufficient religious system to save these individuals. This example illustrates the fact that "Paul is recognizing the possibility that non-Christians may be worshiping the God of Jesus Christ without knowing it," one theologian explains.[5]

Inclusivists believe Scripture teaches that God wants all people to come to know him. They base this view on various passages in the Bible, including the following:

> This is good, and it is pleasing in the sight of God our Savior, who desires all people to be saved and to come to the knowledge of the truth. (1 Tim. 2:3–4)

> The Lord is not slow to fulfill his promise as some count slowness, but is patient toward you, not wishing that any should perish, but that all should reach repentance. (2 Peter 3:9)

Inclusivists point out that the Christian message has not yet reached all people groups, but that God's desire for all people to be saved based on the passages above suggests that God is at work in the lives of people who have never heard about Jesus. They bolster this claim by means of

"There are people in other religions who are being led by God's secret influence to concentrate on those parts of their religion which are in agreement with Christianity, and who thus belong to Christ without knowing it."
—C. S. Lewis

C. S. Lewis, *Mere Christianity* (New York: Macmillan, 1977), 176.

---

4. Clark Pinnock, "An Inclusivist View," in *Four Views on Salvation in a Pluralistic World*, ed. Dennis Okholm and Timothy Philips (Grand Rapids: Zondervan, 1996), 105.

5. Fredericks, *Faith among Faiths*, 14.

Romans 1:19–20, which, they believe, proves that God speaks to individuals and people groups through creation and in their hearts apart from the Christian religion. What's more, inclusivists assert, "God judges people on the basis of the light they have and how they respond to that light."[6]

Advocates of the inclusivist position also construct their views based on the many biblical passages where God works in the lives of non-Israelites. They appeal to Melchizedek (Gen. 14:18–20), who—though a non-Israelite—appeared to have "a sort of knowledge of the God who manifested himself as the Holy One of Israel."[7] They likewise point to many other Old Testament figures, including Naaman the Syrian (2 Kings 5:15), Balaam (Num. 22:18), and Rahab (Josh. 2:8–13). They also cite New Testament figures such as Cornelius, who—though not associated with either the Jewish or the Christian religion—was nonetheless "a devout man who feared God" (Acts 10:2).

One of the best-known Christian advocates of inclusivism was the Catholic theologian Karl Rahner (1904–84), who was instrumental in the formulations concerning non-Christian religions at Vatican II (1962–65). Rahner wrote in a European context where Christianity was no longer a cultural stronghold but a religion that was gradually becoming just one among many others. As Rahner explains:

> Today things have changed. The West is no longer shut up in itself; it can no longer regard itself simply as the centre of the history of this world and as the centre of culture, with a religion which even from this point of view . . . could appear as the obvious and indeed sole way of honouring God to be thought of for a European. . . . [The realities of other religions] have become part of one's own existential situation—no longer merely theoretical but in the concrete—and we experience them therefore as something which puts the absolute claim of our own Christian faith into question.[8]

Despite the varied context of the West, Rahner insists that Christianity is the "absolute religion" of all the religions in the world, for it is the only religion that is intended for all people and "which cannot recognize any other religion besides itself as of equal right."[9] The Christian religion, he

---

6. John Sanders, "Inclusivism," in *What about Those Who Have Never Heard? Three Views of the Destiny of the Unevangelized*, ed. Gabriel Fackre, Ronald Nash, and John Sanders (Downers Grove, IL: InterVarsity Press, 1995), 36–37.

7. Gerald McDermott, *God's Rivals: Why Has God Allowed Different Religions? Insights from the Bible and the Early Church* (Downers Grove, IL: InterVarsity Press, 2007), 32.

8. Karl Rahner, "Christianity and the Non-Christian Religions," in *Christianity and Other Religions: Selected Readings*, ed. John Hick and Brian Hebblethwaite (Oxford: Oneworld, 2001), 21.

9. Ibid., 22.

maintains, is centered on Jesus and on God's entering into a relationship with humankind. Where the Christian religion exists, it is the absolute religion.

At the same time, Rahner argues that because Christianity is a historical religion that began in the first century AD, it was not the religion God used to save people *before* that time. In his words, Christianity "has not always and everywhere been *the* way of salvation for men."[10] Naturally, this opens the door to the view that God can save people of other religions. In fact, Rahner argues, until the gospel is presented to an individual in an objective way, that person's non-Christian religion is a sufficient carrier of God's grace through Christ. In this way, "a non-Christian religion can be recognized as a lawful religion," even though it is tainted with theological and ethical errors.[11] What's more, Rahner asserts, once we understand that even non-Christian religions contain aspects of God's supernatural grace, it is not a stretch to conclude that there are many "anonymous Christians"—past and present—who have had no direct affiliation with the church. He writes:

> The proclamation of the Gospel does not simply turn someone absolutely abandoned by God and Christ into a Christian, but turns an anonymous Christian into someone who now also knows about his Christian belief in the depths of his grace-endowed being by objective reflection and in the profession of faith which is given a social form in the Church.[12]

Rahner's use and meaning of the term "anonymous Christian" gets to the heart of his theology of other religions. As one interpreter of Rahner explains:

> Without ever having heard the name of Jesus, people from all religions . . . can experience the grace of God in Christ and thus become "anonymous Christians" enjoying saving faith. This saving faith comes only through a Christ they do not know, yet can be enjoyed even when the person is not conscious of any of the realities that make him or her a Christian.[13]

The merits of Jesus are extended to individuals and groups by means of other religions. Those who respond faithfully to these merits are "anonymous Christians." Until that time when the Christian message

10. Ibid., 23.
11. Ibid., 25.
12. Ibid., 36.
13. James Lewis and William Travis, *Religious Traditions of the World* (Grand Rapids: Zondervan, 1991), 369.

is explicitly presented to them, God accepts their imperfect response to him—by means of the religion they practice—as a result of the limited revelation they have received.

Exclusivism

Exclusivists believe that Jesus Christ is the only Savior of the world and that explicit faith in Jesus is necessary for salvation.[14] In this way, all religions other than Christianity are false since they do not present Jesus as the Savior of the world. At the same time, the position of exclusivism—sometimes referred to as restrictivism—does not deny that non-Christian religions contain good or even embody important spiritual insights. Nor do its advocates necessarily assert that these religions are demonic. However, exclusivists do believe that all non-Christian religions are ultimately impartial and flawed and that only explicit faith in Jesus Christ can save a person from his or her sins.

The exclusive position appeals to many biblical passages in support of the view that Jesus is the only Savior and that there is salvation in no one else. Some of the most common of these passages come from the Gospels:

> For God so loved the world, that he gave his only Son, that whoever believes in him should not perish but have eternal life. For God did not send his Son into the world to condemn the world, but in order that the world might be saved through him. Whoever believes in him is not condemned, but whoever does not believe is condemned already, because he has not believed in the name of the only Son of God. (John 3:16–18)

Exclusivists say this passage teaches that only belief in Jesus brings about salvation. Not believing in Jesus brings condemnation. Another well-known passage utilized by exclusivists is likewise found in the Gospel of John: "Jesus said . . . 'I am the way, and the truth, and the life. No one comes to the Father except through me'" (14:6). Exclusivists appeal to many other passages in the Bible, such as Acts 4:12, Romans 10:9–10, and 1 John 5:12.

One of the most passionate defenders of exclusivism or restrictivism was the American theologian Ronald Nash (1936–2006). Nash wrote many articles and books on this topic and believed that all the

Exclusivism affirms that people must make a conscious profession of faith in Jesus Christ in this lifetime to be saved.

14. As with each position, there are exceptions and differences of understanding when it comes to the faith of children, the mentally challenged, and those who may never hear the gospel preached. Thus, in this chapter I will focus only on how these positions understand the fate of "morally responsible" adults. See Ronald Nash, "Response to Sanders," in *What about Those Who Have Never Heard?* 118–20.

other positions surveyed in this chapter were incorrect. There are two main aspects of his argument to highlight. The first is that exclusivism is the most biblically faithful of positions and that advocates of other approaches either dismiss or misinterpret biblical passages. The second is that other positions do not properly understand the nature of revelation.

To begin with, Nash criticizes the interpretive practices of both pluralists (discussed below) and inclusivists, which are his primary conversation partners. As for the first, Nash believes that pluralists inadequately deal with Scripture and that—when they do engage the Bible—they use "outdated critical theories and doubtful sources to make [their] case."[15] As for inclusivists, Nash asserts that they misinterpret key passages in the Bible. This especially includes passages such as 1 Timothy 2:4, which reads that God "desires all people to be saved and come to the knowledge of the truth." According to Nash, inclusivists use this passage to make two assertions: "(1) the claim that God wills the salvation of every human being, and (2) the claim that God gives every human a chance to accept his grace."[16] As Nash explains, however, "even if (1) were true, it would not follow that (2) is true."[17] In Nash's opinion, it is not necessary for God to make his special revelation known to all people. This is especially the case since so many people have rejected God's natural revelation.

The discussion about general and special revelation takes us to the other aspect of Nash's arguments for exclusivism. According to Nash, much of the debate between exclusivists and inclusivists, in particular, has to do with a difference in the way in which these two positions understand revelation. As Nash explains:

> A significant disagreement between exclusivists and inclusivists involves the possible role of general revelation in salvation. Inclusivists insist that people outside any sphere of Christian influence may nonetheless be saved by trusting in whatever they may learn from God's general revelation in Creation, conscience, and history. Exclusivists disagree.[18]

In Nash's opinion, exclusivists tend to understand *general revelation* as that knowledge that God gives to all people. They base this view on biblical passages such as Psalm 19 and Romans 1–2. This type of revelation does *not* lead to salvation. It simply communicates to humans that God exists, that God is moral, and that there are universal laws by which humans are meant to

---

15. Ronald Nash, *Is Jesus the Only Savior?* (Grand Rapids: Zondervan, 1994), 91.
16. Ibid., 105.
17. Ibid.
18. Ibid., 20.

abide. Exclusivists understand *special revelation* as that knowledge that God gives to certain people. This type of revelation *does* lead to salvation, given that the person accepts it. Put differently, Nash argues that creation itself and human nature *generally* reveal that God exists, and they even suggest certain characteristics of God. Nonetheless, only Scripture and God's Spirit *specifically* reveal Jesus' identity as the Lord and Savior of human beings.

In contrast with the exclusivist position, Nash believes that inclusiv-ists tend to conflate or outright ignore the categories of general and special revelation. In this way, if we used the categories employed by exclusivists, we might say that inclusivists believe that non-Christians can be saved by *general revelation*, whereas Christians can be saved only by *special revelation*. Indeed, as one advocate of inclusivism explains, "the knowledge of God [what Nash called *general revelation*] is not limited to places where biblical revela-tion [again, what Nash calls *special revelation*] has penetrated."[19] In Nash's estimation, it is only after understanding the difference between general and special revelation that one can properly interpret the role that Jesus and non-Christian religions play in salvation. In the end, Nash concludes, even though special revelation has not reached all people groups, "general revelation does not and cannot save."[20] Thus, only those who receive special revelation about Jesus Christ and accept this revelation will be saved.

Pluralism

Pluralism maintains that all major religions are legitimate expres-sions of humankind's response to the divine. When understood in this way, *religious pluralism* is the view that not only is it a verifiable fact that there are many religions in the world, but each of the major religions should be understood as acceptable and sufficient systems of worship. Pluralists agree with both exclusivists and inclusivists that Jesus pro-vides salvation. However, pluralists differ decidedly from the other two positions in their conviction that Jesus is only *one savior among many*. In this regard, Krishna and Allah, for instance, are also saviors.

Advocates of pluralism generally argue that it is neither necessary nor particularly instructive to appeal to certain passages in the Bible. This is because the different books in the Bible "are all documents of faith."[21] In other words, many pluralists believe that instead of presenting historical

---

19. Clark Pinnock, "The Finality of Jesus Christ in a World of Religions," in *Christian Faith and Practice in the Modern World*, ed. Mark Noll and David Wells (Grand Rapids: Eerdmans, 1988), 159.

20. Nash, *Is Jesus the Only Savior?* 119.

21. John Hick, "A Pluralist View," in Ockholm and Philips, *Four Views on Salvation in a Pluralistic World*, 35.

facts, the Bible offers stories that are spiritually significant but not histori-cally factual. As one advocate of the pluralist position states it:

> We should not think of the four Gospels as if they were eyewitness accounts by reporters on the spot. They were written between forty and seventy years after Jesus' death by people who were not personally present at the events they describe.[22]

Because the biblical books—in this case, the Gospels—were written decades after the events and not, it is asserted, by eyewitnesses, it is likely that they represent later developments in theology that were not representative of the facts. An example is the attribution of divinity to Jesus. As one commentator concludes, "Jesus' divinity is not to be taken as a literal historical fact."[23] Although it is perfectly acceptable for Christians to understand Jesus as *their* Savior, pluralists assert, Jesus should not by any means be understood to be *everyone's* Savior. When pluralists do appeal to specific passages in Scripture, they tend to point out similar themes. A common example is juxtaposing the passages in the Gospels where Jesus is called the "Son of God" with Old Testament passages that refer to Israel (Hos. 11:1) or the king (Ps. 2:7) as God's "son." By placing these passages side by side, pluralists argue that Jesus' title as God's Son did not imply his divinity (since neither the nation of Israel nor the king was perceived to be divine); thus, there is no reason to think that Jesus is the Savior of the entire world or God's Son any more so than another person.

Perhaps the most passionate and well-known Christian defender of pluralism in recent decades has been the British theologian and philoso-pher John Hick (1922–2012). Although he formerly was an able champion of conservative Christianity, over the years he came to fully embrace pluralism. He has written many influential books that have brought the position of pluralism to the center stage of religious thought and practice.

There are two major parts of Hick's argument for pluralism. These include the view that all the major religions are legitimate responses to the ultimate reality as well as the position that they are all virtually equivalent in their ethics and abilities to transform lives and societies. To begin with, Hick defines religion as "belief in the transcendent."[24] By doing so, he takes the nature of the conversation away from Jesus and Christianity and moves it toward belief in an ultimately unknowable divine being, whom Hick often called "the Real." This was Hick's way

Pluralists believe that all major religions lead to "salva-tion," though not necessarily the same salva-tion imagined by Christians.

22. Ibid., 34–35.
23. Fredericks, *Faith among Faiths*, 44.
24. John Hick, *An Interpretation of Religion* (New Haven, CT: Yale University Press, 1989), 12.

of equalizing all major religions and not privileging Christianity over any other. As he wrote in his first book-length treatment of pluralism:

> [I experienced] a shift from the dogma that Christianity is at the centre to the realization that it is *God* who is at the centre, and that all religions of mankind, including [Christianity], serve and revolve around him.[25]

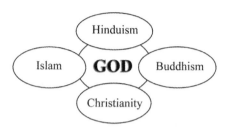

Fig. 7.1. Pluralist view of religion, which believes that all major religions are valid representations of the same universal God.

By moving the locus of the discussion around an ultimately enigmatic deity rather than Jesus Christ, Hick fully opened the door toward pluralism. Now that "the Real" was at the center of the discussion rather than Jesus, it was natural for Hick to understand all major religions as sufficient ways to engage and respond to the divine. In fact, Hick regarded each major religion as falling into one of two groups. The first group, he argued, perceives of the Real "in personal terms."[26] This includes major theistic religions such as Judaism, Christianity, and Islam. Instead of God's being an "it," in other words, God is understood as being a personal deity who interacts with his creation. The second group conceives of the Real in nonpersonal terms. This includes major religions such as Daoism and Hinduism, which view the Dao and Brahman—both impersonal forces—as culturally and historically conditioned expressions of the Real.[27]

The other major part of Hick's argument for pluralism was to propose a test that evaluated the validity of any given religion. Hick's conclusion was that all the major religions (such as all those discussed in this book) were equivalent in ethics and morals, though minor religious systems that practiced human sacrifice and other harmful practices were not sufficient. This was Hick's way of demonstrating how pluralism was not relativism—which is the position that all religions are necessarily valid, since there is no impartial or equitable way to evaluate them. In

One important source for Hick's theology of religions comes from the Hindu Bhagavad Gita (4.11): "Howsoever men may approach me, even so do I accept them; for, on all sides, whatever path they may choose is mine."
—John Hick

John Hick, *God Has Many Names* (Philadelphia: Westminster, 1982), 78.

25. John Hick, *God and the Universe of Faiths: Essays in the Philosophy of Religion* (New York: St. Martin's, 1973), 131.
26. John Hick, "The Theological Challenge of Religious Pluralism," in Hick and Hebblethwaite, *Christianity and Other Religions*, 168.
27. Ibid., 169.

Hick's estimation, all the major religions of the world are theologically similar—since they each seek to express and engage the Real in their own historically and culturally specific ways and since they each contain ethical and moral principles. Therefore, they are all equally useful and beneficial systems of worship.

Theologian Harold Netland notes that Hick's evolution of thought from inclusivism to pluralism coincided with Hick's pastoral position in the religiously and ethnically diverse city of Birmingham, England. As a pastor in that town, Hick increasingly found himself in close contact with many Hindus, Muslims, and Sikhs. Through his attendance at different religious places and dialogue with non-Christians, Hick came to see all major religions as sharing the same general ethical and moral concerns:

> Occasionally attending worship in mosque and synagogue, temple and [Sikh] gurdwara, it was evident to me that essentially the same kind of thing is taking place in them as in a Christian church—namely, human beings opening their minds to a higher divine Reality, known as personal and good and as demanding righteousness and love between man and woman.[28]

Of all the views surveyed in this chapter, pluralism is the view that is perhaps least traditional in Christianity, but it is fast becoming a common view in the church.

Universalism

Universalism is the view that all people will eventually be saved. Like exclusivism and inclusivism, such a position affirms that salvation comes through Jesus Christ. At the same time, universalism differs from these other positions in its belief that people need not make a profession of faith in Christ in this lifetime (as exclusivism necessitates) or even respond appropriately to the limited revelation they may have received during their lifetime (as inclusivism stipulates).

Universalists appeal to various passages in the Bible to support their position. One of the more commonly utilized passages comes from the book of Colossians:

> [Jesus] is the image of the invisible God, the firstborn of all creation. For by him all things were created, in heaven and on earth, visible and

Universalism believes that all people will eventually be gathered into the love of God and experience salvation.

28. John Hick, "God Has Many Names," 17–18, as quoted by Harold Netland, *Encountering Religious Pluralism: The Challenge to Christian Faith and Mission* (Downers Grove, IL: InterVarsity Press, 2001), 177.

invisible, whether thrones or dominions or rulers or authorities—all things were created through him and for him. And he is before all things, and in him all things hold together. And he is the head of the body, the church. He is the beginning, the firstborn from the dead, that in everything he might be preeminent. For in him all the fullness of God was pleased to dwell, and through him to reconcile to himself all things, whether on earth or in heaven, making peace by the blood of his cross. (Col. 1:15–20)

According to self-styled "evangelical universalist" Gregory MacDonald, this passage demonstrates "God's purposes in redemptive history . . . to restore [or reconcile] 'all things' to their proper purpose," which includes recalcitrant sinners.[29] MacDonald argues that the phrase "'all things' is to be taken in its strongest sense" as encompassing everything in heaven and on earth.[30] This means, in particular, that all human beings—even those who rejected the gospel of Jesus Christ when on earth—will be reconciled to God at the consummation. In fact, MacDonald affirms not only that *all people* will eventually be *saved*, but that *all things* will eventually be *restored*. In this way, universalism is the most encompassing of each of the different positions discussed in this chapter, in the sense that it moves the locus of the discussion away from mere personal salvation from sin toward universal restoration of the cosmos.

Two other common passages that universalists utilize to support their position also come from the apostle Paul. The first is based on the Christian hymn that Paul used in Philippians, which reads that "at the name of Jesus every knee should bow, in heaven and on earth and under the earth, and every tongue confess that Jesus Christ is Lord, to the glory of God the Father" (2:10–11). Like Colossians, universalists insist that the word *every* used by Paul makes it plain that all people will eventually confess Jesus Christ as Lord. Similarly, universalists appeal to Romans 5:12–21, where Paul compares and contrasts Adam, the first man, to Jesus, the last man: "As one trespass led to condemnation for all men, so one act of righteousness leads to justification and life for all men" (5:18). Again, it is argued, this passage demonstrates that, in the end, all people—non-Christians included—will be saved by Jesus.

Recently, there have been a growing number of universalists across the theological spectrum. One of the best-known biblical scholars of recent decades who advocated this position was the Scottish commentator William Barclay (1907–78). Although the author of many popular commentaries on Scripture, Barclay presented his argument for universalism most succinctly in his autobiography. In one section of this book

"If the others are going to hell, then I am going along with them. But I do not believe that; on the contrary, I believe that we will all be saved."
—Søren Kierkegaard

Søren Kierkegaard, *Søren Kierkegaard's Journals and Papers*, trans. H. V. and E. H. Hong (Bloomington: Indiana University Press, 1978), 6:557.

29. Gregory MacDonald, *The Evangelical Universalist* (Eugene, OR: Cascade, 2006), 187.
30. Ibid., 187.

Barclay offered four reasons why he was "a convinced universalist."[31] After citing Origen and Gregory of Nyssa as his universalist forebears, his first reason for advocating this position was scriptural:

> First, there is the fact that there are things in the New Testament which more than justify this belief. Jesus said: "I, when I am lifted up from the earth, will draw *all* men to myself" (John 12:32). Paul writes to the Romans: "God has consigned *all* men to disobedience that he may have mercy on *all*" (Rom. 11:32). He writes to the Corinthians: "As in Adam *all* die, so also in Christ shall *all* be made alive" (1 Cor. 15:22); and he looks to the final total triumph when God will be everything to everyone (1 Cor. 15:28). In the First Letter to Timothy we read of God "who desires *all* men to be saved and to come to the knowledge of the truth," and of Christ Jesus "who gave himself as a ransom for *all*" (1 Tim. 2:4–6). The New Testament itself is not in the least afraid of the word *all*.[32]

Two other reasons why Barclay defended the universalist position were his interpretation of Matthew 25:46 and his presupposition that God's grace is boundless. As for the passage in Matthew—"And these will go away into eternal punishment, but the righteous into eternal life"— the Scottish commentator argues that the Greek word that Matthew uses for "punishment" (*kolasis*) always refers to "remedial punishment" but never to eternal torment.[33] In this way, Jesus is understood to mean that sinners will undergo *temporal* punishment after death but will not experience *everlasting* anguish. Correspondingly, God's grace—which is partly revealed on earth—will be fully "effective . . . operative . . . [and] at work" in the age to come.[34]

Finally, Barclay's closing argument for universalism is based on Paul's teaching on the resurrection of human beings and the consummation of the cosmos:

> Then comes the end, when [Jesus] delivers the kingdom to God the Father after destroying every rule and every authority and power. For he must reign until he has put all his enemies under his feet. The last enemy to be destroyed is death. For "God has put all things in subjection under his feet." But when it says, "all things are put in subjection," it is plain that he is excepted who put all things in subjection under him. When all things are subjected to him, then the Son himself will

31. William Barclay, *William Barclay: A Spiritual Autobiography* (Grand Rapids: Eerdmans, 1977), 65.
32. Ibid.
33. Ibid., 66.
34. Ibid.

Particularism
contends that
all religions
have different
aims; therefore,
it is not useful
to speak about
non-Christians'
being "saved,"
since their reli-
gions do not
seek this goal.

also be subjected to him who put all things in subjection under him, that God may be all in all. (1 Cor. 15:24–28)

According to Barclay, this passage confirms that God's love cannot be defeated. Thus, if a person remained "outside of God's love at the end of time, it [would mean that a person] has defeated the love of God—and that is impossible."[35] In Barclay's estimation, the image most appropriate for God is that of Father, while the most fitting attribute for God is love. In Barclay's own words:

> No father could be happy while there were members of his family forever in agony. No father would count it a triumph to obliterate the disobedient members of his family. The only triumph a father can know is to have all his family back home. The only victory love can enjoy is the day when its offer of love is answered by the return of love. The only possible final triumph is a universe loved by and in love with God.[36]

Particularism

The last approach to other religions is what I call *particularism*, which is a term that some reserve for exclusivism. I define particularism as the view that each *particular* religion has a different aim, purpose, and goal. Of all the views in this chapter, particularism is the most recent. The origin of the approach comes from the scholarly engagement of Christians with other religions, especially in the last several decades. Advocates of particularism—though they may not use this exact term— argue that the positions of inclusivism, exclusivism, and pluralism are neither accurate nor particularly instructive when understanding other religions. As theologian Gerald McDermott explains:

> [Particularists] are saying not only that [other] religions teach different goals or salvations, but that there may actually *be* different salvations. These different ends are not for the same person at the same time but for different people, or for the same person at different times. And this reality of different ends may be "providentially" provided by God. In other words, Theravadin Buddhists may indeed experience nirvana, and Muslims may indeed find Paradise. But they won't experience the fullness of the triune God. So, [advocates] say, there are three types of religious fulfillment: lostness, imperfect and partial fulfillment

35. Ibid.
36. Ibid.

through a non-Christian religion, and communion with the triune God—the last of which only Christian faith may provide.[37]

In this understanding, particularists believe that *Christians* will experience salvation by Jesus Christ. But there is no reason to expect that practitioners of *other religions* would experience this—even if they are the "anonymous Christians" that some inclusivists believe exist. This is because no other religion has as its goal the salvation of sinners through the death and resurrection of Jesus Christ. Instead, particularists argue, devoted practitioners of other religions may experience whatever each religion offers as its aim. Still other particularists do not query what happens to practitioners of non-Christian religions after death and only emphasize that all religions are different and that no religion other than Christianity has as its goal the salvation of sinners.

Advocates of particularism, like pluralists, do not appeal to specific biblical passages as readily as exclusivists and inclusivists do. They tend to make philosophical and theological arguments rather than scriptural ones. At the same time, particularists appeal to passages from the Old and New Testaments in support of their position. The first comes from the book of Isaiah:

> The word that Isaiah the son of Amoz saw concerning Judah and Jerusalem. It shall come to pass in the latter days that the mountain of the house of the LORD shall be established as the highest of the mountains, and shall be lifted up above the hills; and all the nations shall flow to it, and many peoples shall come, and say: "Come, let us go up to the mountain of the LORD, to the house of the God of Jacob, that he may teach us his ways and that we may walk in his paths." For out of Zion shall go the law, and the word of the LORD from Jerusalem. He shall judge between the nations, and shall decide disputes for many peoples; and they shall beat their swords into plowshares, and their spears into pruning hooks; nation shall not lift up sword against nation, neither shall they learn war anymore. O house of Jacob, come, let us walk in the light of the LORD. (Isa. 2:1–5)

According to the prophet, the vision for the Jewish nation was for Israel to be joined by the Gentiles in their worship of the one true God on Mount Zion. The aim was not to go to heaven after the Jewish people died, but rather to live peaceably in Jerusalem with other nations. In other words, a particularist understanding of Judaism does not attempt to correlate Judaism with, for instance, Christianity.

37. McDermott, *God's Rivals*, 24–25.

"The differences that distinguish religions need to be recognized and respected." —James Fredericks

Fredericks, *Faith among Faiths*, 163.

The vision that Isaiah saw concerning the nation of Israel is contrasted with one of Paul's last letters. As a passage from Titus reads:

> But when the goodness and loving kindness of God our Savior appeared, he saved us, not because of works done by us in righteousness, but according to his own mercy, by the washing of regeneration and renewal of the Holy Spirit, whom he poured out on us richly through Jesus Christ our Savior, so that being justified by his grace we might become heirs according to the hope of eternal life. (Titus 3:4–7)

This passage in Titus serves as a good summary of the Christian message. Through the work of the Holy Spirit, God justifies a sinner by faith in Jesus Christ. This person's faith in Jesus Christ makes him or her an heir to God's promises of eternal life. According to particularism, the goals of Judaism and Christianity are quite different. Whereas the first has as its goal the worship of God on Mount Zion, the other has as its goal faith in Jesus Christ in the hope of life after death. The two visions should not be melded together but be appreciated for their particularity.

Fig. 7.2.
Representation of particularism, the view emphasizing that all religions have different end points or goals.

One of the most prolific representatives of the particularist position is the contemporary theologian S. Mark Heim. Heim eschews the approaches of inclusivism, exclusivism, and pluralism—though he is most sympathetic with the latter. In his words, these approaches "serve some purposes, but seriously mislead us as the definitive map of our options."[38] Heim thinks

38. S. Mark Heim, *Salvations: Truth and Difference in Religion* (Maryknoll, NY: Orbis, 2001), 4.

they are misleading because they presuppose that all religions seek to offer salvation. Heim recognizes that his approach is the most difficult, since it requires us to make a "painstaking attempt to become acquainted with and in some measure understand the distinctive features of other peoples' faiths."[39]

The main goal of Heim's approach to religions is to establish a way to impartially evaluate all the different religious systems. As he explains:

> [We need to] search for a framework for viewing the religions which is modest enough to recognize its character as one religious perspective among many, yet open enough both to maintain its own universal claims and recognize those of others.[40]

In Heim's estimation, it is not necessary to abandon one's religious convictions to understand that each religion has a unique goal. Even pluralism can do violence to other religions by assuming that they are all the same or that they teach the same goals or aims. According to Heim, all religions are different and should be appreciated for their "particularistic witness" to their own traditions. In this regard, particularism is an attempt to understand other religions on their own terms rather than exclusively on the terms of Christianity.

Conclusion

In his classic book *Christ and Culture*,[41] Christian theologian H. Richard Niebuhr categorizes five major approaches to the relation between Jesus and culture. Despite criticisms leveled against the book, it serves as a useful tool for understanding how our identities as Christians relate to our many other identities within the cultures in which we live. The approaches outlined in this chapter have a similar function. Although not definitive, the five approaches that I have discussed—inclusivism, exclusivism, pluralism, universalism, and particularism—represent varying responses to how Christians are to understand how Jesus may be present in the lives of non-Christians and in non-Christian religions.

As I noted in the beginning of this chapter, there are Christians who promote each of these positions. Apart from particularism, each of these positions is well embedded in the fabric of Christian history. Representatives of each of the other positions claim Christian proponents

---

39. Ibid., 6.
40. Ibid., 144.
41. New York: Harper & Row, 1975.

in virtually every era of the church. Even universalism and pluralism, which are the most controversial positions among evangelicals, have a growing number of Christian supporters in the discussion about Christianity and other religions.

Among evangelical believers, the most traditional and common positions are exclusivism and inclusivism. These two approaches rely heavily on Scripture, and there are advocates from all branches of the Christian tradition for each one. As mentioned, both affirm that Jesus is the Savior of all people. They differ in that exclusivists believe that people must consciously recognize and profess Jesus as Savior, while inclusivists believe that Jesus is able to save people who may never explicitly or entirely profess him as Savior.

Whatever approach we adopt, we must always remember that these are human categories designed to understand the divine. As an oft-quoted passage in the Old Testament reads: "The secret things belong to the LORD our God, but the things that are revealed belong to us and to our children" (Deut. 29:29). We are blessed to serve a kind and compassionate God who has revealed to us many things about himself in the Bible. Most precious is the revelation we have received about the identity of Jesus Christ. And although we will never understand all there is to know about God and how he interacts with his creation, we can confidently sing—along with the psalmist—that "the LORD is good" and that "his steadfast love endures forever" (Ps. 100:5).

Discussion Questions

1. Define each of the five approaches to other religions discussed in this chapter: inclusivism, exclusivism, pluralism, universalism, and particularism. What are the similarities and differences among them?
2. If you had to adopt just one of the approaches described in this chapter, which one would it be? What is the main reason that you would adopt that approach?
3. Paul writes in Romans 11:22 that we are to note both "the kindness and the severity of God." Some Christians emphasize God's kindness over his severity, while others emphasize God's severity over his kindness. How can we allow these seemingly contrasting attributes to stand side by side? Can this passage in Romans help us understand the topic of Christianity and other religions?
4. If someone told you that all religions are the same and that all religions lead to the one God, how would you respond? What biblical passages would you appeal to or other arguments would you make to respond to this statement?

5. Many people have claimed over the years that Jesus appeared to them (whether in person, in a dream, or through a vision) even though they had never heard about Christianity or known any Christians. How would you go about evaluating whether these stories are true? Is it possible for Jesus to save people even though they do not practice Christianity? What biblical passages support or go against this view?

Further Readings

D'Costa, Gavin. *Theology and Religious Pluralism: The Challenge of Other Religions.* New York: Basil Blackwell, 1986.

Fackre, Gabriel, Ronald Nash, and John Sanders, eds. *What about Those Who Have Never Heard? Three Views of the Destiny of the Unevangelized.* Downers Grove, IL: InterVarsity Press, 1995.

Hick, John, and Brian Hebblethwaite, eds. *Christianity and Other Religions: Selected Readings.* Oxford: Oneworld, 2001.

MacDonald, Gregory. *The Evangelical Universalist.* Eugene, OR: Cascade, 2006.

Netland, Harold. *Encountering Religious Pluralism: The Challenge to Christian Faith and Mission.* Downers Grove, IL: InterVarsity Press, 2001.

Okholm, Dennis, and Timothy Philips, eds. *Four Views on Salvation in a Pluralistic World.* Grand Rapids: Zondervan, 1996.

Conclusion

Whether college roommates in an international dormitory, colleagues at work, or participants in the neighborhood carpool, we are discovering people of divergent faiths everywhere we turn.

Daniel Clendenin

Increasingly, Christians will need to stop and reflect on what [religious] diversity will mean for their communities and the future of their own religion.

James Fredericks

W HEN THE FIRST martyr of the Christian faith stood before the Sanhedrin in the year AD 31 to defend his life against the claim that he had blasphemed the Jewish faith by criticizing the temple and the Torah, he did not curse his opponents, attempt an escape, or even demand a fair trial. Instead, he invoked a story. The story he invoked was a familiar one—one that his ancestors had retold generation after generation. It was a story that he had grown up listening to in his home, in the local synagogue, and in the temple. It was the story of how the true God—the LORD God, the maker of heaven and earth—had formed a special people out of one man, Abraham. It was a story recounting how men and women of great faith—Abraham, Sarah, Jacob, Moses, Rahab, and David—had clung to God's promises despite regular setbacks. It was a story of how the nation of Israel had consistently rejected God's prophets in exchange for the ways of the world. It was, in brief, a story.

The Rival Stories of the World

Although it may appear simple and even innocuous to readers today, the story that Stephen told in Acts 7:2–53 was not only provocative—for it brought about his immediate death by stoning—but also immensely instructive for future readers of the Bible. The story is instructive because it highlights the power of storytelling. In this book, we have examined the six rival stories to Christianity: the stories of Hinduism, Buddhism, Confucianism, Daoism, Judaism, and Islam. The importance of these religions' stories or ways of life over the centuries cannot be overestimated. From the perspective of their adherents, the stories of these religions are thoroughly compelling and shaping. They describe the nature of the universe, create an overarching theory of life, define what is right and wrong, prioritize what is important, and seek to fulfill one's inner person.

At the same time, we have learned in this book that each religion tells the story of the world differently. Whereas the story of Confucianism says that the here and now is most important, Islam tells the story of the world from the perspective of heaven. And whereas Buddhism is traditionally the story of no creation accounts—indeed, the existence of a divine being or even of self-existence is questioned—Hinduism is the tale of infinite creation stories. With such diverse and rival stories in the world, what are we to do as Christians?

Acts 17 and Engaging Other Religions

Returning to the discussion of Acts 17 in the introduction, I suggest that Christians have three ways to respond to the stories of other faiths. The first is most basic: We need to cultivate an awareness of and sensitivity to the Holy Spirit. One of the key themes in the book of Acts is the active role that the Holy Spirit plays in the lives of the church in general and specific individuals. The opening line of the story of Paul in Athens informs us that the apostle entered Athens and began interacting with the Athenians at the urging of the Spirit. In short, the author points out, Paul's spirit was "provoked within him" (17:16).

Living by the Spirit, as Paul teaches elsewhere (Gal. 5:25), is a major theme of the Christian life. Sometimes the Spirit tells us to preach the gospel openly, while other times the Spirit tells us to listen carefully but remain silent. Whatever the circumstance, we need to understand that "God gave us a spirit not of fear but of power and love and self-control" (2 Tim. 1:7). It has been my experience as a teacher of world religions that what Christians fear the most about this topic is sharing their faith with non-Christians. But like Paul, we need to act obediently to the Spirit's leading in our lives—including when the Spirit directs us to share our testimony. We can do this not out of our own willpower but by the Spirit's very own "power" (2 Tim. 1:7).

The second way to respond to other faiths is simply by learning the basic tenets and goals of each religion. The book of Acts records, for instance, that when the apostle Paul was at the Areopagus in Athens he "passed along and observed the objects of . . . worship" (17:23). The sense we get is that Paul intently examined how the Athenians practiced their religion. As the New International Version translates the phrase, Paul "looked carefully" at the objects surrounding him as an architect looks at his plans.

Like the apostle in Athens, in the main part of this book we have "looked carefully" at each of the major religions of the world. We examined their origins, histories, practices, scriptures, and basic beliefs. The purpose of this information was empowerment. Now that we are informed about other religions, we are empowered to enter into conversations with non-Christians. When I teach at churches, many people tell me that they could never talk to a Muslim or a Buddhist, for example, because they might say something incorrect or inappropriate. This book, however, has been written to equip each of us with the tools not only to speak intelligently with Christians about other religions but also to communicate accurately to and with practitioners of other faiths.

Finally, the last way I suggest that we may respond to other religions is by learning how to engage them from a Christian perspective. Again, as the apostle Paul said to the religious practitioners in Athens: "I found . . . an altar with this inscription, 'To the unknown god.' What therefore you worship as unknown, this I proclaim to you" (17:23). In the next several verses Paul explains to the Athenians what had *not* been revealed to them in their religion. In fact, Paul was so well informed about *their religion* that he was able to quote from their leading authorities (17:28). Now, it is one thing to be informed about another religion, but another thing to address that religion from a Christian perspective.

In the first part of this book we learned many facts about the world's major religions. But we have also sought to examine these religions from a Christian perspective. In the second part of the book we looked carefully at some biblical and theological reflections on and approaches to other faiths. Whereas one chapter focused on how the Bible appropriated other religions, the other chapter provided a number of approaches to other religions from a theological perspective. What's more, the conclusion to each chapter in the first part of the book addressed one aspect of each of the world's rival religions and attempted to make a "point of contact" between that religion and Christianity.

The Real Mission Field

As we bring our discussion of world religions to a close, I am reminded of a sign I saw last week as I was leaving a church parking lot. It read, "Now you are entering the real mission field." Part of the motivation of writing this book has been to address the changing ethnic and religious dynamics in the world. As I mentioned in the introduction, we live in a shrinking and ever-changing culture. Indeed, as one theologian said in reference to Islam (but any other major religion could be inserted): "Today the Muslim world is no longer somewhere else."[1] To paraphrase this quote for our context, practitioners of religions other than Christianity not only are "somewhere else"; they are likely our coworkers, neighbors, friends, and even family members. Personal experience indicates that the less we know about other religions, the less likely we are to speak with people of other faiths about our beliefs. It is my prayer that we, like the apostle Paul in Athens, will boldly follow the leading of God's Spirit, diligently become informed about other religions, and then engage these religions from a Christian perspective. As we do so, there is no telling what God may do, not only in our lives but also in the lives of others.

Discussion Questions

1. Paul founded many churches, and he wrote letters to a number of them. Based on Paul's speech in Acts 17, what do you make of the fact that the New Testament never mentions a church being established in Athens?
2. What are some practical ways that you might integrate stories of your Christian faith into the workplace and into other informal conversations throughout the day?
3. What do you think "living by the Spirit" (Gal. 5:25) means for you on a daily basis?
4. If you began to think of your primary vocation as that of a missionary, how would your life be different than it is now?

---

1. James Fredericks, *Faith among Faiths: Christian Theology and Non-Christian Religions* (Mahwah, NJ: Paulist Press, 1999), 3.

Appendix A
Projects, Essays, and
Worldview Questions

T O FACILITATE USING this book more effectively in classrooms, homeschools, and independent study, this appendix contains questions for students that (in the words of Bloom's taxonomy—see below) are designed to help them apply, analyze, synthesize, and evaluate what they have learned. There are three types of questions for each chapter—(1) projects, (2) essays, and (3) worldview questions—constructed generally to correspond to the four highest levels of learning in Bloom's taxonomy.

In addition to projects, essays, and worldview questions, there are two other resources available for teachers. The first, discussion questions, is located at the end of each chapter in the book proper. These questions, which also use the highest forms of Bloom's taxonomy, can serve as a good substitute for essay questions or as discussion questions for groups. The other resource, a multiple-choice exam, evaluates students' mastery of the information covered in the book. Thus, it generally corresponds to the lower two levels of knowledge and comprehension in Bloom's taxonomy. The multiple-choice exam can be acquired by e-mailing marketing@prpbooks.com.

Bloom's Taxonomy	Assignment	Location
Application, analysis, synthesis, and evaluation.	Projects, essays, and worldview questions.	In the appendix for each chapter.
Analysis, synthesis, and evaluation.	Discussion questions.	At the end of each chapter.
Knowledge and comprehension.	Multiple-choice exam.	E-mail marketing@prpbooks.com

Chapter 1: Hinduism

Projects

1. Draw a picture of the following Hindu gods: Shiva, Vishnu, Parvati, Hanuman, Ganesha, and Kali. Try to capture their similarities and differences. How do these gods compare with the Christian God?

2. Create a poster of the Hindu caste system. What is it, when did it originate, and why is it so important? Do you think the caste system is more helpful or harmful to society?

3. Locate and visit a Hindu temple in your area. Act like you are a journalist who is preparing an article on the major features of Hinduism. What did you notice? How would you describe your visit? Did anything surprise you? Write a two-page article about your experience and include pictures.

Essays

1. Describe the four major traditions of Hinduism. Based on the differences in these traditions, is it best to describe the religion as Hinduism (singular) or Hinduisms (plural)?

2. Research the two Hindu figures Ramakrishna (d. 1886) and Vivekananda (d. 1902). Who were they? What did they believe? How do their main teachings differ from Christianity?

3. Read chapter 7 from the Bhagavad Gita, one of the most beloved Hindu scriptures. Afterward, compare and contrast the way Krishna is portrayed and the way Jesus is portrayed in the Gospels.

4. Describe the different kinds of yoga in Hinduism. How do these relate to the practice of yoga today in North America as a form of exercise?

5. What are avatars? What are the major avatars of the god Vishnu? What is their role or purpose?

Worldview

1. Worldviews are comprehensive views that human beings have about how the world works. A worldview is often divided into

the *problem* (what is wrong with the world and humanity), *cause* (why the world and humanity are not right), *remedy* (the solution), and *means* (how we access the solution). If we categorized the Christian worldview, for instance, we might say that the *problem* is separation from God and each other, the *cause* is sin, the *remedy* is the death and resurrection of Jesus, and the *means* to this remedy is faith in Jesus. Based on this categorization, how would you classify the worldview of Hinduism?

Problem	Cause	Remedy	Means

2. Rather than provide a single definition of the word *religion* to encompass all the major religions of the world, the history of religions scholar Ninian Smart (d. 2001) argued that each religion displays certain characteristics or dimensions. They are usually called the seven dimensions of religion and are as follows:

   i. Doctrinal—Systematic formulation of the religion and examples of doctrines.

   ii. Narratival—Stories of the religion.

   iii. Ethical—Rules or behavioral guidelines.

   iv. Ritual—Ceremonies performed.

   v. Experiential—The emotions felt as a result of the religion.

   vi. Institutional—Communal system that unites all practitioners of a religion and offers rules for identifying members and encouraging participation.

   vii. Material—Objects, places, and things that symbolize or manifest the sacred or supernatural.

3. Under this rubric, we might classify the seven dimensions of Christianity in the following way:
    i. Doctrinal—Christian confessions and catechisms.
    ii. Narratival—The Bible and Christian tradition.
    iii. Ethical—Ten Commandments or the principle of love.
    iv. Ritual—Baptism, prayer, and other spiritual disciplines and sacraments.
    v. Experiential—Joy, peace, understanding.
    vi. Institutional—Churches and denominations.
    vii. Material—Crucifix, bread and wine from the Lord's Supper.

4. Based on the definitions above and the example for Christianity, how could you classify the seven dimensions of Hinduism?

Chapter 2: Buddhism

Projects

1. Pretend that you have to make a thirty-minute documentary based on your experience and your prior knowledge about Buddhism. You must have the following components: (i) an opening, (ii) brief historical background, (iii) major teachings and practices, (iv) an interview with a Buddhist follower, and (v) a Christian response. How would you design the documentary based on these components?

2. Create a brochure of the Dalai Lama. When did the tradition of the Dalai Lama begin, and what is its importance? What is the relationship between the Dalai Lama and the different forms of Buddhism? Who is the current Dalai Lama? Why is he so famous, and what are his major teachings? (Do an online search for one of his writings and read through it.)

3. Create a pictorial timeline of the life of Siddhartha Gautama. Be sure to include the major features and phases of his life and context.

4. On a large piece of paper, make a diagram of the Wheel of Life. Draw pictures of the different living beings in each realm. Then

draw a picture of the three traditional levels of the Christian realm: heaven, earth, and hell. How do these drawings compare and contrast?

Essays

1. Imagine that you could go back in time and ask the Buddha any question you wanted. What question would that be? Then imagine that you could go back in time and ask Jesus the same question. How do you think their responses would be different?

2. Describe the major teachings of and differences between Zen Buddhism and Tibetan Buddhism.

3. Compare and contrast Mahayana Buddhism with Theravada Buddhism. Where are these two traditions found today? What are their histories? Which is more prevalent? What are their differences?

4. What are the Four Noble Truths? Who first taught them, and what is their importance in the Buddhist tradition? How can one practice or follow these teachings?

5. How would you respond to someone who says that reincarnation is taught in the Bible? Which passages would you use in support of your position? What is the Christian teaching on life and death? What happens to Christians when they die? What is the difference between reincarnation and resurrection?

Worldview

1. Worldviews are comprehensive views that human beings have about how the world works. A worldview is often divided into the *problem* (what is wrong with the world and humanity), *cause* (why the world and humanity are not right), *remedy* (the solution), and *means* (how we access the solution). If we categorized the Christian worldview, for instance, we might say that the *problem* is separation from God and each other, the *cause* is sin, the *remedy* is the death and resurrection of Jesus, and the *means* to this remedy is faith in Jesus. Based on

this categorization, how would you classify the worldview of Buddhism?

Problem	Cause	Remedy	Means

2. Rather than provide a single definition of the word *religion* to encompass all the major religions of the world, history of religions scholar Ninian Smart (d. 2001) argued that each religion displays certain characteristics or dimensions. They are usually called the seven dimensions of religion and are as follows:
   i. Doctrinal—Systematic formulation of the religion and examples of doctrines.
   ii. Narratival—Stories of the religion.
   iii. Ethical—Rules or behavioral guidelines.
   iv. Ritual—Ceremonies performed.
   v. Experiential—The emotions felt as a result of the religion.
   vi. Institutional—Communal system that unites all practitioners of a religion and offers rules for identifying members and encouraging participation.
   vii. Material—Objects, places, and things that symbolize or manifest the sacred or supernatural.

3. Under this rubric, we might classify the seven dimensions of Christianity in the following way:
   i. Doctrinal—Christian confessions and catechisms.
   ii. Narratival—The Bible and Christian tradition.
   iii. Ethical—Ten Commandments or the principle of love.

    iv. Ritual—Baptism, prayer, and other spiritual disciplines and sacraments.

    v. Experiential—Joy, peace, understanding.

    vi. Institutional—Churches and denominations.

    vii. Material—Crucifix, bread and wine from the Lord's Supper.

4. Based on the definitions above and the example for Christianity, how could you classify the seven dimensions of Buddhism?

Chapter 3: Confucianism and Daoism

Projects

1. Research the history of China for a PowerPoint presentation. Classify the major features of its history—including its dynasties, cultures, and religions—into five stages and provide accompanying pictures.

2. Draw a picture or symbol of each of the following terms: yin and yang, the Dao, filial piety, and *chi*. Then provide a brief definition for each term.

3. Create a pictorial timeline of the lives of Confucius and Lao Tzu. Be sure to include major features and phases of their lives and contexts.

4. Draw a diagram of the five major relationships in Confucianism. Then provide an accompanying description of each one.

Essays

1. There were generally four schools of thought in ancient China before the time of Christ. Adherents of these schools of thought were the Mohists, the Legalists (or Realists), the Daoists, and the Confucianists. Research each of these philosophies, and explain their similarities and differences. Which of these philosophies do you believe best deals with the issues of the day?

2. Research the history of Confucianism. Then write a paper arguing for whether Confucianism should best be described as a

religion or a philosophy. Be sure to look at Confucianism from the perspective of different countries, including China, Taiwan, South Korea, Japan, and the United States—all of which may understand Confucianism somewhat differently.

3. What is ancestor veneration? Is it more a religious or a cultural practice? What is its history and purpose? Should Christians practice ancestor veneration, particularly in Asian and African countries?

4. What happened to Confucianism and Daoism after Chairman Mao (d. 1976) became the leader of the People's Republic of China in 1949? How have these two philosophies or religions fared since Mao's death?

5. Read the first ten chapters of the Daodejing (or Tao Te Ching). What exactly is going on? What is the point of the writing, and how does it compare to a section of the New Testament? Now read chapter 4 of the Analects of Confucius. What does this chapter teach about Confucianism? How is it similar to or different from the book of Proverbs in the Bible or the sayings of Jesus in the Gospels?

Worldview

1. Worldviews are comprehensive views that human beings have about how the world works. A worldview is often divided into the *problem* (what is wrong with the world and humanity), *cause* (why the world and humanity are not right), *remedy* (the solution), and *means* (how we access the solution). If we categorized the Christian worldview, for instance, we might say that the *problem* is separation from God and each other, the *cause* is sin, the *remedy* is the death and resurrection of Jesus, and the *means* to this remedy is faith in Jesus. Based on this categorization, how would you classify the worldview of Confucianism and Daoism?

Problem	Cause	Remedy	Means

2. Rather than provide a single definition of the word *religion* to encompass all the major religions of the world, history of religions scholar Ninian Smart (d. 2001) argued that each religion displays certain characteristics or dimensions. They are usually called the seven dimensions of religion and are as follows:
   i. Doctrinal—Systematic formulation of the religion and examples of doctrines.
   ii. Narratival—Stories of the religion.
   iii. Ethical—Rules or behavioral guidelines.
   iv. Ritual—Ceremonies performed.
   v. Experiential—The emotions felt as a result of the religion.
   vi. Institutional—Communal system that unites all practitioners of a religion and offers rules for identifying members and encouraging participation.
   vii. Material—Objects, places, and things that symbolize or manifest the sacred or supernatural.

3. Under this rubric, we might classify the seven dimensions of Christianity in the following way:
   i. Doctrinal—Christian confessions and catechisms.
   ii. Narratival—The Bible and Christian tradition.
   iii. Ethical—Ten Commandments or the principle of love.
   iv. Ritual—Baptism, prayer, and other spiritual disciplines and sacraments.
   v. Experiential—Joy, peace, understanding.

      vi. Institutional—Churches and denominations.

     vii. Material—Crucifix, bread and wine from the Lord's Supper.

4. Based on the definitions above and the example for Christianity, how could you classify the seven dimensions of Confucianism and Daoism?

Chapter 4: Judaism

Projects

1. Create a pictorial diagram of the major events of the Jewish story as found in the Old Testament and in more recent Jewish history.

2. Locate a synagogue in your area and contact the rabbi. Interview him or her, asking questions about why the person became a rabbi, what it means to be a Jew today, what Christians can learn from Judaism as a tradition, and what the major differences are between Jews and Christians today.

3. Have the first two chapters of Genesis read to you slowly aloud (or do a search online to find a reading of the Bible aloud), and then draw a picture of the description of the creation of the world as you hear it. How does this picture help you understand Judaism better?

Essays

1. Read about the different holy days of the Jewish calendar in Leviticus 28. Describe the importance and background of these holy days in the Jewish tradition, and then explain why Christians no longer observe them.

2. Trace the history and development of the major Jewish denominations. Why are they so different? What unites Jews today?

3. Research and locate a synagogue in your area. Visit the synagogue and observe how the service compares to a Christian church's

service. What similarities and differences did you notice? How do these differences indicate the differences in the religions?

4. Research two of the best-known rabbis who lived as contemporaries of Jesus: Hillel (d. AD 10) and Shammai (d. AD 30). Describe these two rabbis and the circumstances of their times. How are their teachings similar to and different from Jesus' in the Gospels? What contributions do their two "schools of thought" make to the study of religion?

5. Describe the core writings of the scriptures of Judaism. What is the difference between the Torah and the Talmud?

Worldview

1. Worldviews are comprehensive views that human beings have about how the world works. A worldview is often divided into the *problem* (what is wrong with the world and humanity), *cause* (why the world and humanity are not right), *remedy* (the solution), and *means* (how we access the solution). If we categorized the Christian worldview, for instance, we might say that the *problem* is separation from God and each other, the *cause* is sin, the *remedy* is the death and resurrection of Jesus, and the *means* to this remedy is faith in Jesus. Based on this categorization, how would you classify the worldview of Judaism?

Problem	Cause	Remedy	Means

2. Rather than provide a single definition of the word *religion* to encompass all the major religions of the world, history of religions

scholar Ninian Smart (d. 2001) argued that each religion displays certain characteristics or dimensions. They are usually called the seven dimensions of religion and are as follows:

   i. Doctrinal—Systematic formulation of the religion and examples of doctrines.

   ii. Narratival—Stories of the religion.

   iii. Ethical—Rules or behavioral guidelines.

   iv. Ritual—Ceremonies performed.

   v. Experiential—The emotions felt as a result of the religion.

   vi. Institutional—Communal system that unites all practitioners of a religion and offers rules for identifying members and encouraging participation.

   vii. Material—Objects, places, and things that symbolize or manifest the sacred or supernatural.

3. Under this rubric, we might classify the seven dimensions of Christianity in the following way:

   i. Doctrinal—Christian confessions and catechisms.

   ii. Narratival—The Bible and Christian tradition.

   iii. Ethical—Ten Commandments or the principle of love.

   iv. Ritual—Baptism, prayer, and other spiritual disciplines and sacraments.

   v. Experiential—Joy, peace, understanding.

   vi. Institutional—Churches and denominations.

   vii. Material—Crucifix, bread and wine from the Lord's Supper.

4. Based on the definitions above and the example for Christianity, how could you classify the seven dimensions of Judaism?

Chapter 5: Islam

Projects

1. Create a pictorial timeline of the life of Muhammad. Be sure to include major phases and features of his life and times.

2. Imagine that you are in a coffee shop and you meet the following three characters: (i) Abdul, a dedicated Muslim, (ii) Peter,

a dedicated Christian, and (iii) an agnostic seeker or group of agnostic seekers. As you enter into conversation with these individuals, the seeker asks whether Christianity or Islam—and the Bible or the Qur'an—is true, and whether the Christians or the Muslims have a more accurate interpretation of Jesus. Then research this topic so that you can create a dialogue that accurately represents what Abdul and Peter would say to this question.

3. Draw a picture that corresponds with each of the six major articles of faith in Islam. Then provide a description of each one.

4. Pretend that you have to make a thirty-minute documentary based on your experience and your prior knowledge about Islam. You must have the following components: (i) an opening, (ii) brief historical background, (iii) major teachings and practices, (iv) an interview with a Muslim follower, and (v) a Christian response. How would you design the documentary based on these components?

5. Research and locate a mosque in your area. Visit the mosque and observe how the service compares to a Christian church's service. What similarities and differences did you notice? How do these differences indicate the differences in the religions?

Essays

1. The Qur'an has a lot to say about Jesus, but not all of it agrees with the message of the New Testament. Please read through the following Qur'anic passages and compare and contrast the way in which Jesus is presented alongside the way in which the New Testament, especially the Gospels, presents Jesus: 2:87; 2:252–53; 3:42–64; 19:16–40; 19:88–95; 43:57–65; 43:81–82.

2. Read the following passages in the Old Testament about Ishmael and the beginning of the Arab people: Genesis 17:20; 21:8–21; and 25:12–18. What do these passages teach us about the relation between Islam and the God of the Bible? What does it mean for God to bless Ishmael and his descendants?

3. Do a search online for Muhammad's last sermon, which he preached in Mecca shortly before he died in Medina in 632. What

are Muhammad's last concerns before his death? What does the sermon inform us about Islam at this time?

4. Research Sufi Islam, the mystical part of the Muslim tradition. When and where did Sufism arise? Who are some major Sufi practitioners throughout the ages? What is distinctive about Sufi Islam in relation to Sunni and Shiite Islam?

Worldview

1. Worldviews are comprehensive views that human beings have about how the world works. A worldview is often divided into the *problem* (what is wrong with the world and humanity), *cause* (why the world and humanity are not right), *remedy* (the solution), and *means* (how we access the solution). If we categorized the Christian worldview, for instance, we might say that the *problem* is separation from God and each other, the *cause* is sin, the *remedy* is the death and resurrection of Jesus, and the *means* to this remedy is faith in Jesus. Based on this categorization, how would you classify the worldview of Islam?

Problem	Cause	Remedy	Means

2. Rather than provide a single definition of the word *religion* to encompass all the major religions of the world, history of religions scholar Ninian Smart (d. 2001) argued that each religion displays certain characteristics or dimensions. They are usually called the seven dimensions of religion and are as follows:

i. Doctrinal—Systematic formulation of the religion and examples of doctrines.

ii. Narratival—Stories of the religion.

iii. Ethical—Rules or behavioral guidelines.

iv. Ritual—Ceremonies performed.

v. Experiential—The emotions felt as a result of the religion.

vi. Institutional—Communal system that unites all practitioners of a religion and offers rules for identifying members and encouraging participation.

vii. Material—Objects, places, and things that symbolize or manifest the sacred or supernatural.

3. Under this rubric, we might classify the seven dimensions of Christianity in the following way:

i. Doctrinal—Christian confessions and catechisms.

ii. Narratival—The Bible and Christian tradition.

iii. Ethical—Ten Commandments or the principle of love.

iv. Ritual—Baptism, prayer, and other spiritual disciplines and sacraments.

v. Experiential—Joy, peace, understanding.

vi. Institutional—Churches and denominations.

vii. Material—Crucifix, bread and wine from the Lord's Supper.

4. Based on the definitions above and the example for Christianity, how could you classify the seven dimensions of Islam?

Chapter 6: Biblical Responses to Other Religions

Projects

1. Create a brochure that deals with the topic of other religions from the perspective of the Bible. On one side of the brochure, summarize the Old Testament's perspective on other religions, and on the other side summarize the New Testament's perspective. Be sure to use images when possible.

2. There are many names used for God in the Old Testament. Research the following names and then draw a picture or sym-

bol for each name: Yahweh, Sabaoth, Adonai, Elohim, and El Shaddai. What do these pictures and names indicate about the nature of God?

Essays

1. Some Christians believe that fallen angels or demons are behind the practices of non-Christian religions and/or reside in specific statues or idols. Other Christians believe that such religions do not have evil spirits or fallen angels at their behest but are empty and misguided. Which of these two do you think best represents the Bible and Christian theology?

2. Read the following quote from John Calvin and discuss its meaning in relation to world religions: "Since the perfection of blessedness consists in the knowledge of God, he has been pleased, in order that none might be excluded from the means of obtaining [happiness], not only to deposit in our minds that seed of religion . . . but so to manifest his perfections in the whole structure of the universe, and daily place himself in our view, that we cannot open our eyes without being compelled to behold him."[1]

3. Do a word study on the term *God* in the Old Testament. How many times does it appear? Glance through as many of the references as you can, and determine how the word is used. Is it uppercase or lowercase? Why? Is it used in reference to the God of the Bible or another god? Is it used in reference to a nondeity? Why?

4. Research the topic of "angels" in the Bible. Use commentaries when possible. What are angels? What is their role? What makes an angel "good" or "bad"? What is the relationship between an angel and a person?

Worldview

1. Read through the book of Proverbs in the Old Testament. Then choose the proverb that you believe best represents the worldview of that book (and perhaps of the Old Testament in general). Why did you choose that proverb instead of another?

1. John Calvin, *Institutes of the Christian Religion*, trans. Henry Beveridge (Grand Rapids: Eerdmans, 1995), 1.5.51.

Proverb	Reason for Choosing This Proverb

2. Read through one of the four Gospels in the New Testament. Then choose a saying of Jesus that you believe best represents the worldview of the book (and perhaps of the New Testament in general). Why did you choose that saying instead of another?

(Gospel) Saying	Reason for Choosing This Saying

Chapter 7: Theological Responses to Other Religions

Projects

1. Draw a picture or a diagram of the different theological positions in relation to God. How do these pictures or diagrams relate to each of the different theological positions?

2. Create a five-minute video titled "What Christians Believe about Other Religions." Choose five people from your church to whom you can ask the following question: "What is Jesus' role or presence, if at all, in non-Christian religions?" Edit the video, provide your own introduction, and locate a song or graphic to accompany it.

Essays

1. Of the five theological positions outlined in this chapter, which do you think is most helpful or accurate? Are any of the positions able to be held at the same time? Are any diametrically opposed to each other?

2. How would you respond to someone who said that all religions are the same? Which theological position is this person maintaining? What biblical passages, Christian figures, or other arguments would you use to support your position against this one?

3. Respond to the following quote by C. S. Lewis in relation to other religions: "There are people in other religions who are being led by God's secret influence to concentrate on those parts of their religion which are in agreement with Christianity, and who thus belong to Christ without knowing it."[2]

Worldview

1. Based on your understanding of each of the major religions discussed in this book, make a diagram of which theological position (exclusivism, inclusivism, etc.) you think best corresponds with each religion.

Religion	Theological Position	Basis for Believing This
Hinduism		
Buddhism		
Confucianism		
Daoism		
Judaism		
Islam		

2. Write a 500- to 1,000-word blog with the heading "The Christian Worldview of Other Religions." How would you organize this content? What major features should be included?

2. C. S. Lewis, *Mere Christianity* (New York: Macmillan, 1977), 176.

Appendix B
Online Links to
Religious Writings[1]

ONE OF MY GOALS in this book has been to interact with primary texts when possible. It has been my experience over the years that many people learn facts about other religions—which certainly has its merits—but that they do not spend much time reading through the primary writings of the various religions. In this appendix, I am including links to various websites so that you may have an opportunity to read through some of the primary writings of the religions discussed in the chapters above. As you read these texts, review the "Religious Writings" sections—each of which is always the third or fourth section of each of the first five chapters of this book—which give context to the writings.[2]

Chapter 1: Hinduism

This link connects you to all the major writings of the Hindu tradition: http://www.sacred-texts.com/hin/. I recommend that you start with the Bhagavad Gita. Then choose Vishnu Purana, the Laws of Manu, and finally the Sama Veda (SV).

1. I have recommendations for further reading at the end of each chapter in the book proper. This appendix highlights only online sources.

2. Again, although this appendix highlights only online texts, I would like to generally recommend some spiritual classics in the SkyLight Illuminations Series by Skylight Paths Publishing in Woodstock, Vermont. The religious books in this series are relatively inexpensive, well translated, and annotated. Primary texts from each of the religions discussed in this book are available in the series, including (1) for Hinduism: *Bhagavad Gita* and *Selections from the Gospel of Sri Ramakrishna*; (2) for Buddhism: *Dhammapada*; (3) for Confucianism and Daoism: *Confucius, the Analects, Chuang-tzu*, and *Tao Te Ching*; (4) for Judaism: *Ethics of the Sages, The Hebrew Prophets, Zohar*, and *Maimonides*; (5) for Islam: *The Qur'an and Sayings of Prophet Muhammad, Rumi and Islam*, and *Ghazali on the Principles of Islamic Spirituality*. They are great resources, and a book that represents each religion could be read by students.

Chapter 2: Buddhism

This link connects you to the Dhammapada, the best place to begin reading Buddhist texts: http://oaks.nvg.org/richards.html.

This link connects you to many Buddhist *sutras*: http://www.cttbusa.org/sutratexts.asp. I recommend that you start with the Heart Sutra.

This link connects you to the Tripitaka: http://www.accesstoinsight.org/tipitaka/index.html. I recommend that you start with the Sutta Pitaka.

This link connects you to the Tibetan Book of the Dead, which is an important book in Tibetan (Vajrayana) Buddhism: http://reluctant-messenger.com/tibetan-book-of-the-dead.htm. I recommend that you use Houston's translation.

This link connects you to the Eight Great Awakenings Sutra, a short Buddhist *sutra* that is easy and quick to read: http://www2.fodian.net/Picture/BaoKu/200692918365987.htm.

Chapter 3: Confucianism and Daoism

This link connects you to the Analects of Confucius, which is the best place to begin reading Confucian texts: http://ebooks.adelaide.edu.au/c/confucius/c748a/.

This link connects you to the Book of Mencius, which was written by an important interpreter of Confucius: http://nothingistic.org/library/mencius/.

This link connects you to the Book of Filial Piety, an important work on understanding the nature of Confucianism: http://www.sacred-texts.com/cfu/bfd/index.htm.

This link connects you to the I Ching or Book of Changes, a classic in both Confucian and Daoist thought: http://www.akirarabelais.com/i/i.html#1.

This link connects you to several Daoist writings: http://www.sacred-texts.com/tao/index.htm. I suggest that you start with the Daodejing (or *Tao Te Ching*). Then read Zhuangzi (or Chuang Tzu), followed by *The Sayings of Lao Tzu*.

Chapter 4: Judaism

This link connects you to a Jewish translation of the Hebrew Bible, with commentary by the Jewish scholar Rashi (d. 1105): http://www.chabad.org/library/bible_cdo/aid/63255/jewish/The-Bible-with-Rashi.htm.

This link connects you to many Jewish writings: http://www.sacred-texts.com/jud/. I suggest that you start with parts of the Talmud, followed by the Zohar. If you would like to read more about the history of the Jews immediately after the time of Christ, read *The Works of Flavius Josephus*, which was written by the former Jewish military commander Josephus (d. AD 100). Finally, read *The Guide for the Perplexed* by Maimonides (d. 1204), a well-respected medieval rabbi who is one of the most capable thinkers in the Jewish tradition.

Chapter 5: Islam

This link connects you to the Qur'an, the best place to begin when reading primary Muslim texts: http://www.dar-us-salam.com/TheNobleQuran/index.html.

This link connects you to the Qur'an read aloud: http://www.listen2quran.com/default.aspx.

This link connects you to various authoritative versions of the Hadith, the most standard of which is by Bukhari: http://hadithcollection.com/.

Appendix C
A Guide to Visiting Non-Christian Worship Spaces

I N THE INTRODUCTION, I stated that you can read and enjoy this book without ever setting foot in a non-Christian religious site. I still stand by that statement! However, I would be very pleased if, over the course of reading this book, you felt inspired to learn more about a non-Christian religion by visiting one of its holy places. If you choose to do so, this guide will help you.

It has been my experience that the first thing you will have to overcome is fear. I have never had anyone try to convert me or keep me prisoner when I visited other places of worship! As is the case with Christian pastors at churches, the religious leadership is eager to talk casually (but not too personally) with visitors.

Visiting a non-Christian temple is a vulnerable act. It takes faith and courage. Although I cannot promise that it will be worth your time, I can tell you that—of the dozens and dozens of students I have taken on tours of non-Christian temples—I have never had any of them inform me that they were disappointed with their experience. On the contrary, I almost always hear students say something like this: "That was an amazing experience. I learned so much!" or "I was scared to come here, but I'm so thankful I did. I have a completely new understanding of this religion and of Christianity."

What's more, I have also discovered that the people who worship at these temples are incredibly warm, generous, and excited about your visit. They often go out of their way to ensure that you are comfortable and that you understand what is going on. They are usually eager to take you aside, help you get situated, and give you literature about their religion.

Things to Do Beforehand

Although the customs of each religious place will vary (even within the same religion), here are some general guidelines when visiting a non-Christian temple:

1. Locate a non-Christian temple by doing an online search or by looking in the phone book. Call or send an e-mail to someone at the temple, letting the person know that you would like to visit. (Having a guide waiting for you beforehand is always better than just showing up.) Inform your contact person that you are studying world religions and that you would like to observe a worship service. Determine a meeting place and time. In general, the best times to visit non-Christian religious places are as follows.

Religious Place	Best Time to Visit
Hindu temple	During religious or cultural festivals; also during weekly service, which will vary.
Buddhist temple	During weekly service, which will vary for each temple.
Confucian or Daoist temple	May be difficult to find one of these temples; if you do, the times will vary.
Jewish synagogue	Sabbath service (Friday night or Saturday morning) or during Bar (or Bat) Mitzvah.
Muslim mosque	Early Friday afternoon service.

2. Pray about your experience. Pray for courage, spiritual protection, wisdom, and humility. Ask God what he wants you to learn through this experience.

3. Make sure that you are dressed modestly. Refrain from wearing "loud" clothing, baseball caps, T-shirts, or shorts. Wear clean socks, since you may be required to remove your shoes. You may be required to stand or sit on the floor for a good portion of the service, so dress comfortably as well.

4. Be sure to bring a pen and a notepad so that you can record your thoughts and observations.

5. Silence your cell phone.

6. Keep the items you bring with you to a minimum.

7. Budget enough time for your stay. Many times people will invite you to stay longer than you may have anticipated.

8. In general, it is best to visit a temple with fewer people rather than more. Entering a non-Christian space by yourself is a humbling act, and the people at the temple will be more inviting if they see that you are few in number. At the same time, do what is most comfortable. If you are younger than a college student, you should be accompanied by an adult. If you are older, I recommend that you attend alone or with one other person.

9. Review the "Worship Practices" section—which is the fifth section of each of the first five chapters—outlined in this book for the service you are about to attend.

General Things to Keep in Mind

1. Observe what other people are doing and fall in line (as long as it is something that you are comfortable doing). Some places require men and women to enter through separate doors, while many others will require you to take off your shoes. Other places may require you to put on a hat or head covering.

2. Never feel that you have to participate in the service. You are an observer. Everyone there will know that you are an observer, so do not feel awkward about not participating. In all probability, the local worshipers from that temple will just be happy that you are there.

3. Do not take pictures unless you first ask permission. If you are given permission, be discreet. The same applies to using a voice recorder.

4. Do not walk in front of someone if that person is standing or praying in front of an object.

5. Do not be antagonistic in the comments you make or questions you ask. You are a guest, so remember to be respectful. Now is the time to observe rather than argue.

Things to Observe during the Service and to Reflect on Afterward

Below are some questions to ask yourself as you observe the service and to think about after your visit.

1. What did the shape, location, and design of the building indicate about the religion and the people?

2. What is the first thing that caught your attention as you arrived and entered the sacred space?

3. How did you feel when you entered? Were you greeted? What were people doing?

4. What space was dedicated for what purpose? What was the focal point of the space? What colors, images, objects, or other things did you notice?

5. How did the space make you feel? How was the lighting? Were there any unique smells, sights, or sounds?

6. What kinds of people were present? Women, men, children? What ethnicity? From what professions do you think the people came?

7. What were the main features of the service? Were any rituals performed, hymns sung, or books read?

8. Did you feel uncomfortable or awkward at any time? Why?

9. Were you surprised by anything? What?

Analyzing Your Experience

After your visit, be sure to respond to the questions above as well as answer the questions below.

1. What did you learn about the religion through your visit?

2. What did the people you interacted with think about Christianity? What did you learn about Christianity?

3. Was there an element of the service that could be incorporated into a Christian service?

4. Did you see God in a different way? How so?

5. Did you experience spiritual warfare? How did you respond? What was helpful or harmful?

6. What questions remain about the service? Do you plan to follow up with these lingering questions?

7. If you had to summarize your experience in one word (and then one sentence), what would it be?

Glossary

Advaita **or Non-dualism**. The Hindu philosophical teaching that all is one and nothing is separate from anything else. In other words, you and I are one, just as a person's soul is one with another living being's soul.

Allah. The name of the Muslim god. It comes from the Arabic word meaning "the God." Because it is the general word for *God* in Arabic, it is used by Arabic-speaking Christians when referring to God the Father.

Anatta. Buddhist term meaning "no self." It refers to the Buddhist teaching that living beings do not have souls and that we do not actually exist. Rather, we are merely an amalgam of transitory components. (This view is a reaction to classical Hindu thought, which believes that all beings have a soul.)

Ancestor Veneration or Ancestor Worship. Common practice in East Asian cultures that believe that the deceased have a continued existence after death and that human relatives (on earth) today should continue to honor their deceased ancestors by making offerings, prostrating themselves at certain times of the year, and observing other important rituals. While some Asian Christians view this practice as merely cultural, others believe it is religious in character and therefore idolatrous for Christians to observe.

Aryan. Hindu Sanskrit term meaning "Noble [Ones]." It refers to the people and culture of some of the earliest Hindus, who may have originated from Europe. Later, in the twentieth century, the term was used by Nazi propagandists.

Asceticism. Greek word meaning "training." It refers to rigorous religious or spiritual practices that neglect the body or actively keep the body from the normal enjoying of natural pleasures or habits.

Atman. Hindu term often translated as *soul*. It refers to the essence of life. All living beings, according to Hinduism, have an *atman*. In philosophical Hinduism, which is based on the Upanishads, the goal of existence is to yoke or attach one's *atman* to Brahman, which is

Pure Awareness, since the two are the same thing anyway. A living being's *atman* is like a drop of water from the larger sea of Brahman.

Bhagavad Gita. Literally "Song of the Lord," it is the most popular and beloved of the Hindu scriptures. It is an excerpt from the much longer epic poem the Mahabharata. The Gita (as it is often called) narrates the story of Arjuna as he prepares to fight against his kinsmen in a great war, and it also contains his conversations with the Hindu god Krishna.

Bhakti. Devotional Hinduism, which is the most popular form of Hinduism today. In *bhakti* Hinduism, a person shows loving devotion to a particular Hindu god by means of prayer and worship.

Bodhisattva. Buddhist saviors who attempt to save living beings from ignorance and suffering by delaying their own attainment of nirvana so that they can be reincarnated to help all beings achieve enlightenment.

Brahma. The creator god in Hinduism who is often associated with Vishnu and Shiva. Although Brahma is the creator god, very few Hindus worship this god and instead have cults of other deities. Brahma is usually depicted with four heads. (Not to be confused with Brahmin or Brahman.)

Brahman. Divine Reality or Pure Awareness. An impersonal force that, from a Western perspective, would be understood as the impersonal god of Hinduism. Brahman is the ultimate essence of existence. (Not to be confused with Brahma or Brahmin.)

Brahmin. Priestly class in Hinduism and the highest within the caste system. Brahmins traditionally were those who performed vital religious and cultural rituals. (Not to be confused with Brahma or Brahman.)

Buddha. Title meaning "Enlightened One" or "Awakened One." Although there are many buddhas, the term is classically used to refer to Siddhartha Gautama, who is believed to have achieved enlightenment as he meditated under the Bodhi Tree in India in the sixth century BC.

Caste System. A complex system of social privilege and restriction in classical Hinduism. Traditionally grouped under four categories: priests (*Brahmins*), warriors (*Kshatriyas*), merchants (*Vaishyas*), and servants (*Shudras*). Under these categories is a noncategory of people referred to as untouchables (*Dhalits*). Classical Hinduism believed that people should act according to their station (caste) in life and perform their *dharma* (duty) according to where they resided within the caste system. The consequences of the caste system in India are still apparent today.

Dao. Sometimes spelled *Tao*, this (Chinese) Daoist term refers to "the way" or impersonal fundamental essence of existence. It signifies the path or direction that one should follow in life in order to live well or "go with the flow" in the best use of the phrase. (It is similar to the concept of *dharma* in Indian thought.)

Daodejing. Sometimes spelled Tao Te Ching, this is the principal philosophical text of Daoist thought often attributed to the classical figure Lao Tzu. The text advocates living according to the Dao.

Dharma. Variously translated as *truth* or *duty* or *law*, it refers to the Indian (thus Buddhist and Hindu) concept of acting according to one's station or vocation in life. (It is similar to the Chinese concept of the Dao.)

Dispersion. Refers to the scattering of the Jewish people outside Judea or Israel after the destruction of the Jewish temple in Jerusalem.

Eight Immortals. A group of eight legendary mortals in the Daoist pantheon who attained immortality by maintaining perfect balance of *chi* or vital energy.

Exclusivism. The religious view that only persons who openly profess faith in Jesus Christ as Lord and Savior will be saved. (All others—those who do not publicly profess Christ—will not be saved.)

Fallen Angel. In the Jewish and Christian traditions, an angel who rebels against God's authority and acts independently of God. (In the Muslim tradition, angels do not have free will and therefore cannot rebel against God.) According to some Christian theologians, fallen angels may be the animating spiritual force behind non-Christian religions. In Judaism and Christianity, Satan is seen as the leader of fallen angels.

Five Pillars of Islam. The basic five practices in (Sunni) Islam, which are binding on Muslims. These are (1) the *Shahada* (professing that there is only one God and that Muhammad is his prophet), (2) *Salah* (five daily prayers determined by a Muslim calendar), (3) *Zakat* (almsgiving, traditionally about 2.5 percent of one's income), (4) *Ramadan* (observing a monthlong fast during the ninth month of the Muslim calendar), and (5) the *Hajj* (a pilgrimage to Mecca once in a person's lifetime).

Four Noble Truths. The four classic tenets of Buddhist thought taught by the Buddha after his enlightenment in the sixth century BC. They are (1) the reality of suffering, (2) the cause of suffering, (3) the cessation of suffering, and (4) the practice of the Noble Eightfold Path, which leads to the cessation of suffering.

General Revelation. Revelation from God in nature and human reasoning that is available to all people regardless of their geographical location, spiritual character, or religious preference. Christian theologians generally believe that this reveals God's existence and certain moral qualities. Most theologians do not believe that general revelation leads to salvation; for salvation, special revelation from God (through God's Spirit by means of a miracle or through the Bible) must be granted.

Great Signs. The crucial events of Siddhartha Gautama's life when he encountered the realities of sickness, aging, death, and liberation, respectively, on his private journeys with his chariot driver outside his father's kingdom. These trips inspired and challenged Siddhartha to reject his luxurious lifestyle and to embrace a life of exploration with the goal of enlightenment.

Guru. Sanskrit word meaning "teacher" in Indian religions (thus Hinduism and Buddhism). Gurus have important roles in Hindu and Buddhist thought and practice and seek to guide their pupils toward enlightenment.

Hadith. "Traditions" or sayings in Islam that record the sayings and customs of the prophet Muhammad. There are many standard collections of the Hadith (both the Sunni and the Shiite Muslims have their own versions), and they are used to make judgments on various matters related to Islam. Sometimes used synonymously with the word *Sunna*.

Haggadah. Hebrew term meaning "narrative," used in rabbinic Judaism to describe the interpretation of nonlegal portions of Torah.

Halakha. Hebrew term often translated as *Jewish law*. It refers to the laws or *mitzvot* of the Torah, which Jews (today, principally Orthodox Jews) believe are binding.

Hindu Trinity. Referring to the three principal Hindu deities of Brahma (the creator god), Vishnu (the preserver), and Shiva (the destroyer).

Imam. Arabic word meaning "one who stands before," it is used in reference to the spiritual leaders of individual mosques. In Shia Islam, imams are given special honor. This is because in Shia Islam imams are believed to have been appointed by God, whereas in Sunni Islam the imams tend to be chosen by the community.

Inclusivism. The religious view that Jesus Christ alone saves people from their sins, but that people do not necessarily have to practice Christianity or even profess Jesus as Lord and Savior to be saved. People of non-Christian religions (or no religion at all), therefore, can potentially be saved by Jesus.

Karma. Often translated as "action" or "deed," this Indian (and thus Hindu and Buddhist) term refers to the universal notion of cause and effect. One's karma, which includes thoughts, deeds, and actions, remains with a living being (through the course of one's death and rebirth) until one reaches nirvana or extinction. Afterward, a being is no longer bound by cause and effect or karma.

Mahayana Buddhism. The dominant tradition or denomination of Buddhism. It provides a greater role for laypeople in the process of liberation (in contrast with Theravada Buddhism, which emphasizes the role of monks), and also focuses on the role of *bodhisattvas* in helping other living beings attain enlightenment. It is the most prevalent form of Buddhism outside Southeast Asia.

Moksha. Hindu term meaning "liberation," it refers to the release or liberation that living beings may attain from the shackles of *samsara*, the endless cycle of birth, death, and rebirth. (It is similar to the Buddhist term *nirvana*.)

Murti. An image or representation of a Hindu god. Many Hindus have home shrines of *murtis* that they take care of on a daily basis. *Murtis* also reside in Hindu temples, where they are taken care of on a daily basis by priests. *Murtis* are imbued with the divine through formal rituals by a priest and are then able to be used to worship the god represented. *Murtis* vary in size and are not considered idols by Hindu devotees.

Nirvana. Buddhist term meaning "extinction." It is the end of existence as we know it, which frees living beings from suffering or *samsara*. (It is similar to the Hindu term *moksha*.)

Noble Eightfold Path. The eight paths that one must follow in classic Buddhist thought in order to end suffering and achieve enlightenment. They are traditionally categorized under wisdom (right view and right intention), ethics (right speech, right action, and right livelihood), and concentration (right effort, right mindfulness, and right concentration).

Pantheon. Greek term meaning "temple of all gods," it refers to the standard set of gods in any given religion. For instance, the pantheon of Hindu gods refers to all Hindu divinities, including Shiva, Parvati, Ganesha, Vishnu, Kali, Hanuman, etc.

Particularism. The religious view that each world religion has its own aims and goals, and that these aims differ from one religion to another. For instance, while the goal of Christianity is to be saved from one's sin by means of Jesus' death and resurrection, the goal of Islam is to submit to Allah, observe the practices set forth by the *Ummah* or Muslim community, and live in Paradise after death.

Pluralism. The view that all major world religions lead to the same one deity. Although they have different backgrounds, traditions, and beliefs, all world religions are believed to have similar goals (namely, uniting with the divine and living morally and ethically while on earth).

Puja. The worship of a Hindu deity, often by bowing in front of a *murti* or offering food or flowers to the divinity. *Pujas* can be done at home or in temples. There is no set day to make *pujas*.

Pure Awareness or Supreme Reality. The ultimate existence in Hindu thought, sometimes referred to simply as Brahman. It is an impersonal force.

Qur'an. Arabic word meaning "recitation." It is the holy book of Muslims, believed to have been given to Muhammad from AD 610–32 by the angel Gabriel. Muhammad did not write any of the Qur'an. Muslims believe that God is the author of the book, and that it was later perfectly written down in Arabic by Muhammad's followers.

Rabbinic Judaism. The mainstream form of Judaism since the codification of the Talmud. It traces its origin indirectly to Nehemiah and more directly to the first century after the destruction of the Jewish temple in AD 70. It is traditionally centered on the observance of the Torah and not the sacrificial system (as is the Old Testament).

Rectification of Names. Confucian teaching arguing that what is needed for societal stability and proper governance and order is for things to be designated by their right names and then for people to act accordingly. This is believed to bring order to society and to prevent chaos and instability. It is hierarchical in nature and assumes that one's personal choices are subservient to the stability of society.

Rightly Guided Caliphate. Muslim term referring to the first four caliphs or (Sunni) Muslim leaders after the death of Muhammad in 632. These are Abu Bakr (d. 634), Umar (d. 633), Uthman (d. 656), and Ali (d. 661). The Rightly Guided Caliphate ends after Ali is assassinated in 661, which leads to formation of the Umayyad Dynasty under Muawiya (d. 680) from 661–750.

Samsara. Literally meaning "continuous flow," it is an Indian religious term (and thus used in Hinduism and Buddhism as well as other Indian religions) referring to the repeated cycle of birth, life, death, and rebirth (or reincarnation). All living beings are trapped in *samsara*, and the goal of Indian religions is to escape *samsara* by achieving *moksha* or liberation.

Sangha. The Buddhist community, which was originally monastic but is now more inclusive, especially in Mahayana Buddhism. In this tradition it is virtually synonymous with the term *church* for Christians.

Shia or Shiite (Islam). Minority form of Islam today, representing about 15 percent of the Muslim population. Shias (otherwise known as Shiites) believe that the first true successor of Muhammad was Ali (d. 661), the son-in-law of the prophet, who was assassinated shortly after gaining the caliphate in 656. Shias differ from the dominant Sunnis by their high regard for imams and ayatollahs (high-ranking leaders in Twelver Shiasm), their own distinct Hadith, and their further divisions according to how many rightful successors of Muhammad reigned before the last one was killed: Fivers, Seveners, and Twelvers. The Shia are most prevalent in Iran, Iraq, Lebanon, and Yemen. The Twelver Shias, the largest of the Shia groups, believe that the "last imam" is in occultation and will appear as the Messiah before the day of judgment.

Special Revelation. Revelation from God that leads to salvation. Christian theologians use this term in contrast to *general revelation*, which is basic knowledge about God that is available to all people and does not lead to salvation. Theologians assert that special revelation must come supernaturally from God's Spirit.

Sunna. Arabic term meaning "trodden path," it refers to the customs or habits of the prophet Muhammad. It is sometimes used synonymously with the word *Hadith*.

Sunni (Islam). Most prevalent form of Islam today, representing about 85 percent of the Muslim population. Sunnis believe that succession to Muhammad rightly fell to the most competent leaders, not those who were physically related to the prophet (as in Shia Islam or Shiasm). The Sunni have their own Hadith or tradition, which differs somewhat from Shiasm. The Sunni concentrate their authority on the *ulama* (Muslim scholars) and the *Ummah* (Muslim community), while the Shias concentrate their power on their own imams or ayatollahs (in Twelver Shiasm).

Tanakh. Jewish term used for the Hebrew Bible. It derives from an acrostic of the three Hebrew terms *Torah* (the Pentateuch or first five books of the Hebrew Bible), *Nevi'im* (the prophetic books), and *Ketuvim* (or remaining writings).

Theravada Buddhism. The oldest and most traditional form of the Buddhist traditions or denominations. Emphasizes the role of the monk to achieve nirvana and is most prevalent in Southeast Asia.

Torah. Jewish term literally meaning "teaching" or "instruction," it can refer to the first five books of the Old Testament or Hebrew Bible, to the entire Hebrew Bible, or to the Talmud. In Orthodox Judaism, there is a "written" Torah (which includes the Hebrew Bible) and an "oral" Torah (which includes the Talmud). Both were believed to have been given to Moses on Mount Sinai.

Ulama. Arabic term meaning "scholar." It refers to the Muslim legal scholars and religious leaders who engage in Islamic studies.

Ummah. Arabic term meaning "community." It refers to a collective Muslim nation (such as the *Ummah* of Saudi Arabia) or more broadly to the global Muslim community.

Universalism. The religious view that all people will eventually (that is, after death) come under the lordship of Jesus Christ and will be saved. In fact, in addition to all people eventually being saved, all things will eventually be restored.

Vedas. Hindu term meaning "knowledge." It refers to the oldest Hindu scriptures. Traditionally, the term designated the Rig Veda (RV), Yajur Veda (YV), Sama Veda (SV), and Atharva Veda (AV), but it can also more broadly encompass later Hindu writings.

Wheel of Life. The different realms of Buddhist existence, including the realms of the gods, titans (demigods and demons), animals, hell beings, ghosts, and humans. All living beings are born in one of these realms and may be reborn in another realm in a different lifetime.

Yin and Yang. Chinese (thus Daoist and Confucian) philosophical terms teaching that everything originates from the interaction of opposite and complementary principles. Yin and yang represent the fundamental elements of the universe. Yin is associated with earth, cold, wet, passive, dark, mysterious, and feminine. Yang is associated with heaven, hot, dry, active, bright, clear, and masculine.

Yoga. Coming from the Sanskrit word meaning "yoke," it refers to the Hindu concept of yoking one's soul or *atman* to the Supreme Reality by means of specific practices. There are a variety of ways to practice yoga in Hinduism, including the following: *raja yoga* (rigorous meditation and asceticism), *karma yoga* (the path of action or duty), *jnana yoga* (the philosophical study of distinguishing between what is real and unreal), and *bhakti yoga* (lovingly devoting oneself to a Hindu god).

Credits

Introduction
Figure 1.1 © llfede / dreamstime.com

Chapter 1
Figure 1.1 © F9photos / dreamstime.com
Figure 1.4 © Kirat Jadeja / dreamstime.com
Figure 1.5 © Photowee / dreamstime.com

Chapter 2
Figure 2.2 © Erinpackardphotography / dreamstime.com
Figure 2.4 © Chatchai Somwat / dreamstime.com

Chapter 3
Figure 3.1 © Lieska / dreamstime.com
Figure 3.3 © liiiiimax / dreamstime.com

Chapter 4
Figure 4.1 © Chert61 / dreamstime.com

Chapter 5
Figure 5.5 © Pniesen / dreamstime.com
Figure 5.6 © Aidar Ayazbayev / dreamstime.com

Chapter 7
Figure 7.2 © Iqoncept / dreamstime.com

Index of Subjects and Names